TEMPLE OF DREAMS

THE CHANGING FACE OF IBROX

IAIN DUFF

First published in Great Britain in 2008 by The Breedon Books
Publishing Company Limited, 3 The Parker Centre, Derby, DE21 4SZ.

Paperback published in Great Britain in 2010 by The Derby Books
Publishing Company Limited, 3 The Parker Centre, Derby, DE21 4SZ.

ACKNOWLEDGEMENTS

My deepest thanks for their assistance go to Mike Stanger, John Weedy, Sam Moore, Andy
Ellis, Tom Cunningham, Stevie Tyrie, Mark Dingwall, Murdo Fraser, John Robertson, Hugh
Barrow, Stuart MacQuarrie, Gordon Urquhart and Rob Hadgraft. A special thanks also to
Clino D'Eletto for allowing me to use his historic postcards of Ibrox in the book.

Thank you also to Catherine MacPhail for giving permission to use Jack Kirkland's
account of the Ibrox disaster.

Finally, many thanks to Ross Matheson for providing the photographs taken by his
father, Farquhar, during the redevelopment of Ibrox in the 1970s.

ISBN 978-1-85983-815-0

Printed and bound by Cromwell Press Group, Trowbridge, Wiltshire.

CONTENTS

FOREWORD

Every other Saturday is my half-day off,
And it's off to the match I go.

Happily we wander down the Copland Road,
Me and my wee pal Joe...

The song dates back to the the 1960s but still gets a regular airing by the Rangers fans at Ibrox. Times have certainly changed since it was first sung four decades ago. For one thing, these days fans do not normally have to put in half a day's shift before heading off to the game. And thanks to the power of television, Saturday afternoon matches are about as rare as hen's teeth. But on every match day (whenever it might be) you will still find thousands of supporters happily wandering down Copland Road with their wee pal, making their way to Ibrox.

In the modern world of football it can be difficult for fans to relate to their club in the way that they did in the past. Players and managers come and go with such alarming regularity that forming any sort of bond can be impossible. And it is difficult to relate to someone who is paid as much in a week as you are in a year. For many fans, it is the match-day routine – meeting up with their mates, having a pre-game pint in the pub, discussing the team news with the guy who sits next to them in the stand – that keeps them interested in going to the football. Central to the experience is the one thing that remains constant throughout all the changes on the pitch: the stadium.

Mind you, Ibrox has undergone a dramatic change in appearance over the last 30 years. The moment the bulldozers moved in to flatten the old Rangers End terracing in the summer of 1978, the whole match-day experience was transformed forever. After 50 years in which the look of the stadium had remained largely unchanged, suddenly the sweeping banks of terracing were gone, to be replaced by bright, modern stands. What was lost in character and tradition was replaced by comfort and safety. In a stadium where more than 90 people had lost their lives in a series of tragic accidents, crowd safety was now more important than anything.

But for all the modernisation of Ibrox, many aspects of the match-day experience remain much the same as they have for decades. Just as their predecessors did at the start of the last century, thousands of supporters still travel to the stadium by underground, although these days the station is known as Ibrox rather than Copland Road. After disembarking from the train, shuffling along the packed platforms and negotiating the spare-ticket sellers at the top of the stairs, they emerge into Copland Road itself. Resisting the temptation to cross to the Stadium Bar directly across the road, they turn right into the throng heading towards the stadium, passing the fanzine seller with the bright orange and blue scarf, who competes for business with the official programme vendor. Beyond them, a street trader displays a vast selection of unofficial flags, scarves and T-shirts.

The smell of vinegar and chip fat wafts down the street from the Sportsman chippy. There is always a huge queue stretching out onto the pavement, no matter how long it is until kick-off. On the corner of Copland Road and Mafeking Street is a branch of the bookies William Hill, where the original Rangers Shop once stood. It is here that they catch their first glimpse of Ibrox. Turning right into Mafeking Street, past the stall selling vintage programmes on the left and the Masonic Lodge on the right, the Copland Road and Govan stands loom on the horizon.

They might stop for a bite to eat at one of the many burger vans that line the road up to the stadium concourse, or maybe meet up with friends before swiping their smart card on the electronic pad and going through the turnstiles into the ground. Everyone has their own ritual. Others might choose to meet up in one of the pubs on Paisley Road West before hot-footing it to the ground with a few minutes to spare. Many others gather at the iconic statue of former club captain John Greig that stands outside the magnificent Main Stand in tribute to those who died at the stadium in the tragedies of 1902, 1961 and 1971.

For more than 100 years, Ibrox has been the home of Rangers Football Club. No other football stadium in Europe, possibly the world, has such a rich history of triumph and tragedy. It boasts state-of-the-art modern facilities that rank alongside the best in the world. But its wood-panelled entrance lobby and famous marble staircase evoke memories of a distant era, while the glittering trophy room inside the magnificent Main Stand tells the story of the club better than any words could.

Although Rangers have managed to preserve the traditions of the famous old stadium, much of the Ibrox of today bears little resemblance to the ground that opened in December 1899. This book charts, in words and pictures, the history of Ibrox from the early days through the creation of Archibald Leitch's stunning Main Stand in 1929, with its Masonic imagery, to the present-day five-star facilities. Using official records and eye-witness accounts, it tells the story of the two Ibrox disasters and how the second tragedy in 1971 resulted in a complete overhaul of the stadium and the creation of the most modern football ground in Britain, years ahead of its time.

As well as the many football triumphs, the stadium has witnessed dozens of other events over the years, including the famous annual Ibrox Sports meeting created by the legendary manager Bill Struth. On one spectacular afternoon, seven world records were broken in one race on the Ibrox cinder track. The book also reveals the part played by famous figures like Buffalo Bill Cody, King George V, Winston Churchill, *Chariots of Fire* athlete Eric Liddell, evangelist Billy Graham, Frank Sinatra and Elton John in the history of the stadium.

Ibrox holds the record attendance for a League match in Britain, and it would be nothing more than a pile of bricks and mortar without the fans who breathe life into it every other Saturday. Rangers have consistently been the best supported club in Scotland. In the 85 official seasons between 1905 and 1999, when Celtic Park's capacity was increased above Ibrox's, Rangers had the highest average League attendance on 67 occasions. This includes several seasons during the period when Celtic won nine consecutive League titles in the 1960s and in the early 1980s when Rangers performances on the pitch were at an all-time low.

From the days when fans lit bonfires on the vast terraces to keep warm in the depths of winter and donned customised hard-hats as protection from flying beer bottles in the 1960s to the spectacular Champions League nights of the 21st century, this book tells the glorious and often poignant story of the changing face of Ibrox.

THE BEGINNING

On any given Saturday afternoon, Glasgow Green is alive with the sound of football. Hundreds of players, of varying ages and abilities, take to the pitches on the large expanse of parkland just to the east of Glasgow city centre every weekend. On the banks of the River Clyde, they brave wind, rain and hail, all for the love of the game. Turn the clock back 135 years, and things were not too different.

In the early 1870s, among those vying for a spare patch of ground to kick a ball around in the Fleshers' Haugh area of the Green, was a group of young men who were to call themselves the Rangers. The team was formed by Peter Campbell, William McBeath and brothers Peter and Moses McNeil, who were studying in Glasgow. Keen sportsmen, they were smitten by the fast-growing new sport of football and decided they would give it a go.

Beyond those basic facts, the origins of Rangers FC remain a matter of some debate. The first official club history, written in 1923 by John Allan, tells a romantic tale of a group of young rowers from the Gare Loch area of Argyll coming ashore at Glasgow Green on the summer evenings of 1873 and being enraptured by football through watching the 'giants' of the Eastern Football Club, who played their games on Fleshers' Haugh.

The much lauded book, titled *The Story Of The Rangers*, goes on to chronicle in some detail a match that took place on 15 July 1873 between two teams called Argyle and Clyde. The match is portrayed as little more than a kick-around between a group of players who arbitrarily split themselves into two teams, but it is granted some significance by the fact that the Argyle team featured the McNeil brothers, McBeath and Campbell, as well as Tom Vallance, who would go on to be a Rangers player and administrator for many years.

According to this official history, the match was quickly followed by a meeting at which it was proposed that a club should be formed and that a subscription should be paid by members to secure the purchase of a ball. Sixteen-year-old Moses McNeil was credited with christening the new club Rangers after taking a fancy to the name of an English rugby team he had spotted in a book.

So pretty unequivocal then – Rangers were formed in the summer of 1873. Except an entirely different version of the club's formation has emerged in more recent years. Recent history books suggest that the four founders came up with the idea of forming a club as they went for a stroll in Glasgow's west end in February 1872. After several weeks of training at Fleshers' Haugh, they played their first match against Callander FC in May of that year at the same venue. A full year before Allan's young pioneers had supposedly even thought about football, they had actually played their first game.

The reason for such widely differing versions of history is not entirely clear. One would have thought that the original historian would have had some factual evidence to back up his story, but equally the painstaking research of the dedicated modern-day historian is surely beyond questioning. It certainly reads as more reliable than the somewhat flowery story told in the first official history.

Whichever version one chooses to believe, there is no doubt that the story of the Rangers is a classic rags to riches tale. Those young founders, all aged under 20, started out from humble origins with nothing but a love of the game and created what has gone on to become a sporting institution, known and revered throughout the world, as well as a vast multi-million pound business.

After numerous matches at Fleshers' Haugh against some of the other up-and-coming new teams, Rangers joined the Scottish Football Association in 1873 and took part in the national Cup competition for the first time the following year. Still based at Glasgow Green, the young Rangers had begun to attract a lot of interest, and their games were often attended by large crowds. Having defeated Oxford 2–0 in the first round of the Scottish Cup, Rangers faced Dumbarton in their first (and, as it turned out, last) competitive match at Fleshers' Haugh in November 1874. The match ended goalless, and Rangers lost to a single goal in the replay – their only defeat in what had been a very promising season.

BURNBANK

Fleshers' Haugh had served the fledgling club well, but as interest in the game heightened and Rangers continued to impress on the field, the committee decided it was time they had their own enclosed ground. In leaving Glasgow Green there were certainly some 'pangs of regret', according to *The Story of the Rangers*. The author wrote 'Many cherished memories were woven about the old birthplace, and for years afterwards these were fondly debated by those to whom the early adventures were the richest incidents in their career.' Nevertheless, the search began for a permanent home. A ground at Shawfield, close to Glasgow Green, was considered and almost agreed on. But surprisingly, for a club that is now synonymous with Glasgow's south side, they chose to make Rangers' first enclosed ground in the west end of the city.

The new Burnbank ground was sited on the north side of Great Western Road, close to St Mary's Episcopal Cathedral. Maps show the playing field sitting between Dunearn Street and Blythswood Drive, now North Kelvinside Drive. Nearby was the famous Arlington Baths, which opened in 1870 and remains a Glasgow institution to this day.

The ground was owned by the 1st Lanark Rifle Volunteers, and their drill hall was also close by. William Alexander Smith, the founder of the Boys' Brigade, was a member of the 1st LRV, as was John Mellish, a future president of both Rangers and the Clydesdale Harriers Athletic Club. Both the BB and Clydesdale would go on to have close ties with Rangers and would use the future Ibrox Park on more than one occasion.

In Rangers' day, the Burnbank area would have appeared almost rural, but today it is heavily built up – a bustling residential and commercial sector of the city, with red sandstone tenements now occupying what was the site of the ground. A few years after Rangers departed for pastures new, the cathedral gained a spectacular new spire. Great Western Road was a major thoroughfare then and of course remains so today, although the stretch where Rangers were based bears little resemblance to how it looked 130 years ago.

The road is now lined with pubs, cafés and shops, many catering for the ethnic communities that have moved into the neighbourhood. Sadly, there is no sign that this was ever a significant site in the history of one of Europe's leading football clubs, and even one eminent local historian, specialising in Glasgow's west end, confessed he had no knowledge of Rangers' links with the area.

The first match at Burnbank took place on 11 September 1875 and was a 1–1 draw with Vale of Leven, one of the early powerhouses of Scottish football. Unfortunately, the records do not show who scored the first goal. The first competitive game came a few weeks later in the Scottish Cup, as fate would have it, against 1st LRV, with Rangers securing a comfortable 7–0 victory. Rangers stayed in the west end for just one season, playing only a handful of home games before moving south across the Clyde, where they have remained ever since.

KINNING PARK

In the mid-19th century, Kinning Park was a rural outpost on the very edge of Glasgow, a world away from the noise and smoke of the city. Its hedge-lined fields on the south side of the river were the ideal location for sporting activity, and in 1849 the newly formed Clydesdale Cricket Club leased fields from a Mr Meiklewham, just west of the General Terminus Railway. The land sat to the south of West Scotland Street, close to the location of the current Kinning Park subway station and only a couple of hundred yards from what was, until recently, the site of *The Scottish Sun* newspaper's head office.

Within two years of opening, Kinning Park had hosted a crowd of 8,000 for a cricket international between Scotland and England. In the 1860s, Clydesdale's players began to play football during the winter months, and they soon became one of Scotland's 'Big Four' football teams, along with Queen's Park, Third Lanark and Vale of Leven. The fledgling Rangers considered it a major achievement when they went to Kinning Park in 1873 and came away with a 1–1 draw.

In 1875 Clydesdale made the decision to move to the Pollokshields area (having turned down the offer of a ground on Paisley Road in Ibrox), and they remain there to this day as one of Glasgow's leading cricket clubs. The final cricket match was played at Kinning Park in September 1875 and was followed by a slap-up dinner in the pavilion. Clydesdale's footballers used the pitch for one more winter before Rangers, clearly impressed by their visit two years earlier, moved in.

By the time of Rangers' arrival in the autumn of 1876, the neighbourhood had already begun to change. Kinning Park was no longer in the countryside but had become a heavily built-up residential and industrial area. The football ground sat on West Scotland Street behind a row of tenements and a church, between Craig Street and Broomhall Street, with the fourth side of the ground backing onto a railway depot.

Rangers and their groundsman of the time, 'Geordie' Cameron, were now the proud possessors of a 'beautiful green playing field'. No pictures of the ground appear to have survived; however, a diagram that appeared in The Story Of The Rangers by John Allan shows there was a grandstand on the north side that ran the entire length of the touchline. On the opposite side of the pitch was a club house. Supporters accessed the ground through entrances behind the goals on Craig Street and Broomhall Street, and wire ropes and boards around the pitch kept them off the playing field. The lucky residents of Craig Street had no need to bother paying the entrance fee though – they had a grandstand view of the matches from their tenement windows.

Just as with Burnbank, Vale of Leven were the first opponents for Rangers at Kinning Park on 2 September 1876, and this time the home team marked the occasion with a victory, as Marshall and Dunlop scored in a 2–1 win. The attendance at that inaugural match has been recorded as 1,500, but as the game's popularity grew so did the crowds.

Kinning Park remained home for 10 years, during which time Rangers became one of Scotland's most popular teams, even though they were by no means the dominant force that they would eventually become. League football still hadn't come around, but the young Rangers team performed reasonably well in the prestigious Scottish Cup, reaching two Finals and a semi-final in the club's first 10 years. In fact, the only trophy won in the first 20 years was the Glasgow Charity Cup of 1879. Despite this lack of success, Rangers saw attendances at Kinning Park gradually rise to 6,000, 7,000 or even 8,000 for big matches. By the mid-1880s, they had outgrown their home, and a five-man committee was set up to look into the possibility of finding a new ground. This became a matter of urgency when the ground's factor arrived one day in early 1887 with the news that Kinning Park had to be vacated by 1 March.

Honorary secretary Walter Crichton was the driving force behind the hunt for a new home. In the face of some scepticism, he was in favour of a move further west toward the bucolic Ibrox district. He predicted that Glasgow's population would spread in that direction along with the city's tram network, providing a large, ready-made local supporter base and a transport infrastructure capable of bringing spectators from further afield. Crichton won the argument, and history proved him right. Rangers made the decision to move to Ibrox and went from strength to strength.

Before vacating Kinning Park, Rangers had some unfinished business to complete, not least an exciting run in the English FA Cup. Having joined the Football Association in 1885, the Scots were entitled to play in the Cup competition south of the border. In October 1886 – a week after being knocked out of the Scottish Cup – Rangers travelled to Liverpool to beat Everton 1–0 in front of 6,000 in the first round. The subsequent draws were kind to

Rangers, giving them four successive ties at Kinning Park against Church, Cowlairs, Lincoln City and Old Westminsters, each one resulting in home victory.

The sixth-round match against Old Westminsters on 19 February 1887 was the last official game at Kinning Park, and the 5–1 victory was a fitting finale. In the semi-final, Rangers went down 3–1 to Aston Villa at Crewe, and it was to be their last-ever match in the competition. The SFA were alarmed at the number of Scottish clubs playing in the English tournament and in May of that year banned their members from taking part.

The curtain finally came down on the ground with a challenge match between the Ancients and Moderns on 26 February 1887, with Rangers playing their last few home games of the season at Third Lanark's home ground, Cathkin Park.

Following Rangers' departure, the Kinning Park ground became the site of timber merchant Anderson and Henderson's saw mills, which were later destroyed by fire. Other businesses later used the site, and it was also the location of Lambhill Street Primary school. In the mid-1970s, the whole area was changed forever with the building of the M8 motorway. Craig Street and Broomhall Street (which had become Cowie Street and Heather Street respectively) disappeared under the asphalt along with the primary school and any remaining trace of Rangers' old ground. The irony is that thousands of Rangers fans drive to the stadium along the M8 every match day at Ibrox, blissfully unaware that the motorway passes over the site of what was once the club's home ground and the scene of some of its earliest triumphs.

FIRST IBROX

Having followed the advice of Walter Crichton, Rangers looked a mile west along Paisley Road towards the Ibrox area and identified a site in what was then perceived as a distant, rural outpost for their new home. A 10-year lease was signed on the land at Copland Road, slightly to the north-east of the present-day Ibrox, and work began to ready the new ground in time for the start of the 1887 season. The well-known metalworks firm Frederick Braby and Co, based in Springburn, was appointed to do the building work.

The company billed itself as 'contractors for pavilions, stands, barricades and other requisites for football and cricket enclosures'. For Rangers, Braby provided a 300ft-long, 1,200-capacity grandstand. The firm also built a 'commodious' and extremely well-appointed pavilion in the north-east corner of the ground, featuring a dressing room and committee room. Diagrams of the structure, stored at the Mitchell Library in Glasgow, show a basic building with six narrow pillars at the front, supporting an overhanging balcony roof. Inside were two locker rooms (one with a stove), a committee room and a bathroom.

The pitch was surrounded by a 3ft-high wooden fence, painted white, and around this ran an athletics track. The whole ground was enclosed by perimeter fencing of corrugated iron sheets fixed to timber, which, according to Braby, made it 'strong and unclimbable from outside'. Entry was gained via five gates on Copland Road, which gave access to the area behind the terracing at the eastern end of the ground.

Although Ibrox was largely surrounded by farmland when Rangers made the move, factories and chimneys soon dominated the skyline around the ground, towering over the terracing. A map of the Ibrox area from 1895 reveals some of Rangers' neighbours. To the west of the Copland Road End, immediately behind the houses on Ibrox Terrace, which still stand today, was a pick handle factory. To the north-west of the ground was Govan Match Works, the Broomloan Weaving factory and something described, rather unpleasantly, as a 'hair works'. Another surprising neighbour to the west of the ground was a curling pond.

The ground was officially opened on 20 August 1887 with a match between Rangers and the 'Invincibles' of Preston North End, regarded as the best team in England at the time. According to *The Story Of The Rangers*, Tom Vallance, the club president, struck a deal with the Lancashire club that would see them pick up a £50 fee, with Rangers keeping the remainder. It proved to be a good piece of business, as the club pocketed a tidy £290 from the estimated 18,000 crowd – thought to have been a record attendance in Scotland at the time. The income was gratefully received: the cost of building the new ground had put a great deal of pressure on Rangers' finances, and it required a great deal of 'consideration' to be shown by Frederick Braby and Co. for the club to meet its obligations.

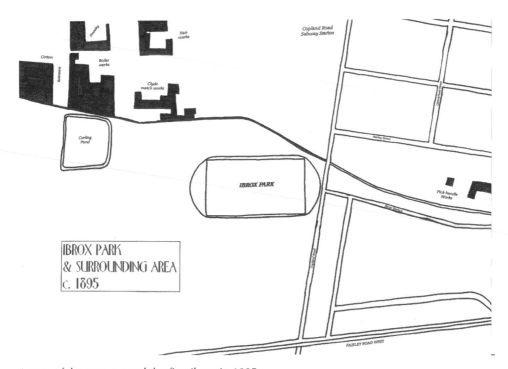

A map of the area around the first Ibrox in 1895.

A drawing of the John Gordon grandstand at the first Ibrox from an 1898 newspaper.

On a 'delightfully fine' summer's afternoon, crowds began to besiege the new ground long before the advertised 3.45pm kick-off time. As the spectators flooded in, they were entertained by a brass band from the local Fairfield's shipyard and the Govan Police Band. With 18,000 crammed into the ground, A.B. McKenzie had the honour of kicking-off the first-ever match at Ibrox for Rangers, 15 minutes later than planned. Unfortunately, it was not a pleasant experience for the home team or their exuberant followers. By half-time Rangers were 5–0 down, having been swamped by the English side, who would go on to win the first-ever Football League Championship the following season.

In the second half, Rangers fought back and thrilled their supporters when they pulled back a goal through Andrew Peacock. Urged on by the raucous crowd, Rangers pressed forward but were unable to turn their attacks into goals. Preston, though, had no such problems – and by the time they scored their eighth goal with a few minutes to go, some of the crowd had seen enough. The game was brought to a premature end as a large number of local youths invaded the pitch – a rather disappointing end to what was considered to have been a successful opening day.

It was an inauspicious start to life at their new home to say the least, and it would be some time before Rangers really settled in. The first season at Ibrox saw a second-round exit from the Scottish Cup at the hands of Partick Thistle, followed by defeat in the Final of the Glasgow Cup to Cambuslang. On the positive side, the run to the Final – which included a series of draws and a replay against Cowlairs, after they made allegations of professionalism against a Rangers player – brought a welcome boost to the Ibrox coffers.

The following March, Rangers played under floodlights at Ibrox for the first time, in a practice match against the Scotland international team. Braby and Co, who had built the ground, supplied the 'sunlight' system that illuminated the pitch during the evening game. The lights were described as 'flaring beams' by the *Evening Times* and were seemingly a success, with the Light Blues recording decisive victory. Other clubs also experimented with floodlights around this era, but strangely the idea of playing under artificial light did not seem to catch the imagination. It would be more than 60 years before floodlights became a permanent feature at Ibrox.

On 28 May 1888 Rangers visited a new club formed for the Roman Catholic population of the city's east end. The 5–2 defeat at the hands of Celtic in the last game of the season was the beginning of one of football's most intense, and arguably most bitter, rivalries. Another heavy defeat to Celtic, this time at Ibrox, was a low point of the following season, probably the worst in the club's short history. Rangers lost 19 and drew seven of their 39 matches and were knocked out of the Scottish Cup early by Clyde, before a demoralising 6–1 home defeat to Celtic in the Glasgow Cup.

WILLIAM WILTON

Behind the scenes, moves were afoot that would change the club's fortunes forever. An incredibly important figure during this time – arguably the key person in the development of the fledgling club – was William Wilton, who joined Rangers in September 1883 and quickly rose through the ranks. He became match secretary in May 1889 at the age of 23 – a role that effectively saw him become the club's first-ever team manager. He was a key player in the development of the first Ibrox and was instrumental in the creation of its successor – the Ibrox of today.

His role in Rangers' history cannot be overstated. For 30 years, until his untimely death in a boating accident on the Clyde in 1920, he was the dominant figure at the club, and without his guiding influence it is unlikely that Rangers would have gone on to become the force in Scottish football.

With his balding pate, wire-rimmed glasses and neatly trimmed moustache, photographs of Wilton give the impression that he was an austere, headmasterly sort and hardly the type one would associate with the rowdy game of football. His membership of a prominent Glasgow choir seems rather more appropriate, but impressions can be deceiving, for football was his life's passion. Contrary to appearances, it seems he was actually a keen player and made a handful of appearances for one of Rangers' minor XIs. But he apparently never had the talent to progress any further, and it was as an administrator that he was to make his mark.

Soon after joining the club he became match secretary for the Shields XI before joining the general committee, which oversaw all aspects of the running of the club. Unlike most of today's football clubs, which are essentially run by a chairman or chief executive appointed by the owner, the Rangers of the 1880s were a far more democratic body, run along similar lines to a bowling or golf club. Wilton quickly found himself on several of the key committees, including team selection, finance and ground development, before being elected match secretary.

One of Wilton's earliest achievements was the creation of the annual Rangers Sports at Ibrox. The event first took place in 1889, and for six decades it was arguably Scotland's most prestigious meeting. Wilton was particularly proud of the fact that the event was held in such high regard, and he has been given credit for the quality of the running track that surrounded the pitch.

The introduction of the athletics meeting demonstrated Wilton's wider influence at the club. He may have been the match secretary but this title did not do justice to the role that Wilton fulfilled. The remit of his job seemed to touch on every aspect of the running of Rangers, not least the development of Ibrox.

A LEAGUE APART

As a leading football administrator, Wilton was heavily involved in the formation of the Scottish League in 1890. After the huge disappointments of the two preceding seasons, Rangers would have gone into the inaugural League campaign with low expectations. However, their opening match – a 5–2 home victory over Hearts in front of 3,400 – gave some cause for optimism, and a 6–1 defeat of Cambuslang followed by an impressive 4–1 win against the highly fancied Renton filled the Ibrox men with confidence. A first-round defeat to Celtic in the Scottish Cup was a setback, as was a heavy loss to Dumbarton at Boghead the following week. With pre-season favourites Renton expelled from the League for a breach of the amateurism rules that still prevailed in the Scottish game, Dumbarton were emerging as the team most likely to win the first League title.

However, inspired by the goals of one of their greatest servants, John McPherson, Rangers recovered and the Ibrox men and the 'sons of the rock' were battling it out for first place as the season drew to a close. In an exciting climax, first Dumbarton then Rangers held the initiative, both succumbing to damaging defeats to Celtic. The two clubs finished the season tied on 29 points each, and it was ruled that a one-off match should be played at neutral Cathkin Park to decide the Championship. A crowd of 10,000 witnessed a titanic struggle that saw a cavalier Rangers take a two-goal lead in the first half before being pegged back level after half-time. The match ended 2–2 and the League committee decided that the only option was for the two clubs to share the title.

As the players received their joint winners' medals at a reception the following season, John McPherson declared 'Gentlemen, we are joint champions but we will not be satisfied until we become the real champions.' He surely couldn't have predicted it would be another seven years before he would be able to fulfil that promise.

In May 1892 Rangers held their first cycling meeting at Ibrox, which proved hugely popular. Two years later the first professional meeting in Scotland took place at the ground in front of a crowd of 14,000. World-renowned racers from England, America and Europe took part in the 'thrilling contests', which brought the crowds to a 'high pitch of enthusiasm'.

Despite repeated disappointment in the League, Rangers finally managed their first-ever Scottish Cup triumph in 1894 after two decades of trying, with a 3–1 win over Celtic at Hampden. Earlier in the season Rangers had defeated their city rivals 5–0 at Ibrox in the League. Interest in the game was enormous, with an 18,000 crowd paying a record £360 at the gate. Brake clubs – named after the horse-drawn carriages that carried fans to the games – were the equivalent of the modern-day supporters' club, and already Rangers were attracting support from all over Glasgow. The pulling power of the club was even more apparent the following week, when seven brake loads of Rangers supporters travelled to Renton for the next League match.

THE WILD WEST COMES TO IBROX

As football became increasingly popular towards the end of the century, crowds continued to rise. Ibrox was also fast becoming the place to be seen for those in the upper echelons of Glasgow society. On one memorable afternoon in November 1891 the *Scottish Referee* newspaper reported how the pavilion housed 'a real live colonel, a budding member of Parliament, and two Greater Glasgow Bailies'. It so happened that the colonel in question was also the most famous person on earth at the time, a certain Buffalo Bill Cody.

Cody was an American civil war veteran and former frontiersman, who became an entertainer and created Buffalo Bill's Wild West show in the 1880s. It was an international sensation. He spent the next two decades touring the USA and Europe with his cowboy-themed extravaganza, performing in front of hundreds of thousands of fans. The showman enjoyed astonishing levels of fame, particularly in an age when there was no television and no cinema. To much excitement, in the autumn of 1891, he and his entourage rolled into Glasgow for a three-month run at the 7,000-capacity East End Exhibition Buildings in Dennistoun.

Having brought his own brand of American culture to Scotland, Cody obviously felt the need to enjoy some local entertainment during his stay, and on 7 November he took in a match between two of the city's leading football clubs, the Rangers and Queen's Park. The occasion was a Glasgow Cup quarter-final at Ibrox Park. According to *Scottish Sport*, the gate reached the 'handsome total' of £280. The stand would mean £20 more. The paper went on to point out 'What with membership, season ticket holders, and free admissions, there could not be less than 12,500 persons present. Not bad for a Glasgow tie.'

There was a congratulatory mood around Ibrox before the match. Among the VIPs present were Bailies Ure Primrose and Guthrie, both 'staunch friends and loyal supporters' of the club. Sir John Ure Primrose would go on to be a Lord Provost of Glasgow, as well as chairman of Rangers and a key figure in the development of the club. Added to the exalted company was a Mr A. Stewart, the Unionist parliamentary candidate for the Hutchesontown constituency in Glasgow, as well as local artist W.A. Donnelly. The two Bailies were given a rousing ovation by the crowd to mark their recent 'creation', as was Rangers' goalkeeper, Haddow, who had got married the previous evening.

In true showbiz style, Buffalo Bill and his party ensured they made a grand entrance by turning up after the match had already started. Wild West enthusiast Tom Cunningham, who has written a book chronicling Cody's trips to Scotland, is in no doubt that this was a ruse to gain as much attention as possible. In fact he believes their entire presence at the match was more to do with generating publicity for the show than a desire to take in a game.

As they were placed in reserved seats in front of the pavilion by club secretary Mr Dunbar, the celebrities received a warm welcome from most of their fellow spectators. But for one of the Ibrox faithful the American's flamboyant appearance – 'long hair, lean jaw, keen eye, and billy-goat beard', as the *Scottish Referee* put it – was too much. 'Get your hair cut!' came the cry. It was a lone voice of dissent.

Cody, described as wearing a white sombrero and a very large patronising smile, was taken into the pavilion at half-time and introduced to both teams. It is unlikely that he had much idea what had been happening on the pitch, but according to reports he was quite taken by the 'blue shirts' and invited the Rangers players to visit his own show. On the other hand, the Queen's players were less than starstruck at the prospect of meeting the entertainer, and received him coldly. They clearly came round to him in the end, though, taking up an invitation to attend the Wild West show on Christmas Eve.

The most surreal take on the American's appearance at Ibrox came from the *Scottish Referee* writer, who was inspired to pen some verse in honour of the occasion.

I'm Buffalo Bill from 'cross the sea,
I guess this game's quite new to me:
I fancy the boys that's dressed in blue
Will give the other side their cue.

I hope the better team will win,
But, snakes alive, I can't but grin
To see the players jump about:
I'd like my "bucks" to have a shout.

I guess thar's sumthing in this game,
When such a crowd looks at the same;
I hope you all will see my show,
For I have been at yours, you know.

As for the match itself, despite being under the cosh for most of the game, Queen's Park eventually ran out 3–0 winners. A combination of bad luck – Rangers hit the woodwork six times – and resolute defending conspired against the home team. A few sharpshooting lessons from Cody would not have gone amiss. An interesting side note was the appearance of former Celtic defender Tom Dunbar in the Rangers line up. The *Scottish Sport* said of his performance 'We have seen him play better, but a first appearance should not be judged harshly.'

There was a tragic aftermath to the match, one that demonstrated the difficulties the authorities faced when it came to coping with the knock-on effects of the ever-growing popularity of the game. The magazine *Quiz* described on 13 November how a supporter drowned at a busy ferry landing stage after the game. The shocked contributor wrote:

That a life should be lost by drowning in the sight, and within two yards of above one hundred persons, is a deplorable fact, I witnessed at Kelvinhaugh Clutha landing-stage on Saturday, after the football match at Ibrox. The reckless rushing and scrambling of the hundreds who crowd the cluthas and ferries after these matches will not cease till some better provision is made to meet the extra traffic, or some terrible accident on a large scale takes place.

IBROX EXPANDS

Although Ibrox crowds were steadily growing for Rangers matches, the really big attendances were seen at international games and Cup Finals. Celtic Park was increasingly being used to host Scotland matches, so Wilton was determined to improve Ibrox to make it an arena capable of doing likewise.

In 1892 plans were submitted for an uncovered stand in the south-west corner of the ground and for a new grandstand. The south-west stand was an uninspiring affair, but the grandstand, designed by Glasgow architect John Gordon, was a fine structure. It featured a curved roof with a gable centrepiece, flanked on either side with elaborate cast-iron cresting, depicting three thistles and two stars. A terraced enclosure in front of the seated area was built up on a bank of engine ash. Four pay boxes provided public access for supporters, while both the home and away teams enjoyed lavish facilities for the day: two large dressing rooms, with communal baths and changing areas, were created on either side of the main entrance.

CUP FINAL CHAOS

Rangers were rewarded when the 1892 Scottish Cup Final between Queen's Park and Celtic, who had beaten the Light Blues in the semis, was held at Ibrox on 12 March. A massive crowd was anticipated for the match, and in a bid to cope with the demand, additional banks of terracing were installed at Ibrox along with the two new stands. The work took the capacity up to an estimated 36,000 but even this was inadequate in the end.

No fewer than 13 special trains were laid on for supporters in addition to the numerous scheduled services, and an estimated 12,000 fans arrived at Ibrox station. At noon, four hours before kick-off, supporters began arriving at the ground and by 2pm it was almost full. By 3pm the decision was taken to close the gates, but thousands had already managed to break into the ground for free while many more were turned away. The *Evening Times* described the rush as an 'eager, palpitating sea of humanity'. Under the directions of a Captain Hamilton, more than 100 police officers were on duty in addition to four mounted police – the first time police horses had been deployed at a Scottish football match.

The large police presence turned out to be essential, as supporters piled onto the pitch before kick-off. The horses had to be sent out onto the playing field to restore order before the game could get under way. The pitch invasions continued even after play started, and eventually the players decided they could not take any more. After a quick consultation with the referee it was agreed that the game would continue as a friendly, which Celtic won 1–0. The Final was rearranged for 9 April, again at Ibrox. This time the SFA insisted that the admission prices should be doubled in an attempt to limit the numbers. Second time around the Final passed off peacefully, with Celtic winning convincingly.

Hosting the game had proved a lucrative enterprise for Rangers. Takings totalled around £1,900, with £500 of that coming from the stand, which the club was entitled to keep. The remaining gate money was split between the SFA and the clubs.

THE GREATEST-EVER RANGERS?

Although the League title was still proving elusive, Rangers were growing in strength as the century drew to a close. In the 1896–97 season Rangers won their second Scottish Cup, as well as the Glasgow Cup and the Glasgow Charity Cup. A third-place finish in the League did not diminish the achievements of the 'three-Cup team' in an era when Cup competitions were held in greater esteem than today. The Scottish and Glasgow Cups were retained the following season, and only a 1–0 defeat to Third Lanark in the Final of the Charity Cup prevented a repeat of the achievement.

But it was the 1898–99 season that saw Rangers reach unprecedented heights and achieve a unique record that remains to this day. Captained by the legendary R.C. Hamilton, the team won all 18 of their League matches – a perfect record. It bettered the Preston North End team of 1888–89, which went undefeated but drew four matches, not to mention Celtic's achievement the previous season of also going through a campaign without losing – but again drawing several matches. The title was wrapped up with a 7–0 win over Dundee at Ibrox in the 14th match of the run, but there was no slacking in the remaining matches, with Hibernian – title challengers at one stage – being destroyed 10–0 the following week.

Even at the time, arguments raged as to whether this was the greatest Rangers team. The three-Cup achievement was seen by some as even more impressive. Ayrshireman Alec Smith was one of the stars of both teams – a legendary outside-left, who played for the club for 21 seasons. His view was that the 1896–97 team 'showed the most brilliant football I have ever seen.' He elaborated 'The 1898–99 team was a marvellously good side, but for purity of football, easy, confident, swinging combination, I think our three-Cup team was the better.'

It can also be argued that with only 18 games played, it is difficult to compare the performance with the achievements of the modern era, when the demands are so much greater. During 1992–93, for example, Rangers went 44 matches undefeated in all competitions, but the far smaller size of squad used by clubs in that earlier era can negate that argument – five players were ever present throughout the run – and the fact is that no other team of the time had come close to a 100 per cent record. No matter how it is judged in the modern era, the season remains the high point of Rangers' first three decades.

As predicted, Greater Glasgow's population was growing at a rapid rate and the Ibrox area was becoming a popular place to live. A railway station on the Glasgow to Paisley line served the district, and in December 1896 the city's underground railway system was opened with a station on Copland Road. The surface level station has long since disappeared, but supporters continue to use the subway to travel to and from the stadium more than 100 years on.

By the end of the 1890s the Ibrox capacity had grown and was attracting crowds of up to 30,000 for big games but it was still not enough, and with the end of the 10-year lease on the ground approaching fast, it was obvious that a new site was needed. Furthermore, the landlords needed part of the land for a new development.

In early 1899 Rangers began the quest for a new home. The land was easy enough to find – there was a site adjacent to the existing ground that fitted the bill perfectly – but Rangers needed to have their new ground ready for use within months, so to complete the task they turned to a man who would go on to become one of the most important, and at times controversial, figures in the history of the club, Archibald Leitch.

NEW IBROX EMERGES

Hidden away in the footnotes of football history is a name that will barely register with most followers of the sport. Even among keen students of the game's history, it may only prompt a flicker of recognition and some of those will probably have only the vaguest notion of why the name sounds faintly familiar. But for almost half a century, Archie Leitch – not to be confused with Archie Leach, the real name of silver screen idol Cary Grant – was one of the most important figures in British football. He was not a player, a manager or a trainer. He was not a chairman, an administrator or even a journalist. But people in all of those professions had reasons to be grateful to Leitch for his work. His talents did not lie on the playing field or in the pavilion but in the drawing office.

In the early part of the 20th century this Glasgow-born architect and engineer was the football stadium designer par excellence, the creator of the most famous grounds in Britain. As football rapidly grew in popularity, new stands and terraces were needed to house the massive crowds, and Leitch carved out a niche for himself as the man the club chairmen turned to first when they wanted to develop their grounds. Over the years, Manchester United, Chelsea, Aston Villa, Everton, Tottenham Hotspur, Sheffield Wednesday, Wolves, Dundee, Hearts and Kilmarnock were among the many clubs who called on his services. But it was at Rangers where he made his name and at Ibrox where he enjoyed his greatest moments, as well as his darkest hour.

Leitch's background is painstakingly detailed in the book *Engineering Archie* by stadium devotee Simon Inglis. Leitch was born in the heart of Glasgow's industrial east end, in the shadow of the Parkhead Forge. His father, originally from Lochgilphead in Argyll, was a blacksmith, a skilled profession but one without much in the way of social standing. Like many others of his background, though, young Archie was to rise. At the age of 11, he won a scholarship at Hutcheson's Grammar and on leaving school attended Anderson's College, where he studied science before becoming a draughtsman in 1887. After training as a marine engineer, he returned to Glasgow in 1890, where he married at the age of 25 and served with some of the city's most respected companies before setting up on his own in 1896.

By the end of the century, Leitch and his partner, Henry S. Davies, had set up an office at 40 St Enoch's Square, Glasgow, where they described themselves as 'consulting engineers and factory architects'. They had already picked up numerous lucrative contracts, but it was a meeting with officials from Rangers in March 1899 that would shape Leitch's future. Among the city firms Leitch worked for in the 1890s was sugar machinery manufacturers Mirrlees, Watson & Yaryan. A certain William Wilton was also employed by the company until 1899, and although it is not 100 per cent certain that they were there at the same time, it is probably reasonable to speculate that the pair knew each other. Perhaps it was even Wilton's influence that saw Leitch get his foot in the door at Rangers.

ARCHIE'S VISION

The club wanted a new ground to match their growing ambitions; and at that first meeting, Leitch – apparently a keen supporter – came up with a dramatic, some might have even said fanciful, scheme to create the biggest football ground in the world. Evidently he was able to persuade the club's committee that his plans were the way forward, but Leitch had to overcome the instinctive cynicism of the membership before he could turn his vision for New Ibrox into reality. He attempted this at a special general meeting on 13 March at the Trades Hall in Glasgow, where the members were asked to consider a committee proposal to form the club into a limited company. The aim was to raise enough funds to pay for the new ground's development.

Club president James Henderson set out the terms of the formation of the new ground and the liabilities that the club had entered into. It amounted to a 10-year lease with an annual rent of £200 for the first five years and £250 for the next five. In addition it would cost £2,500 to remove the present grandstand and terracing.

Then it was Leitch's turn to take to the stage. Bearing in mind that even the biggest club attendances of the day were around the 30,000 mark, his proposal for a ground that could accommodate 140,000 spectators must have sounded somewhat ambitious to say the least. The predicted cost of up to £15,000 – roughly the equivalent of around £1 million in today's money – did little to win over the sceptics. Leitch later outlined smaller alternatives, explaining that grounds to hold 60,000 and 80,000 could be constructed for £10,000 and £12,500 respectively. No matter which option was agreed on, there would be disappointment for one group of sportsmen. Celtic Park had a well-used cycling track, but the *Evening Times* pointed out that 'Cyclists, especially racing men, should note that the committee and almost the entire membership are determined that there should be no cycle track on the New Ibrox.'

Following Leitch's presentation, a heated discussion took place about the committee's suggestion that each member should get a fully paid-up £1 share. Various amendments were put forward, some calling for 10 £1 shares per member and others wanting five £1 shares. With no sign of any sort of unanimous agreement imminent, the meeting was adjourned for a fortnight, during which time Leitch's plans for the ground were made available for inspection in the Ibrox pavilion.

Two weeks later, the 500 members reconvened at the same venue to make another attempt at agreeing on a financial plan for the club and at settling on plans for a new ground. This time, Leitch pulled out all the stops. Instead of merely pinning his plans to the wall, he used the latest technology – a lime-light projector, sometimes referred to as a magic lantern – to throw images of the plans onto a screen erected on the platform. It was the 19th-century equivalent of a Powerpoint presentation and the *Evening Times* was suitably impressed, describing it as a 'unique and highly effective method of presenting the various plans'. It may have impressed the watching journalists, but of far greater

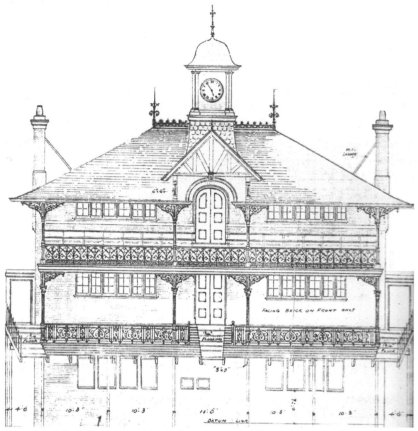

Front view of Archibald Leitch's original plans for the pavilion at the new Ibrox. The clock tower featured in the design was never built.

importance was the verdict of the membership. This time, they were convinced and agreed to go ahead with the construction of a ground to hold 80,000 spectators at a cost of about £12,000. A decision was also taken on limited liability, which provided the funding and resulted in a new name for the club, The Rangers Football Club Ltd.

The board, now with Wilton in the new position of club manager and secretary, met on 1 June to formally rubber-stamp the architect's proposals. The minutes read 'An offer was considered from Leitch the engineer with regard to the new ground, the terms being 4 per cent on the amount expended, this to include the services of a competent Master of Works.'

Leitch's partner, Davies, was duly appointed master of works, and their plans for New Ibrox were submitted to the Govan borough surveyor, Frederick Holmes, on 1 July and gained approval within two weeks. The new ground would be sited just 150 yards south-west of the club's existing home, with part of the new structure overlapping the old. Leitch had come up with an oval design, with an 11,000-capacity grandstand and standing enclosure occupying the south side of the pitch and another covered enclosure directly opposite.

John Gordon's stand from the original ground was kept and moved to the new Ibrox, where it was used as a cover for the north terrace. In later years, a large and prominent advertisement for the football fan's favourite half-time drink was added to the gable centrepiece, which earned the structure its nickname of the Bovril Stand.

An ornate pavilion featuring seating for 1,700 spectators, dressing rooms and the manager's office was planned for the south-east corner of the ground. Behind each goal, completing the oval, was a large, curved wooden terracing that towered 50ft above ground level, supported by an intricate iron latticework frame. A wooden terrace was favoured ahead of a steel structure because Rangers only had a 10-year lease on the ground.

Having settled on the design, it was now time for Rangers to find the contractors who would make Leitch's vision a reality. One of the winning tenders came from Partick-based timber merchant and saw miller Alexander McDougall. At a meeting on 1 August 1899 the committee accepted his offer to complete various timberworks specified in Leitch's

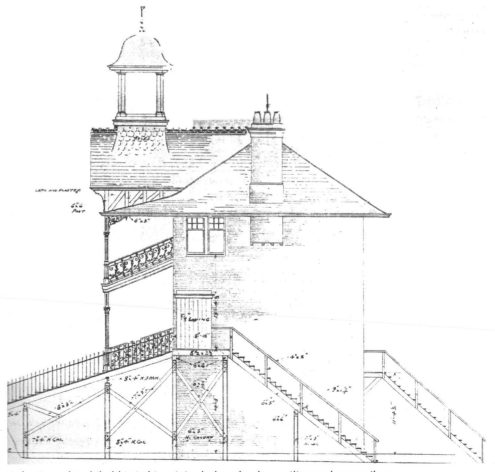

Side view of Archibald Leitch's original plans for the pavilion at the new Ibrox.

plans, including the woodwork in the construction of the new grandstand, the north stand enclosures and the pavilion. By far the biggest job, though, was the building of the two end terracings, stairways and entrances, which were estimated to cost the club £3,486 – around a quarter of the cost of the whole ground.

The work got under way in October 1899, with Wilton, Leitch and Davies taking an active involvement at every stage. All three men were on site almost every day and Davies in particular was heavily involved in the supervision of the construction work.

The final match at the old Ibrox took place on 9 December when a crowd of 5,000 witnessed a resounding 6–1 League victory over Kilmarnock. It was their 34th consecutive League match without defeat and was a fitting end to a remarkable period for the club. During their time at the first Ibrox, Rangers won the League twice, the Scottish Cup three times and five Glasgow Cups. As John Allan put it in *The Story of the Rangers*, 'The club, like a lusty, vigorous boy, had outgrown its old garments.'

THE NEW IBROX EMERGES

On 30 December – just two days before the start of the 20th century – the new Ibrox was open for business, with Heart of Midlothian the first visitors for an Inter-City League match. The inclement Glasgow weather didn't seem to deter the crowds, with a healthy 12,000 grabbing the chance for a first glimpse of the partially completed ground. The *Glasgow Herald* noted 'As it was, a goodly number took advantage of the chairman's invitation and the opening ceremony passed off very well indeed.' The paper went on to point out 'The new ground gave all a fair idea of the hugeness of the undertaking and there was a feeling that the Rangers had tackled with success the problem of accommodating the greatest crowds with the greatest comfort.'

Captain R.C. Hamilton was handed a brand new ball to kick-off the match, and he led Rangers to a 'rousing' 3–1 victory marked by what the *Herald* described as 'beautiful combinations and unerring shooting' by the forwards. John Wilkie had the honour of scoring the first-ever goal at the new ground and went on to celebrate the opening with a hat-trick. One well-to-do supporter marked the occasion by supplying a gold watch to the scorer of the first goal, but as the defenders and goalkeeper were unlikely to be able to take advantage of the offer, the players unanimously agreed that the goalscorer would gift the timepiece to trainer James Wilson.

In the early days of the new ground, there were alarming stories of the terracing swaying as supporters defied warning notices and a rope fence to get into areas that were not yet completed. It was assumed that the issue was resolved once the structure was braced. As Rangers powered towards their second successive League title, construction work continued, finally being completed in the spring of 1900. By the time the 80,000-capacity ground was finished, costs had soared to around £20,000, leaving Rangers with debts of around £9,000.

The next two years saw Rangers go from strength to strength on the field under the guidance of Wilton. The Ibrox men were League champions again the following season, winning the title by six clear points from runners-up Celtic. A fourth successive Championship was secured at Ibrox on 29 March 1902, when Rangers beat Dundee 3–1. With five matches to go it seemed Celtic had an unassailable lead, but they collapsed dramatically, allowing Rangers to come up on the inside.

Throughout this glorious period, Ibrox attendances had remained constantly high, if unspectacular, ranging between 10,000 and 30,000 depending on the opponents. Rangers were the country's best-attended club, but it was international games that attracted the really big crowds. That was why Ibrox had been built so big and partly why the club were desperate to bring the national team to Govan on a regular basis. It was hoped the Scotland games would go some way towards paying off the remaining heavy debts, although the status these matches would have bestowed on the club were also an important factor.

In 1902 Rangers lobbied hard to host the Scotland v England clash – the most prestigious international in the football calendar. The match was played annually as part of the British Home International Championship, with the venue alternating each year between Scotland and England. The proposed match on 5 April was to be the 27th meeting between the old rivals, and Celtic Park had staged the showpiece match on the last four occasions that it had taken place north of the border. It clearly rankled with Rangers that they had only once had the honour, in 1892.

Five days before the SFA was due to rule on where the 1902 game would be played, Archibald Leitch requested the assistance of the surveyor, Frederick Holmes, to boost Rangers' case. He wrote:

In order to strengthen their hands when applying, it might be advisable that you should inspect their ground with a view to giving them a report, that it is quite suitable for accommodating all the spectators who may be able to find footing. It is quite probable that a crowd of about 60,000 people may attend. Personally I have no doubt that everything is in order, still it might be better that both of us should go on the structure in order to have all possible precautions made for the safety of spectators.

Holmes duly obliged, visiting Ibrox and passing it fit for such a large crowd. In a letter that formed part of Rangers' submission to the football authority, he declared 'During the erection of the structure I inspected it regularly and have also inspected it on other occasions since completion and my inspection yesterday confirmed the opinion previously formed that not only is the ground suitable in all respects for all matches drawing large crowds, but that the structure is also perfectly safe for any crowd which can be accommodated on it.' In addition, in his letter to the SFA committee, William Wilton wrote 'In further pressing our claims for recognition, we beg leave to say that not only has our elaborate ground scheme left us heavily in debt, but would respectfully remind you of the fact that in the course of our long membership of your association, we have only once had the honour of housing this – the premier international.' Rangers obviously made a strong case, as the committee met on Tuesday 11 March and agreed by one vote that the game should take place at Ibrox rather than Celtic Park. It was a decision that was to have fateful consequences.

DAY OF TRAGEDY

At 1.30pm on Saturday 5 April 1902 James Smith and John McLelland set off from the north of Glasgow for the big match, Scotland against England at Ibrox. After a hard working week, the football would be a welcome escape. John was the younger cousin of James's wife, Elizabeth. He worked as a warehouse porter in the hat department of the wholesalers Arthur & Co and was single and living in Duke Street in the east end of the city at the age of 25.

Elizabeth prepared dinner for her cousin and her husband, which they ate before heading out in good spirits. From the Smiths' home in Petershill Road, the journey to the ground would have been a fair trek. First they would have to make their way into the centre of Glasgow, before crossing to the south side of the river and travelling the two or so miles to Govan. At Ibrox, they paid their one shilling entrance fee for the western terracing and made their way inside. The ground was filling up fast, especially at the front, and the two men decided to make their way to the rear of the terraces, where the crowds were thinner. It was to prove a fateful decision, as the pair got separated at some point. James never saw John again.

Shortly after the match got under way in front of a crowd of 68,000, the wooden terracing collapsed and swallowed up hundred of fans. James was safe, but when he returned home at 7pm that evening he told his wife that he feared her cousin may have been among the injured.

John had indeed been standing on the spot where the joists gave way, and he plunged 50ft to the ground below. He fractured the base of his skull in the fall and, although he was rushed to the Western Infirmary, never regained consciousness and died at 4.45 the following morning. His cousin had the heartbreaking task of identifying his body.

John was one of 25 people who died as a result of the catastrophic collapse of part of the Ibrox terracing. At least 500 more were injured. Alexander MacDougall, the contractor who supplied the timber and built the wooden structure, was charged with culpable homicide – the Scottish equivalent of manslaughter – but was acquitted after a trial at the high court in Glasgow. His defence pointed the finger of blame at the original design of the ground by Archibald Leitch, declaring that his plans were not up to the job.

An artist's interpretation of the aftermath of the Ibrox disaster of 1902.

THE FALL OF A STAND

From all over Scotland, football fans had descended on the south side of Glasgow for the game. More than 3,000 supporters travelled from Aberdeen alone, and hundreds more made the journey south from Tayside and Fife. Trains from Lanarkshire, Renfrewshire,

Ayrshire and Dunbartonshire also carried many fans through for the game.

Ibrox had never seen a crowd like it. The new stadium's capacity was given as 80,000 but it had never been more than half full until that day. To cope with the vast numbers, some 200 members of the Govan constabulary were on duty and the Scottish Football Association supplied 50 stewards. The stewards were generally friends of SFA members, and it was suggested that some of them actually gave up their role on the day, as the task of marshalling the crowds became increasingly difficult as the numbers swelled towards kick-off time. Thousands of fans may have gained entry after the stewards departed.

On the western terracing, the fans were growing increasingly excited as the start of the match approached. Among those in the ground was Ernest Tait, a joiner by trade, who lived in George Drive, Govan. Although the stadium was close to capacity, he recalled having plenty of room around his position at the back of the terrace. 'We could light our pipes quite easily,' he told the high court during McDougall's trial. Other witnesses also declared that the front of the terracing had been far busier than the rear. Although the ground was by no means full, pressure built up on the terracing and, even before kick-off, some of the crowd burst over the iron perimeter fence that Rangers had specially installed for the match.

At around 3.30pm the match got under way, with thousands of fans lining the edge of the pitch, kept off the playing surface by police officers. The fans remaining on the terraces were soon engrossed in the play. From his vantage point in the pavilion in the south-west corner of the ground, William Wilton had a good view of the terracing as the game progressed. He recalled later that 'The crowd was in a very excited condition and they followed the points of the game, stamping and swaying according to their interest in the different parts of the field.'

Scotland were shooting into the goal in front of the western terrace, and around 10 minutes into the game the home team had a good opportunity to score. The chance came to nothing, but reports at the time suggested that it may have been a contributory factor in the accident. *The Scotsman* described how the crowd surged down the terracing as the Scots pressed forward, with the fans moving back into their old position when the attack came to an end. Supporters pressing up from the packed stairway quickly filled the open spaces and 'an extraordinary congestion' took place, which put an unbearable pressure on the flooring.

Ernest Tait was standing on precisely the point where the terrace gave way. In his evidence to the trial, he told of the moment of disaster. 'The floor gave no warning before it gave way,' he said. 'There was a sudden crack below us. I had time to look down and see the joists split up and then we fell among them through the gap.' A huge hole 70ft long by 10ft wide opened up, sending hundreds plummeting into the abyss through a criss-cross of pine joists and steelwork onto the solid concrete below. The rescuers who arrived at the scene were met with 'a sickening spectacle', according to *The Scotsman*. The paper described how the moans of the maimed and dying mingled with the cheers of the

A cigarette card that marked the Ibrox disaster of 1902.

unknowing crowd in other parts of the ground. The wounds suffered by some of the victims left hardened ambulance men physically sick. Injured fans were removed from the wreckage and laid out on pathways behind the stand, awaiting the arrival of ambulance wagons. Metal sheeting had to be ripped out to get access to the victims, and this was used by rescuers as makeshift stretchers. Parts of the wooden debris were used as splints to hold broken limbs in place.

Meanwhile, back on the terracing, the panicked supporters in the vicinity of the gap pushed forward, causing another incursion onto the playing field. It was this that caused the match to be brought to a halt. It quickly became clear to those in the pavilion that something serious had taken place. Wilton recalled:

About 15 minutes after the game had begun I observed that something had happened on the western terracing and I left the pavilion to find out what was wrong. When I got to the ground I was told that there had been an accident and that ambulance vans were required. I was told that part of the terracing had given way and people thrown to the ground, but no details were given. I at once went and did everything I could to assist, sending for ambulance vans and for medical assistance also.

After a 20-minute delay, the decision was taken by SFA officials that the game should continue. Judged by today's standards, it can be seen as a mind-boggling decision given the extent of the carnage; however, this was an era when there would have been no way of intimating to the crowd what had happened. Had the game not gone on, the risk of further trouble was real. William Wilton was not involved in the decision-making but he backed the SFA. 'In the whole circumstances, looking to the danger of riot or disturbance, it was decided that it was better just to continue the game, and I personally thought that was the wisest thing to do,' he said. To the astonishment of witnesses, the area of the terracing around the scene of the accident continued to be occupied.

As the game continued, so did the rescue operation. The area at the back of the west terracing began to resemble a miniature battlefield, as the victims were slowly removed from the tangle of bodies below the structure. With clothes ripped to shreds, survivors emerged dazed and bloodied, some with their arms and legs 'hanging limp and broken', according to a newspaper report.

In one particularly gruesome account, *The Scotsman* described some of the injured as 'ghastly sights, one man having a big gash in the throat sustained in the fall, another with an eye gouged out and other mutilations of various descriptions'. Many of the injured were carried to the Ibrox pavilion, where they were treated before being taken to hospital. Some of the most seriously hurt were taken across the river by ferry to the Western Infirmary. The list of the dead and injured was pinned to the hospital gates, and a large crowd arrived to find out news of their relatives. Among them was the wife of George McAuslane from Cathcart, who had been married for just six months. She had visited all of the city's hospitals in search of her husband. At the Western, she was taken to the mortuary, where she was shown his lifeless body. Ernest Tait, however, was one of the lucky ones. He suffered severe injuries to his arms, several broken ribs and a sprained ankle, spending two weeks in hospital.

Special editions of evening newspapers were produced, bringing the first news of the disaster to the wider public. In Aberdeen the news filtered through by early evening that one local man had died and six were injured, and the following morning crowds gathered at the railway station to await the return of the special trains that were carrying fans home from Glasgow. There was a similar reaction in Kirkcaldy, Arbroath, Alexandria, Paisley and Ayr. In fact this would have been repeated in towns all over Scotland. It was truly a national tragedy.

A NATION GRIEVES

Messages of condolence flooded into Glasgow from all round Britain in the days following the disaster. King Edward VII led the grieving from the Scilly Isles, where he was onboard the Royal Yacht, passing on his sympathies to the relatives of victims and survivors. His message, signed by his private secretary, read 'The King has been deeply grieved to hear of the terrible disaster which happened at the football match, and wishes you to convey the expression of his most sincere sympathy with the sufferers in the accident and with the relatives of those who lost their lives on the occasion. His Majesty would like to know how the injured are progressing.'

A telegram was also sent to Glasgow's Lord Provost, Samuel Chisholm, from the Duchess of Sutherland, who wrote 'We are so grieved at the terrible disaster in Glasgow. Trust sufferers are progressing favourably.' Another telegram came from the Glasgow grocer and tea baron Thomas J Lipton. His message read 'My heart is full of sorrow for all who have suffered and I hope your Lordship will allow me to express my feeling of deep sympathy with yourself and all my fellow citizens.' Similar messages came from civic leaders around the country, along with offers of financial assistance.

A common relief fund was quickly set up by the Lord Provost to raise money for those who had lost breadwinners in the tragedy. It was estimated that 60 heads of families and around 100 single people who supported their household were among the dead and injured. In the days before the welfare state, all of these families would have suffered great financial hardship as a result of the loss of income.

Among the many who donated to the fund were the officers of the Govan Police who were on duty at the game. They generously agreed to hand over the fees they were paid by Rangers for their services on the day. The total may have only amounted to £30 but would have been gratefully received. The heavily indebted Rangers declared that they had no money to donate to the fund as a club but pledged that individual members would give whatever they could afford in a personal capacity. The Scottish Football Association had around £3,000 in their account and promised the whole amount to the fund, as long as they were relieved of all liability.

A public meeting took place six days after the disaster in the banqueting hall at Glasgow City Chambers. More than 300, including town councillors, clergymen, business leaders, members of the SFA and representatives of several football clubs, turned up to express their sympathies and help organise the relief fund. The Lord Provost revealed that £1,000 had already been raised. Among those listed as donators to the fund was Archie Leitch. Over the next few weeks the coffers would be swollen further by numerous fund-raising concerts and theatre performances, as well as football benefit matches.

As well as the grief that had engulfed the city and the country, there was a palpable sense of anger. The Lord Provost told the same meeting of one letter he had received, which read 'Somebody doubtless ought to be hanged, but that is too good to hope for.' Such a reaction might have been extreme, but there was a huge public desire to find out what had gone wrong and who was to blame.

THE INVESTIGATION BEGINS

Within days of the accident, newspapers reported it had been decided by the Lord Advocate, Scotland's chief prosecutor, and the Secretary of State for Scotland that there would be an official inquiry into what had happened, but this was not the case. Instead a criminal investigation was launched, centring on claims that the timberwork contractor, Alexander McDougall, had used an inferior type of wood in building the terraces. Leitch and Rangers had requested red pine be used, but it was alleged that the cheaper, yellow pine (also known as 'bastard pine') was used instead.

Evidence gathering began immediately, with a delegation of experts from the building trade carrying out an inspection of Ibrox under the supervision of Sheriff J.N. Hart, the procurator fiscal for Lanarkshire. As architect for the project, Leitch also attended, as did McDougall and SFA officials. Safety inspections were also ordered to take place at Celtic Park, Cathkin Park and Hampden Park before any other games were allowed to take place.

The investigators' reports were sent to the Lord Advocate, who had to take a decision on whether charges should be brought. In a memo, he stated that the legal papers 'disclose a grave case of fault in the matter of the yellow pine'. He made it clear that if Leitch and Rangers had specified the use of red pine then they could not be held criminally liable. Likewise, the Govan borough surveyor, who had granted approval for the structure, was not responsible in the eyes of the law, although his certificate 'may have been negligently given'. Following discussion with the Solicitor General, the Lord Advocate concluded 'It seems to us that all points to the responsibility lying on the contractor.'

Two weeks after the tragedy McDougall was charged with culpable homicide and served with an indictment. The charge alleged that McDougall 'culpably and recklessly and in violation or neglect of your duty' failed to erect the timberwork of the terracings 'in a substantial and tradesmanlike manner'. Specifically, he was accused of using 'wood of an inferior quality' and of fitting the joists 'all short' instead of the required alternate long and short method, 'as was proper and tradesmanlike'. As a result, 'the terracings were rendered insecure and dangerous to the lives of spectators'. For his part, McDougall's defence was based around his assertion that Leitch's terracing 'was too light in structure and design and that it was in consequence of these defects that it fell with the result stated in the indictment.'

THE PROSECUTION

On Monday 7 July 1902 Alexander McDougall went on trial in Glasgow before Lord Kyllachy, accused of causing the deaths of 25 football supporters. His defence team said prosecutors had failed to draw any link between the timber used and the failure that caused the deaths and injuries, but their attempts to have the case thrown out before it began failed.

William Wilton, whose address was given as 107 Pollok Street in Glasgow, was the first witness called for the prosecution. Having gone through the events of the day, he told the court how he had reached the scene of the accident at the end of the match. He said 'I visited the terrace about 6pm, and saw a part 70ft long x 10ft wide had given way. I noticed that the wood that had given way seemed to be an inferior quality of wood. I knew the kind of wood that should have been there was red pine and I noted that this was not red pine – it was what is called bastard yellow pine.'

Other witnesses concurred with Wilton's view that the wood used was not up to standard. Spectator Ernest Tait, a joiner by trade with 15 years' experience, told how he had gone back to the ground a month after the accident and saw some of the pine used was, indeed, 'inferior quality'. Ambulanceman George Wilson also told how he was a joiner by trade and had never seen such yellow pine used for bearing joists. He added 'The wood was perfectly fresh. It was just wood of very bad quality.'

On the afternoon of the opening day of the trial, Leitch took to the witness stand. He told how he had raised concerns with McDougall and his foreman about the use of inferior pine on numerous occasions during the construction of the ground. On the Monday after the accident he discovered that yellow pine had been substituted for red pine and that the joists had not been laid in the specified manner. In his view, had the wood been of the quality demanded, the accident would not have happened.

Despite the tragedy, Leitch was firmly of the view that his design was perfectly suitable for the task and that he saw no reason to alter his plans, as long as the correct timber was used.

The next day Frederick Holmes, the Govan borough surveyor, told the court that he had approved the plans on the basis that the joists were to be of first-class red pine and that he was satisfied, therefore, that the design was adequate. On his frequent visits to the site he was more concerned that the steel columns were in order, assuming that the correct materials were being used elsewhere. After the disaster he discovered that the broken joists were brittle and of an inferior quality. He told the court 'I have no doubt whatever about the cause, because the only portion that fell was where the bad wood was. The timber at that point was only from a fourth to a fifth of the strength of the timber specified.' The final expert witness, Neil McKinnon, also agreed that the wood used for the joists was of poor quality. Indeed he went as far as to say the wood was only 'fit for making packing boxes'.

THE DEFENCE

If Alexander McDougall was at all concerned at how the case was progressing, he must have taken some comfort in knowing who was going to enter the witness stand on his behalf. In the context of the case, it is difficult to imagine a more impressive person to have in your corner than Sir Benjamin Baker. He was a past president of the Institute of Civil Engineers, a laureate of the Academie des Sciences, a doctor of science at Cambridge and Fellow of the Royal Society. His greatest achievements were designing the Forth Rail Bridge and supervising the design of a scheme to dam the Nile. In his 40-year engineering career, he had been involved in around £20 million worth of public works, at home and abroad.

Baker was in no doubt that it was Leitch's design rather than McDougall's workmanship that was to blame for the accident. Having inspected the stand and the plans, he told the court 'I had no difficulty in saying at once that this was very much below the usual standard of strength. I mean that just as anyone who saw an omnibus fitted with the wheels off a cab would say that the wheels were light for the work, so in the same way one accustomed to building construction can tell whether a thing is light or not.' Damningly for Leitch, he added 'I should not think that the design and structure were safe for a crowd such as would be at a football match.'

Baker's evidence also reflected badly on the Govan borough surveyor. 'If these plans had been submitted to me as plans of a terracing for a crowd during a match, I would not have sanctioned them and no one would,' he declared. 'It has got to be rebuilt or strengthened. No one dare sanction it.' In conclusion he told the court 'If this thing had been all red pine of the best quality instead of the white pine that is there, the accident in my judgement would have taken place all the same.'

THE VERDICT

After a succession of defence witnesses who all cast aspersions on Leitch's design, Lord Kyllachy summed up the evidence for the jury on the third and final day of the trial. Tellingly, he told them that no matter how reprehensible they felt McDougall's conduct had been in using yellow pine instead of red, if they took the view that one was as strong as the other then they must acquit him. Half an hour after retiring to consider their verdict, they did just that, to cheers from the public gallery.

Leitch's professional reputation had been dragged through the mud during the trial, not least by the production of a private letter he had written to Rangers' chairman, James Henderson. In it he complained that the club had employed another architect, John Gordon, to strengthen the Ibrox terracings for a fee of £2,000. He felt that this would reflect badly on him personally and could jeopardise the case against McDougall. Ironically, the disclosure of the letter itself probably did more harm to the Crown than Rangers' decision.

The Scotsman welcomed the acquittal and said that the real cause of the accident was 'distributed on many shoulders', including the supporters who crowded onto an already fully occupied terracing. The paper concluded that the deaths and injuries 'constitute too serious a catastrophe to permit longer toleration of the rough and ready methods of calculation employed in the erection of such stands as that which collapsed at Ibrox Park.' The writer insisted that it was the 'duty' of the authorities to ensure such a disaster was never repeated.

THE REBIRTH OF IBROX

The 1902 disaster had a devastating effect on Rangers, both on and off the field. The club's reputation had taken a severe battering, and having run up debts of £9,000 building the new Ibrox, the board had to sanction the spending of another £2,000 on emergency works to strengthen the wooden terracing. In the longer term, though, the club knew that they would have to completely overhaul the ground to improve safety and that this was going to require major investment.

As a result, the club was reluctantly forced to put 2? professional players on the transfer market, so the 'four-in-a-row' team started to break up, bringing a glorious era to an end. Against the odds, Rangers won the Scottish Cup in 1903 but it was to be their last triumph in the premier Cup competition for 25 years. The League also proved beyond the Ibrox club, and their demise allowed a revitalised Celtic to take advantage, winning six successive titles.

Despite the criticism of Archibald Leitch during the high court trial that followed the disaster, the engineer was not abandoned by Rangers. In fact, when it came to redeveloping Ibrox in the early part of the 20th century, he was the man William Wilton and his committee turned to. In 1904 Rangers bought the Ibrox site for £15,000 and began the process of demolishing the discredited wooden terraces and replacing them with solid embankments the following year. Coincidentally, a railway freight line was being laid alongside the ground at this time, and the earth dug up to create the cutting was perfect for creating the massive embankments. Although this piece of good fortune would have kept costs down, the improvements still brought the total spend on the ground to around £45,000 – almost 300 per cent up on the original estimate of £12,000.

Thankfully for the club's bank balance, Rangers had never been more popular among the paying public, despite their lack of success on the pitch. For big games, attendances would regularly reach 30,000, and during the first decade the average League crowd ranged between 10,500 and 16,750. More often than not, Rangers' season average was the highest in Scotland, bettering even Celtic, who were enjoying an unprecedented period of supremacy on the pitch.

CROWD TROUBLE

By this time, Rangers and Celtic had already established themselves as Scotland's two biggest clubs and had developed into rivals as a result. While there was no sign of the religious and political tensions that would affect the fixture in later years, the games between the two clubs were always the best attended and often featured the worst behaviour among the supporters. Off the field, the two clubs remained friendly, gaining the infamous nickname the 'Old Firm' from a 1904 magazine cartoon, which suggested the teams 'manufactured' draws in Cup ties in order to play more lucrative replays.

In 1909 the Scottish Cup Final replay between Rangers and Celtic at Hampden was marred by a pitch invasion and riot. The match had ended level again, and there was some confusion as to whether there would be extra-time or another replay. When it became clear that another match would be required, the fans reacted angrily in the belief that the clubs had conspired to generate another pay day at the expense of the hard-pressed supporters.

Dreadful scenes ensued as supporters of both sides ran amok, ripping down fences, hurling bottles and starting fires. Police officers and firemen were also attacked as they attempted to do their job. It was the worst hooliganism ever seen at a Scottish football ground, but crowd trouble was in no way a new thing. An academic study published in the 1970s, widely considered to be the low point of football-crowd behaviour in Scotland, concluded that 'riots, unruly behaviour, violence, assault and vandalism appear to have been a well-established, but not necessarily dominant, pattern of crowd behaviour at football matches at least since the 1870s.'

Undoubtedly, the violence that blighted football in the 1960s, 70s and 80s was a reflection of wider social issues, so it should not be a surprise that the sport was similarly affected in the Victorian era, particularly in Glasgow. Scotland's biggest city has always had something of a reputation for drunkenness and violence, and at the time when football was becoming a popular spectator sport, it was certainly no place for the faint-hearted. Book editor and journalist Sir John Hammerton wrote in his memoirs, *Books and Myself*, that in 1889 Glasgow was 'probably the most drink-sodden city in Great Britain'. He said the Trongate, Argyle Street and, worst of all, the High Street were scenes of 'disgusting debauchery'. 'Many of the younger generation thought it manly to get "paralytic" and "dead to the world",' he wrote. *Plus ça change.* Hammerton also described drunken brawls on every street corner and told how 'sheer loathsome, swinish, inebriation prevailed'.

Rangers, with their large working-class fan base, had suffered as much as any other Scottish club from bad behaviour. At Kinning Park there were occasionally reports of unruly elements within the support, and of course the opening of the first Ibrox was marred by a pitch invasion. A newspaper report of the inaugural Ibrox game against Preston pointed out that a large number of the 'better classes' from the local area had attended the match, and the club was urged to do their utmost to retain their support. But to do this, the paper warned, Rangers would have to keep the 'rowdier portion of the crowd' under control. All a far cry from the almost genteel early days of the club's existence.

The traditional New Year derby match was often the catalyst for crowd trouble in the early days. On 2 January 1902 Ibrox played host to a meeting of the soon-to-be christened Old Firm. The ground was already comfortably filled an hour before the scheduled kick-off time, with thousands more waiting outside. According to the *Evening Times* the crowds stood 10-deep in Edmiston Drive and queued all the way back onto Copland Road. Passage to the Copland Road entrances from the subway was impossible due to the weight of numbers. With 30 minutes to go, police decided to allow thousands of boys to move onto the cinder track around the pitch, as both stands and the east terracing were absolutely packed to the limit. Supporters continued to arrive in huge numbers, and soon they spilled onto the turf behind the goals to escape the crushing.

The match finally got under way without any serious injuries, but 'mob law prevailed' among a section of the support and the referee was forced to bring the match to an early conclusion. The *Evening Times* pointed the finger of blame firmly in Rangers' direction. 'Two mistakes were made by the Ibrox management,' the paper declared. 'They had no sufficient policemen to control the crowd and they allowed more people through the turnstiles than could view the game in comfort.' Worryingly, it seemed that some of the lessons of 1902, still so fresh in the memory, had not been learned.

It would be unfair to tar all supporters with the same brush. Troublemakers were in the minority, and flashpoints were still relatively rare. Crowds continued to rise dramatically, and Rangers cemented their position as the country's best-supported club. Matches against Celtic were now attracting attendances of up to 60,000, and vast crowds were also turning up for games against other clubs. A Scottish Cup replay in February 1908 saw a massive 54,000 inside Ibrox. Crowds were still inconsistent, though. The same season's Ne'erday derby at Ibrox attracted 60,000 – but just 5,000 passed through the turnstiles for a home match against Partick Thistle the very next day.

After eight seasons, the League title was finally regained in 1911 with a record 52 points. The average Ibrox attendance was more than 16,000, and it broke through the 20,000 barrier for the first time the following season as Rangers powered to another Championship win. To meet the increased demand, dozens of new turnstiles were ordered and the terracing was extended. In 1913–14, the last season before the outbreak of World War One, the average rose to around 21,400.

THE LITTLE WONDER OF THE TRACK

In the early days, sporting achievement at Ibrox was by no means limited to football. By the start of the 20th century, Rangers' own athletics meeting was established as one of the most prestigious events on the sporting calendar. The city's athletics clubs also staged regular meetings at Ibrox, and it was one such event, hosted by West of Scotland Harriers in November 1904, that produced one of the greatest-ever performances in the history of British athletics.

The unlikely hero was a wiry, 'snake-thin' distance runner from Sussex called Alfred Shrubb, also known as the 'Little Wonder'. During his glittering career Shrubb won more than

Alfred Shrubb, who broke seven world records on the Ibrox running track.

Newspaper cartoons to mark athlete Alfred Shrubb's record-breaking performance at Ibrox in 1904.

" They carried me shoulder high off the ground."

1,000 races, but it was on the firm Ibrox track that he performed his greatest feat. With the backing of a vociferous crowd, he set a new world record for 10 miles, beating another six world-best times in the process.

Shrubb had arrived in Glasgow a week in advance of his big race and stayed at the home of Harriers official Jack Primrose Brown in Darnley Street, Pollokshields. He was treated like a returning son by the Browns, receiving what he called 'wonderful hospitality and cheer'. Mrs Brown helped his preparations by providing good, wholesome food that she deemed to be suitable for an athlete.

Conditions on the afternoon of the race were typical of a dreich Glasgow autumn day, but Shrubb had prepared well and was not disheartened by the grey, rain-filled skies. Nor apparently was the Glasgow public – a big crowd paid the sixpence admission to see if the Englishman could beat the 20-year-old record for 10 miles. He was running in Event Three, a race that was openly billed in the official programme as a world-record attempt.

In his biography of Shrubb, *Little Wonder*, Rob Hadgraft wrote 'When he emerged from the dressing room just before 4pm, the skies were dark and forbidding, but Shrubb was uplifted as the crowd

" The way the music of the piper relieved the monoton' of running round the track was magical."

ignored the joyless Glasgow weather and gave him a spine-tingling welcome. "The cheers almost lifted me off my feet and my hair seemed to go upright with excitement," he recalled.'

At Shrubb's request, the organisers had laid on pipers to provide a musical backdrop to the race, and the bagpipes were in full swing as the Little Wonder surged round the track. The crowd roared him on as he picked up the pace. The banked track was wet and

" Shrubb disna' break records—he cuts 'em doon like a harvester cuttin' corn wi' a scythe."

Another cartoon to mark athlete Alfred Shrubb's record-breaking performance at Ibrox in 1904.

the wind was blowing, but the running surface was considered one of the best in the business and Shrubb knew it well from his previous appearances. He was averaging less than five minutes per mile, and as he powered towards his target, the records began to tumble. First he beat the world's best for six miles, then seven, eight and nine. As well as the roars of the crowd, the skirl of the pipes inspired Shrubb towards his goal. 'In the last two miles, the help I received from those gallant pipers was greater than anybody can understand,' he said later. 'It put gladness in my heart and mettle into my heels. Never has music had greater charm for me than at such a time as that.'

To a huge roar, Shrubb crossed the finish line in 50 minutes and 40.6 seconds, obliterating the amateur record by 39.4 seconds and the professional mark by 25. But his work was not yet over. After the slightest of hesitations, he carried on running to the hour mark, breaking the 11-mile world record in the process. By the time 60 minutes had passed and he could finally come to a halt, he had travelled 11 miles and 1,137 yards – yet another record. The Ibrox crowd was ecstatic. Shrubb was hoisted aloft by spectators and carried to the pavilion to a chorus of *Will Ye No' Come Back Again?* The runner recalled later that 'They carried me off the ground amid such a storm of cheering as I never heard before or since anywhere.'

A year later, Shrubb was banned for life for accepting expenses, and he headed to North America to run professionally. He died in 1964 and his achievement in Glasgow on Guy Fawkes Day 1904 is now largely forgotten, but there is no doubt he deserves his place in the Ibrox hall of fame.

Another top athlete who competed at Ibrox in the first decade of the century was the first Scottish winner of an Olympic gold medal, Wyndham Halswelle. He was awarded his medal in controversial circumstances at the London games of 1908. Having qualified for the 400-yards Final with an Olympic record time, he was blocked by American rival Carpenter as the pair vied for first place in the closing stages of the race. The officials ordered the race to be rerun but the American athlete refused, and Halswelle was awarded the gold with a walkover.

In July 1908 the Scot recorded a time of 48.4 seconds for 440 yards at Ibrox, setting a British record that stood for 26 years. The event was St John's Young Men's Catholic Union Sports. Halswelle's final athletics appearance also came at Ibrox during the Rangers Sports, later the same year. Seven years later, the Boer War veteran lost his life during World War One.

WRESTLING

The athletics meeting that provided Alfie Shrubb with his greatest hour also featured a wrestling sideshow, featuring kilt-clad Scots grappling with each other in the middle of the Ibrox pitch. But a year later the stadium hosted an altogether more serious bout, as Scotland's champion Alex Munro took on the Estonian-born world champion George Hackenschmidt. Wrestling's popularity was at its peak in the early part of the 20th century, and Hackenschmidt was the undisputed star of the sport. He took part in a long list of engagements at packed British music halls before finally coming up against Munro at Ibrox on 25 October 1905.

Local hero Munro was a fine specimen. Standing at 6ft tall and weighing more than 15st, he was a full two and a half inches taller than Hackenschmidt and 11 pounds heavier. But other measurements showed just what power the Estonian possessed. Hackenschmidt's neck measured 22 inches, and his chest was a frightening 52 inches. His forearms and biceps were also both a good inch bigger than the Scot's.

A crowd of 16,000 braved the inevitable rain, and were treated to a bruising encounter. The first bout lasted almost 23 minutes before Munro finally succumbed to a half nelson. The second bout was shorter but no less intense, with both men adopting attacking tactics. Again, Hackenschmidt took the honours, rolling Munro over with another half nelson to win the contest.

That night, Hackenschmidt turned out at the Palace Theatre, just outside Glasgow, for another of his music hall engagements. He recalled 'The audience called for a speech, and after my saying a few words they stood up as one man and gave me one of the biggest ovations I had ever experienced in Great Britain. The kindly enthusiasm with which they acclaimed me as "a jolly good fellow" was such as I shall never forget for the rest of my life.'

THE ARRIVAL OF MR STRUTH

If William Wilton was the dominant force in turning Rangers into the country's leading football club, it was his successor as manager who took the club to the next level. William Struth was born in 1875 and grew up in Edinburgh, where he followed the fortunes of his local club, Hearts. His sporting interests were varied but it was as a runner that he excelled. A stonemason by trade, he became a professional athlete in his teens, picking up medals and cash prizes in races all over Scotland and the rest of the UK.

After a brief period helping Hearts players improve their fitness, he successfully applied for the job as full-time trainer at Clyde at the age of 32. His reputation was greatly enhanced by his time at Shawfield, so much so that Rangers tried to bring him to Ibrox as trainer in 1910. He declined the offer, but when veteran trainer James Wilson died four years later, he was the obvious choice to take over. Months later, Britain was plunged into crisis as war broke out, but Struth's arrival at Ibrox ensured that Rangers would go from strength to strength in the post-war years, dominating the Scottish game for decades.

A PLACE FOR HEROES

With millions of men dispatched to the horrors of the western front, it was hardly surprising that football crowds dropped dramatically during the war. Quite apart from anything else, there were simply fewer people around to attend matches. The impact on football clubs like Rangers was quite dramatic, with income sharply affected. In the first year of the war, Ibrox League attendances fell by more than 6,000 per match – around a quarter less than pre-war levels.

As the fighting continued, attendances carried on falling, although considering what most families were going through it is remarkable that crowd levels remained as high as they did. For many, football was an escape; a place where the horrible realities of the war could be forgotten about, for 90 minutes at least. After initially favouring a complete shut-down of the game, the authorities recognised the positive benefits football could have on the morale of the nation.

Although the Scottish Cup was scrapped, the League continued throughout the war years, but teams suffered from the loss of players who joined up for the war effort. Many Rangers players signed up and went off to the front, and on one occasion they had only nine available men for a match against Falkirk. Other players remained to work locally in the key industries that surrounded Ibrox, while William Wilton and Bill Struth also contributed to the war effort by working with the Red Cross, developing close links with the local Bellahouston Hospital, where wounded soldiers were treated. The Rangers board also agreed to make space available within Ibrox to accommodate casualties, if required.

Rangers only managed to win the League once during the war, but the foundations were laid for the incredible success that followed the cessation of hostilities. Numerous players who would go on to play key roles in the all-conquering team of the 1920s arrived during the war, including Ulsterman Bert Manderson, Sandy Archibald, Andy Cunningham and Tommy Muirhead.

A ROYAL VISIT

In 1917 King George V decided to visit Glasgow to honour heroes of the war, both military and civilian, at a massive outdoor ceremony at Ibrox. It was appropriate that Rangers' home should have been chosen as the venue for the investiture. The working-class industrial districts that surrounded the arena were key to the war effort, and the empire owed a huge debt to those who lived in the area's tenements and worked close by. As *The Scotsman* pointed out, 'Within easy hail are the great docks and the yards, where the busy hammers are clanging the death-knell of enemy hopes, and shell factories, where night and day many toilers are aiding the defeat of the German military machine.' Several thousand women workers from local munitions factories were packed into the north stand, and a choir made up of factory workers from Cardonald provided musical entertainment to the crowd.

After a morning touring the city, the king travelled to Ibrox from the city chambers in his royal car, along streets lined by crowds. By the time he arrived, at least three-quarters of the vast bowl was filled. In size, it was the sort of crowd normally only seen at football matches but it differed greatly in make-up. With thousands of men still serving in combat, many of those attending were women, and they dressed for the occasion. Rather than the usual monotonous, row after row of drab flat caps, the steep Ibrox slopes were filled with colour from brightly hued hats and dresses. Entrance to the stadium was 'first come first served', and there were huge queues outside Ibrox when the gates were opened two hours before the ceremony was due to start.

It was not just the crowds that brought colour to the scene. The ground was festooned with a multitude of flags from all the Allied countries. Notably, the US Stars and Stripes flew alongside the Union Jack on the roof of the north stand, and a long line of small flags hung above the terracings. The royal platform, which had a prominent position on the green playing field, was covered with crimson cloth and was surrounded by brightly coloured flower arrangements. The *Glasgow Herald* wrote 'The famous enclosure has housed many crowds, but seldom has it presented such a scene as today, when the sombre monotony of the football spectators' bonnets gave way to the blaze of colour provided by the military display.'

To the sound of a bugle, the king entered the arena in his horse-drawn carriage at 3.30pm and was greeted by deafening cheers from the crowd. The *Herald* described the scene in glowing terms, 'They waved tiny flags and handkerchiefs and cheered as though they would never cease. The demonstration was as a whole of the most superb character,' while *The Scotsman* said the welcome 'reinforced the spirit of loyalty and personal regard' for the monarch.

HEROES HONOURED

A company of wounded soldiers from local hospitals faced the king as he took to the dais on the royal platform, while the recipients of the day's honours were seated to his right. The greatest ovations were reserved for the three soldiers who were presented with the Victoria Cross, particularly Private Harry Christian of the Royal Lancaster Regiment. He had been brought north from a hospital in the North of England but was so ill that he had to be carried to the stage on a chair by members of the St Andrew's Ambulance Association. The official description of his deeds read as follows:

He was holding a crater with five or six men in front of our trenches. The enemy commenced a very heavy bombardment of the positions with heavy 'minenwerfer' bombs, forcing a temporary withdrawal. When he found that three men were missing, Private Christian at once returned alone to the crater, and although bombs were continually bursting actually on the crater, he found, dug out and carried one by one into safety all three men, thereby undoubtedly saving their lives. Later he placed himself where he could see the bombs coming and directed his comrades when and where to seek cover.

Private Christian was followed onto the stage by a cheerful Highlander, Private George Mackintosh of the Gordon Highlanders. His commendation read:

During the consolidation of a position, his company came under machine gun fire at close range. Private Mackintosh immediately rushed forward under heavy fire, and, reaching the emplacement, he threw a Mill's grenade into it, killing two of the enemy and wounding a third. Subsequently entering the dug-out, he found two light machine guns, which he carried back with him. His quick grasp of the situation and the utter fearlessness and rapidity with which he acted undoubtedly saved many of his comrades and enabled the consolidation to proceed unhindered by machine gun fire.

The third and final VC was received by ANZAC Lance Corporal Sam Frickleton, of the New Zealand rifle brigade. As well as the injuries he suffered carrying out his act of bravery, it also transpired that he had been gassed. The official description of his actions read:

For most conspicuous bravery and determination when with attacking troops which came under heavy fire and were checked. Although slightly wounded, Corporal Frickleton dashed forward at the head of his section and pushed into the barrage and personally destroyed with bombs an enemy machine gun and crew which was causing heavy casualties. He then attacked a second gun, killing the whole of the crew of 12. By the destruction of these two guns he undoubtedly saved his own and other units from very severe casualties and his magnificent courage and gallantry ensured the capture of the objective. During the consolidation of the position he received a second severe wound. He set throughout a great example of heroism.

The most poignant moments of the investiture came when the mourning widows of fallen soldiers stepped forward to receive posthumous awards on behalf of their late husbands. Among them was the widow of Lieutenant J. Giffen of the Cameron Highlanders, who collected her husband's Military Cross amid sympathetic applause from the crowd. Their two young sons and daughter watched the ceremony from the grandstand.

William Wilton and Rangers president Sir John Ure Primrose were introduced to the king as the day's events drew to a close. By all accounts it was a good-humoured exchange, with the monarch laughingly suggesting that most of the crowd at Ibrox that day would rather have been watching a football match. After the playing of the national anthem, the royal party left the ground to yet more cheers from the crowd and a chorus of *Rule Britannia* from the munitions girls. For the Ibrox men it was the perfect end to what had been a historic day – and a hugely successful one for the club, which cemented its reputation as one of Scotland's greatest sporting and social institutions.

THE LOSS OF A LEGEND

When the war finally ended in November 1918 the crowds flocked back to football, with Rangers again proving the biggest attraction. Average Ibrox attendances were back to pre-war levels and, although Rangers narrowly lost out to Celtic for the League title, there was no doubt that William Wilton had assembled a team that had merited such adulation.

The following season was yet another of triumph and tragedy at Ibrox. A dramatic end to an exhausting season brought the League title back to Govan – the 10th time Rangers had won the Championship. After the final match against Morton on 1 May 1920, Wilton told Sir John Ure Primrose how he had been 'feeling fatigued by the season's heavy work' and planned to recharge with a relaxing weekend breathing in the sea air. Immediately after the game, he travelled to Gourock with club director Joseph Buchan to spend a few days on the yacht of former Rangers committee member James Marr.

During the first night, with the boat tied to a buoy in Cardwell Bay, a storm blew up, breaking the vessel free from its mooring and sending it hurtling into the pier. The five men decided to climb the mast so they could escape on to the pier wall. Four of them managed to get ashore to safety, with Wilton the last to attempt to get off. As the boat was tossed around on the waves, he was thrown into the water. Despite the desperate attempts of Marr, who dived in to rescue him, he disappeared under the water and drowned.

It was a devastating loss to the club and to Scottish football. Ure Primrose described him as 'a prince among football managers'. Wilton was the first-ever manager of Rangers, and his contribution to the club's development is immeasurable. Not only did he preside over the move to League football but he created at least two great teams and signed some of the most famous players ever to wear the blue jerseys. Wilton's personal darkest time would certainly have been the Ibrox disaster of 1902 and the criticism he and the club received in its aftermath. But he led the club through that period and emerged from it with a great deal of credit, not least due to his co-ordination of fund-raising efforts that generated £4,000 for victims' families. And, ironically, it could be argued that his greatest legacy to Rangers may just have been Ibrox Park itself.

Wilton's other great legacy was the man who was to take over his management role, Bill Struth. He was the natural successor and, as it turned out, was just as successful, if not more so, than Wilton. The two men shared common principles of discipline and respect, as well as a common belief that nothing was too good for Rangers. Like his predecessor, Struth's vision of 'nothing but the best' extended far beyond the playing field. The players were famously expected to be meticulously turned out at all times and would incur Struth's wrath if they failed to meet his strict standards. At the same time, he was fiercely protective of his 'boys' and ensured that they always received the best of treatment.

Struth's man-management techniques were an immediate success. Rangers won the League in his first season as manager, beginning a period of domination that was unprecedented in the Scottish game and has never been repeated.

DEATH OF A GOALKEEPER

Another tragic day in the history of Ibrox came on 12 November 1921. Rangers took on Dumbarton and a promising 24-year-old former Scotland Schoolboy international named Joshua Wilkinson was in goal for the Sons. He had already packed a lot into his young life. More commonly known as Joe, he spent three years at sea during the war where, according to newspaper reports, he had his 'fair share of adventure', including being torpedoed twice. On his return to Scotland, he spent a season with Rangers and another at Renton before signing up for his home-town team, while studying for an honours degree in the arts at Glasgow University. According to his father, William, he was 'a young man of robust constitution'.

Dumbarton were no longer the force they had been when they shared the very first League Championship with Rangers 30 years earlier. They were destined to be relegated at the end of the season, but they played above themselves on the day and managed to secure a draw against the champions. Despite telling one member of the Rangers training staff he hadn't been feeling 'up to the mark' before the start of the match, Wilkinson had a brilliant game and managed to limit Rangers to just one goal, from Tommy Cairns. In the style of the day, Cairns had shoulder-challenged the 'keeper as he stood on the line with the ball in his hands. Wilkinson carried the ball over the line and a goal was given. Dumbarton players claimed the challenge was illegal, but the referee was in no doubt it was fair.

What very few realised at the time was that Wilkinson was already suffering from an internal injury, which he had picked up earlier in the game. infection set in, and within 48 hours he had died in hospital. At the Fatal Accident Inquiry into his death, several incidents were suggested were he might have suffered the injury. Dumbarton right-back Donald Colman, who had travelled to the game with Wilkinson on the subway from Partick to Govan, told the court that the goalkeeper asked him to take goal-kicks because he was in too much pain to take them himself. Despite his pain, he played on until half-time, when he complained his injury was 'pretty bad'. But he went back out for the second half and completed the game. Colman recalled 'He played extraordinarily well, right through the game.'

After the game, Wilkinson was violently sick. He went to White and Smith's, the restaurant where the Dumbarton team had tea after the game, but according to the club's director, John Carrick, he crouched down beside the fire instead of joining his teammates at the table. When Carrick asked him how he was, he pointed to his left side and said 'I have an awful pain here.' He said he got the injury when he 'knocked against' the Rangers forward Andy Cunningham. For his part, Cunningham told the inquiry he was certain he had not had any sort of collision with Wilkinson during the game.

As his condition worsened, Wilkinson was put in a taxi and driven home to Dumbarton. He was seen by a local doctor, who immediately diagnosed peritonitis. He was rushed back to Glasgow the next day and underwent emergency surgery at the Western Infirmary. Bill Struth visited him in hospital after the operation, and although Wilkinson recognised the Rangers manager, he lost consciousness soon after and never woke up again. His devastated parents were at his bedside when he died on the Monday morning. His father's last words to him were 'You have played the game too well'.

Mr Wilkinson may well have been right. Doctors discovered that his son had suffered a ruptured intestine during the game, which had caused infection to set in. The cause of the rupture was never established, but one expert speculated that the intestine might have been damaged early in the game but did not fully rupture until later, possibly as a result of his own exertions in goal.

Wilkinson told his mother that nothing out of the ordinary had happened at Ibrox and that he had not been kicked. His family were at pains to exonerate Rangers from any blame attached to his death and, as a mark of respect, the Glasgow club paid for his headstone.

It was a tragic loss of life, and it is sad that the death of such a promising and popular young footballer has gone largely forgotten. But in those more stoic days, the sort of collective, public grieving that is commonplace today was largely unheard of. Life simply went on and so did football, with both Rangers and Dumbarton fulfilling their respective fixtures the following Saturday.

ON THE TERRACES

The Ibrox of the 1920s had changed very little from the ground that emerged in the wake of the 1902 disaster. The only obvious differences from the early part of the century were the two solid earth embankments at either end, which had replaced the wood and steel terracings. Over the period, these embankments had gradually expanded and now featured Archibald Leitch-designed crush barriers. One iconic feature appeared at Ibrox around this time – the half-time scoreboard. In the days before loudspeaker announcements or Jumbotron screens, most British football grounds had these peculiar contraptions to keep fans updated on how their rivals were getting on, and many remained in place until the 1970s. At Ibrox the board rose up from behind the east terracing, and featured the letters A to P (but not the letter O, in case it was confused with 0). Each letter applied to a specified match, and there was a space alongside for the relevant score to be inserted.

Due to the huge, tightly packed crowds, stewarding was non-existent on the terraces and very few police officers ventured into the seething mass to keep order. In the circumstances it is astonishing just how few serious incidents there were, but self-policing

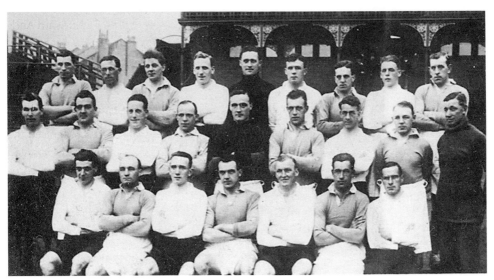

The Rangers squad of 1922 line up in front of the Ibrox pavilion.

seemed to work. As detailed earlier, only occasionally did trouble break out, although there were plenty of minor injuries suffered.

Thanks to the expansion of the terracings, the Ibrox capacity was now back up to around 80,000, and although average attendances throughout the 1920s hovered around the 20,000 mark, Ibrox regularly housed crowds upwards of 60,000 for big games, especially against Celtic. On these occasions the terraces would be a sea of bodies, almost exclusively male and of working age. Football colours were not yet worn; instead, the vast majority of the supporters would be wearing the working-class 'uniform' of dark suit, white shirt and flat cap, although the odd bowler hat or trilby would make an appearance to break the monotony.

Although many football historians suggest that community singing only became a feature of the terraces in the 1960s, there is some evidence that fans in Glasgow had been belting out their anthems since the early part of the century. Whereas the Liverpool supporters of the 1960s sang their versions of chart hits by the Beatles, the Rangers followers in the 1920s preferred traditional Scots or Irish songs or would even put their own words to hymns. It is thought the club anthem *Follow, Follow*, which is based around the hymn *We Will Follow Jesus,* may have been first sung around this time.

The boxy and somewhat characterless south stand, with its press box on the corrugated iron roof, remained in place, providing bench seating for just under 6,000 spectators. There was a large amount of empty land between the rear of the stand and the pay boxes on the perimeter wall, which ran along the length of Edmiston Drive. The only splash of colour on the structure came from three large Bovril adverts, which were emblazoned on the back of the stand. Its relatively uninspired design could be explained by the fact that in 1899 Rangers were still not convinced that they would remain at Ibrox for the long term. Only when they bought the land in 1905 could they be sure of a lengthy stay.

Alongside the south stand stood the pavilion, a relic of a bygone age. It remained an ornate structure, but its facilities were outdated and it simply did not fit in with the modern era. On the opposite side of the ground, John Gordon's salvaged stand from the old Ibrox remained on the north terracing, although the area was never especially popular among fans, despite the fact it provided protection from the elements.

Aerial photographs from the time show how the railway line, which had provided the tonnes of earth used in the terracing embankments, now ran right behind the north stand, which seemed to teeter precariously above the tracks. The pictures also reveal the amount of development that had gone on in the area around Ibrox since Rangers moved in, back in 1887. Tenements now lined Copland Road (Bill Struth lived with his wife at No. 193, which overlooked the ground), and a block of flats had been built on the land where the original Ibrox Park once stood. Where once there had been farmland, now there were factories and the skyline was dominated by the Clydeside shipyards further afield. These yards were increasingly providing Ibrox with a good proportion of its audience, including many workers who had come over from Northern Ireland when the Belfast shipbuilders, Harland and Wolff, moved to Govan in 1912.

The migration across the Irish Sea brought a new dimension to the rivalry between Rangers and Celtic. Although Celtic were formed as a Roman Catholic club and had always played on their Irish roots, Rangers were never defined by religion. The club's founders were of good Presbyterian stock but this was hardly surprising, as most Scots were of a similar background in those days. But in the early part of the 20th century, the politics of Ireland, with all its religious associations, arrived in Glasgow with a vengeance and changed the dynamics of the Old Firm. Reports from the era describe the Rangers supporters singing the Protestant folk song *The Boyne Water*, which celebrates William of Orange's victory at the Battle of the Boyne in 1690.

Celtic's mostly Catholic supporters openly flaunted their support for Irish nationalism, predictably drawing a backlash from the wider Scottish population, who were more inclined to be sympathetic to the Unionist cause. It has never been entirely clear why Rangers specifically became the 'Protestant club', but the arrival of Ulster shipyard workers in Govan would certainly have been significant. Equally important was the simple fact that Rangers were already Celtic's biggest football rivals, so it was natural that they became the focus for those who disliked the Parkhead club's mix of religion and politics. What is certain is that the sectarian lines were drawn then, and the religious divide between the two clubs has been a unique and often defining feature of their rivalry ever since.

Ironically, in the 1920s and 1930s Celtic were rarely capable of challenging Rangers on the field. Struth's team won eight of the 10 League titles available during the decade, and legendary players like David Meiklejohn, George Brown, Alan Morton and Bob McPhail were brought in to augment the team that Wilton had created. This new all-conquering team deserved a home befitting their status, and as the decade drew to a close, Rangers again turned to Archie Leitch to create what was billed as the finest grandstand in the world.

GRAND DESIGN

The plans to revamp Ibrox had their origins several years before the new stand saw the light of day. In 1924 a delegation from Rangers visited Aston Villa's ground, Villa Park, to view the newly opened Trinity Road Stand, designed by Archie Leitch. It was an impressive structure, widely considered to be the finest stand in Britain at the time. Leitch's design reflected Villa's status as one of England's most pre-eminent clubs, with its red-brick frontage, including a grand central stairway and balcony, resembling a Victorian civic building rather than a sports venue.

Rangers obviously liked what they saw, because Leitch was commissioned to redevelop Ibrox. Leitch, who was by now established as the country's leading football ground designer, divided his time between his offices at 30 Buchanan Street, Glasgow, and Victoria Street, London. It was there that he drew up his plans to replace the old south stand, which he had created the previous century. If the original stand was a utilitarian triumph of function over style, his new work would truly put the 'grand' into 'grandstand', both inside and out. The imposing Ibrox Main Stand would come to represent the power and dominance of Rangers, just as the Trinity Road Stand was a reflection of Aston Villa's stature in the game.

The plans submitted to the Govan Dean of Guild Court in May 1926 specified that the stand would have seating for 10,419 spectators plus space for a further 15,496 in the standing enclosure at the front. The original design also included a self-contained flat on

An aerial view of Ibrox from 1924. The picture shows the old south stand that preceded Leitch's main stand. The pavilion can also just be seen in the top-right corner.

the first floor, which featured two bedrooms, a parlour, a kitchen and a bathroom. The first phase of the redevelopment got under way in the spring of 1926 and involved the construction of a two-storey, red-brick office and dressing room block on the spare land between the old stand and Edmiston Drive.

When the heavy timber doors were opened to the press on 4 August 1927, they revealed levels of opulence never seen before in a football ground. Entering from Edmiston Drive, visitors were halted at the enquiry bureau before crossing the threshold into the oak-panelled entrance hallway. Across the chequered floor, beyond two prominent pillars, they would see a marble staircase leading up to the administrative offices. The scene remains almost identical to this day, a circular reception desk being the only significant addition in the last 80 years.

What probably will not register with most modern-day visitors, however, is the Masonic imagery incorporated into the design. The pillars, the chequered flooring and the staircase are all symbols of King Solomon's Temple, a key part of Freemasonry, and references can be found in every Masonic Lodge around the world. There is no record anywhere that Leitch himself was a Freemason, but at that time it would have been almost inconceivable that someone in his line of work and social circle would not have been in the craft. Whether the use of the imagery was deliberate or not has to be a matter of conjecture, but it would certainly be a remarkable coincidence if it was not included in the design on purpose. The symbolism of the design definitely would not have been lost on the Rangers players, as the majority, if not all, would have been Masons in that era.

Elsewhere on the ground floor were two large players' dressing rooms, both fitted out with plunge baths, a gymnasium and a medical room, which one observer described as 'an operating theatre on a modified scale'. The referee's quarters were more spacious and better equipped than most clubs provided for their own players. According to the *Evening Times*, 'Referees will miss the "Bird's Cage" heater of the old room, but revel in the facilities offered in the new.' Completing the lower level were state-of-the-art heating and laundry systems.

At the top of the marble staircase was the boardroom, a reception hall and the offices of the manager and secretary. A tea room and a ladies room were also to be found on the first floor, along with numerous admin offices. It seemed like the office suite of a modern, successful commercial firm, rather than a sports club. The furnishings took the business parallel further, with the *Evening Times* pointing out 'The inevitable table telephone, the orthodox "roll top" and the comfortable chair all speak of the prevailing mode of furnishings – stylish – but underlying it all, the note of utility.'

Centrally heated and electrically lit throughout, the building provided the most up-to-date accommodation possible. The wood panelling theme was continued throughout, with joiners Hamilton, Marr and Co. installing 2,000sq ft of mahogany, 3,000sq ft of oak and 3,000sq ft of Port Orford cedar. The marble work was completed by John Youden.

The woodwork was also a feature of Bill Struth's office, where he would work long into the night for the club he loved. Often his only companion in the huge south stand would have been his canary, which lived in a cage hanging from the ceiling of his office. Legend has it that Struth kept a wardrobe full of suits in the office to allow him to maintain his dapper appearance, even after a long day behind the desk. A notice on the shiny, mahogany desk read 'The club is greater than the man', a mantra that Struth lived by. Hanging on the wall was another motto, 'Be brief, I prithee, for time is short with me.' Warmth came from the large central-heating radiator below the window overlooking Edmiston Drive, as well as from the fireplace in the corner. On the wall outside the office was a small box with a button that the players would have to press if they were summoned up the marble stairs to see the manager. The box would light up either for them to enter or for them to wait. As Ralph Brand – who played under Struth in the 1950s – recalled, no one ever got the entry sign straight away. 'The longer you had to stand outside the office waiting, the more you knew something sharp was going to be said to you. Any Rangers player from those times would remember that. In fact it was just one of those small things about Ibrox that made it special.'

The press were full of praise after being given their first glimpse behind the scenes. *The Scotsman* described the entrance hallway as 'palatial', while the *Daily Record*'s view was that it was 'the last word in football appointments'. The paper's correspondent, Waverley, gushed 'Everything that mere man can think of has been brought in by the Ibrox people to make their administrative and training block the most sumptuous thing extant.' The *Glasgow Herald* was a little more sober in its description, although no less fulsome with its praise. 'The entire work has been carried out in a pleasing and practical manner by the contractors – the wood panelling and marble being particularly attractive,' wrote its reporter.

It was all a far cry from the club's roots at Fleshers' Haugh, where the players changed behind bushes and had to arrive several hours early to guarantee access to a pitch. The *Daily Record* summed up the progress made over the last five decades: 'What those dead and gone pioneers who launched the club on Glasgow Green, or even those who were at old Kinning Park, would say could they gaze upon the work of their twentieth century success one can only conjecture.'

If William Wilton had taken much of the credit for the development of Ibrox in the early years of the century, it was his successor, Struth, who was the driving force behind the new Main Stand. Board member Duncan Graham paid tribute to the manager, stating he had more to do with the new offices than any of the directors. 'His work had been unceasing,' according to the director.

The new facilities were first put to the test on Saturday 6 August, when 30,000 attended the 41st Rangers Sports at Ibrox. During the meeting, the League flag was unfurled by the wife of chairman Joseph Buchanan to the cheers of the crowd and the sound of *Scots Wha' Hae*. On completion of the new admin block, the much-loved pavilion was demolished and replaced with a new section of terracing, housing 6,000 supporters. Work could then begin on the remainder of the new stand.

Although times were hard between the wars, football was a relatively inexpensive form of entertainment. Entry to a First Division match in the 1920s was around one shilling, with transfer to the stand another shilling. In comparison, entrance to the Plaza's grand Hogmanay ball was six bob in 1929. To meet the growing crowds and predicted increased demand, at around the time of the new stand's construction, Glasgow Corporation agreed to lay lines and run tramcars past the club gates, meaning Ibrox could now be easily accessed by tram, train and subway.

With work continuing apace, Rangers had to decide what to do with the old stand, and on 12 April 1928 an advertisement appeared in *The Scotsman* headed 'Grandstand For Sale'. It invited offers for the 5,000-capacity structure, with the 'period of demolition and removal to be mutually arranged'. An indication of the influence of Struth on all aspects of the club was the fact that he was the point of contact for anyone interested in viewing or making an offer for the stand. It is difficult to imagine even the most dominating of modern-day managers, such as Sir Alex Ferguson, taking such a hands-on role.

At £95,000 the new stand was the most expensive built on these shores. The cost may have caused some eyebrows to be raised, but Struth was convinced that the club was getting value for money. 'It's all good Welsh brick and moreover it will be here long after the others have gone,' he declared. History would prove him correct. And it is not as if they were letting things slip on the field; apart from one inexplicably awful season when they finished sixth, 14 points behind champions Celtic, the 1920s was undoubtedly Rangers' decade. In 1928 they even managed to finally break their Scottish Cup hoodoo, winning the trophy for the first time in 25 years in front of more than 118,000 fans at Hampden.

Struth's management techniques may have been unorthodox but they were certainly effective. He never talked tactics with his players and never instructed them on how they should play. His belief was that if he gathered together the best group of players possible and got them disciplined, fit and motivated then they would do the rest. Morning visitors to Ibrox would have been met with the unusual sight of the Rangers squad walking round the pitch in their suits. Every day, the players would arrive for training at 10.30am, remove their hats and coats and step out onto the track for a lap of deep breathing.

During the 1928–29 season the backdrop to these morning walks was gradually changing. The old south stand was removed and work began on its replacement, finally being completed in time for the New Year's Day Old Firm clash. There were some similarities between the structure and Villa's Trinity Road stand, although the Ibrox stand was certainly more understated. Both were built with red brick and had large, arched windows along their length. Like Villa Park, the Ibrox stand had mosaic crests on both end walls, bearing the club motto, 'Ready,' and above the main entrance on Edmiston Drive, an imposing white sign bore the legend RANGERS FC in blue lettering.

Leitch's Ibrox design called for 19 rows of tip-up seats – supplied by the Bennet

Furnishing Co – providing accommodation for 10,500 spectators. In front of the seated area, the standing enclosure was deceptively large, holding almost 16,000. In between the two levels, running the full 476ft length of the stand, was the criss-cross detailing that was one of the trademark features of Leitch's sports ground designs. Although free-standing cantilever stands were coming into fashion, Leitch still preferred to use traditional upright beams to support the roof. There were six pillars along the length of the stand, which meant a restricted view for some unfortunate fans.

Perched precariously on the stand's roof was the press box, which gave reporters a bird's-eye view of proceedings on the pitch, although a head for heights would have been essential. Occupants also had a panoramic view over Glasgow, taking in the huge cranes of the shipyards, the spire of the university and the hills that surround the city. The box, which also carried the same lion crest and motto that featured on the outside walls of the stand, had a distinctive, if slightly peculiar, castellated design, adding something of a royal flavour to the structure. Leitch's original plans had called for a far more sober design for the press box, so one can speculate that the Rangers directors may have had a say in its final look.

Inside the stand, the concourses were bathed in natural light from the arched windows and overlooked a large indoor warm-up area where the players could train before matches, particularly when the weather was bad. Exposed steel beams and uprights gave the concourses an industrial feel, which reflected Leitch's roots as a designer of factories.

The statistics relating to the construction of the stand were impressive. More than one million red bricks and 536 tonnes of cement were used by the masons, Wilson Bros, in the building. The Glasgow Steel Roofing Co. installed around 1,000 tonnes of steel, while

Ibrox in 1910 featuring the famous 'Bovril Stand' that had been moved from the old ground.

joiners Lawson and Co used nine and a half miles of timber battens and two acres of flooring and linings. The wooden boards used would have stretched almost 38 miles if laid end to end. On the opposite side of the ground, the old Bovril stand that had been imported from the first Ibrox was finally removed and replaced with a smaller barrel-shaped roof, which provided cover for the rear half of the north terrace.

The official opening came as Rangers were powering their way towards yet another title. The dark days at the turn of the century were a distant memory, and the Ne'erday match with Celtic would signal that Rangers had completely moved on from the disaster, both on and off the field.

A dense fog had descended on Glasgow on the day of the opening, prompting one wag at Kelvinbridge Subway Station to tell the *Evening Times* reporter, Olympic, that they would not be able to see far enough to open a bottle at Ibrox, never mind a grandstand. On a bitterly cold day, when the sand-covered Ibrox pitch resembled 'an Arctic waste', the Govan Burgh Band raised a few laughs with their rendition of the old wartime tune, *Never Mind The Weather*. A group of wounded and limbless veterans of the war were among the guests in the new stand.

So thick was the fog that reporters could not see far enough from their vantage point in the new press box to accurately estimate the size of the crowd. The crowd could certainly be heard, though. Or some of them at least. The *Evening Times* reported 'Noise never means anything. I mean by that, that the Ibrox "sea lions" were already singing their club songs. Not a whisper sailed over the fog from the Celtic end of the field.' A desperate plea from the *Daily Record* that 'bugles, ricketties and noise makers' should be left at home was apparently ignored.

Before the match the Rangers directors were all presented with watches to mark the occasion, while the ever-dapper Bill Struth was given a diamond ring. At half-time, Glasgow Lord Provost Sir David Mason officially declared the grandstand open, telling the crowd via specially installed Marconi loudspeakers that 'the history of the Rangers was the epitome of the game in Scotland'. He went on:

A month or two ago the Rangers had their 55th birthday, but I have not heard that it was celebrated by a birthday cake. As we are gathered here today for another purpose, we may quite well celebrate the birthday as well...Fifty-five years ago the Rangers began an adventurous career on the Fleshers' Haugh on Glasgow Green. They had just enough space to play on and nobody paid the slightest attention to them. Today they possess a ground which comprises over 15 acres and which will accommodate over 120,000 persons...From the Glasgow Green they transferred their activities to their first private ground in Great Western Road, just opposite St Mary's Episcopal Church. From there they flitted across the river to Kinning Park and in August 1887 made the shorter journey down here to Ibrox...At that time even the most farseeing members of the club could not, I feel certain, have visualised the growth in popularity of the game, which has been the constant impetus behind the steady expansion of Ibrox Park, culminating in this handsome and spacious enclosure which you see today…A few simple facts and comparisons will best illustrate the wonderful progress of our great national game and the manner in which the Rangers Club have kept pace with the advance…Eight thousand spectators witnessed the first Scottish Cup Final in which Rangers took part in 1876 against Vale of Leven. At Ibrox Park in 1920, when Rangers and Celtic met in the fourth round of the Scottish Cup competition, the attendance was 85,000…Rangers' very first League match was played at Ibrox Park against the Heart of Midlothian in 1890. The attendance was 3,400. In season 1919–20, 75,000 witnessed the League game, Rangers v Celtic, at Ibrox Park…This handsome pavilion and grandstand, with accommodation for 10,500 enthusiasts, and a tip-up chair for each and every one, must stand as a monument to the enterprise of the Rangers directors. They are due the thanks and congratulations of all devotees of our fine old game, for it must add immensely to the pleasure of the spectators to be able to watch the play in ease and comfort.

Rangers director and former player Jimmy Bowie put it more succinctly: 'This is our magnificent new Main Stand. It holds 10,000 people and we could fill it 10 times over with young boys who want to play for the Rangers.'

Rangers went on to complete a comprehensive 3–0 victory over their city rivals. As well

Ibrox during an Old Firm game in the 1930s, with its new barrel roof over the north enclosure, which replaced the Bovril stand.

as pushing them closer to the League title, it was a milestone victory. For the first time since the creation of the Scottish League in 1890, Rangers overtook Celtic in the number of League wins achieved in the derby. The clubs had met in 78 matches, and the Light Blues had now defeated Celtic 26 times, compared to Celtic's 25 victories.

The balance of power in this football-mad city of Glasgow was now officially in Rangers' favour, and their stunning new stand stood as a symbol of their prestige. It would be decades before any rival would seriously challenge Rangers' standing as Scotland's pre-eminent football club.

A DARK DAY

On a spring morning in 1967, around 100 mourners gathered to say their final farewells to a former footballer. Sam English had fought a long and painful battle with motor neurone disease, but in his day he had been a phenomenal player. In his first season with Rangers in 1931–32, the young Ulsterman set a League goalscoring record that still stands today, more than 75 years later. Such exploits would normally be enough to secure a player legendary status. But not Sam English. His funeral at Cardross Crematorium in Dunbartonshire merited a tiny article, just 23 words long, in the *Daily Record* of 14 April.

In September 1931 another footballer was laid to rest in very different circumstances. Tens of thousands lined the streets of the Fife mining village of Cardenen to pay tribute to the 22-year-old Celtic and Scotland goalkeeper, John Thomson. Hundreds more attended a memorial service in Glasgow. Among them was a weeping Sam English.

Thomson lost his life after a sickening, accidental collision on the Ibrox turf on yet another day of tragedy at the ground. He had bravely thrown himself at a Rangers forward's feet to stop a certain goal, but in the process his head impacted with the opponent's knee. His skull was fractured, and despite the efforts of doctors at the Victoria Infirmary, he never regained consciousness.

Thomson's death prompted a huge outpouring of public grief, and he remains a legendary figure among Celtic fans. The loss was a tragedy for Thomson's family and for the football world in general. But for the unfortunate opposition player involved in the accident, it was the beginning of a personal nightmare that would shatter his career and haunt him for the rest of his life. That player was Sam English.

THE FORGOTTEN VICTIM

Born in Coleraine, Northern Ireland, English joined Rangers in July 1931 from junior club Yoker Athletic, where he had been a prolific scorer. At just 5ft 8in he was quite small for a centre-forward but possessed electric pace and an eye for goal. His impact was immediate. On his League debut, in the first match of the season, he scored two headers in a 4–1 win over Dundee at Ibrox. In his second game he scored five as Rangers beat

Morton 7–3. By the start of September, English had already scored 12 goals in six League games and had formed a highly effective partnership with Bob McPhail.

On 5 September 1931 English had his first chance to demonstrate his undoubted talents in the red-hot atmosphere of a Rangers v Celtic derby. By Old Firm standards, the first half at Ibrox was relatively uneventful for the crowd of 80,000, and both teams retired to the dressing rooms at the interval with the deadlock unbroken. Five minutes after the restart, Jimmy Fleming broke away down the right wing for Rangers and sent a tempting cross into the penalty area. As English ran onto the ball, Thomson came charging out of his goal in his trademark style and threw himself at the forward's feet. The pair collided, but the 'keeper managed to divert the ball away to safety. As he limped over to check on Thomson, English immediately realised the goalie was seriously injured and gestured for the medics to come on to the field.

Typically of a partisan football crowd, both then and now, the first reaction of the Rangers fans behind the goal was was to jeer. But they quickly silenced themselves as captain Dave Meiklejohn signalled to the terraces that this was serious. Watching from the stands was a Dr Kivlichan, a casualty surgeon at the central police station in Glasgow. He examined Thomson in the Ibrox medical room and diagnosed that he was suffering from a depressed fracture of the skull. He later told the fatal accident inquiry 'At the time, I thought the goalkeeper was going to die.' His opinion was passed on to officials of both clubs but the decision was taken to continue the match, and Celtic left-half Chic Geatons took over in goal. As the teams played out a meaningless 0–0 draw, surgeons at the Victoria Infirmary desperately tried to save Thomson's life. But at 9.25pm that night he was declared dead. The official cause of death was a depressed fracture of the skull, haemorrhage and laceration of the brain.

The entire Rangers squad attended John Thomson's funeral in his home village of Cardenden, along with an estimated 30,000 mourners. There were chaotic scenes at a memorial service at the Trinity Church in Glasgow, where thousands of men and women wanted to pay their final respects. Police trying to keep control were overwhelmed as the church doors were opened and the crowds tried to get access. When order was finally restored, Dave Meiklejohn read a lesson. Sam English sat with his head buried in a handkerchief throughout the proceedings, and he was seen crying as the *Death March* was played.

The service was conducted by Rev H.S. McClelland, a football follower who had witnessed the fatal accident first-hand. During the service, he paid tribute to Thomson for his bravery as a player, but he turned his ire on the supporters whose 'shameless jeering was the last sound that ever reached John Thomson's dying brain'. With barely disguised disgust, Rev McClelland told the congregation 'By chance it was a Rangers crowd that howled with fiendish glee as that silent figure, that had done such a splendid thing, lay broken on the ground. But if the Rangers goalkeeper had been lying there, as loud a roar would have risen from Celtic throats.' His hope was that the shock of the tragedy would bring an end to such 'ghoulish gloating'. Others hoped that the way the Old Firm supporters and players united in grief would bring an end to the bitter divide between followers of the two clubs. For a short while, it seemed that might be the case, but it was not long before normal service was resumed.

At the fatal accident inquiry at Glasgow Sheriff Court, English was entirely absolved of any blame for Thomson's death. But during the proceedings, Celtic manager Willie Maley caused outrage through ill-judged comments, which suggested that English may have deliberately injured the goalkeeper. Maley had been in the stand and did not actually see the incident. But, asked by the procurator fiscal whether he had formed a view on whether it was an accident, he responded 'I hope it was an accident. I cannot form any opinion as to what happened, because I did not actually see the accident.' Many years later, in his autobiography, Bob McPhail told how he could never forgive Maley for what he said. 'There was never the slightest doubt in the minds of every player on the field at Ibrox that day, that it had been an accident. It was a shocking statement to make in front of a court of inquiry.'

Despite being entirely blameless, English was vilified and persecuted for his part in the tragedy. Somehow he went on to score a total of 53 goals in all competitions that season, 44 of them coming in the League, but he had to do it to the sound of cruel taunts from the terraces. During his first match at Parkhead after the incident, he was met with shouts of 'murderer' and 'killer' every time he went near the ball. He stayed at Rangers for another season and even gained two international caps for Ireland, but he remained a marked man and in the summer of 1933 he moved to Liverpool in an attempt to escape the abuse. Even in England he could not escape his past, with opposition supporters and players taunting him. Two years later he moved to Queen of the South then on to Hartlepools United, but at the age of 28 he had had enough and quit the game altogether.

In a newspaper interview in the 1960s, English, by now living back in Clydebank and employed as a sheet metal worker, described himself as 'the second unluckiest footballer in the world'. Based on the electric start to his Rangers career, many believed he could have gone on to become one of the club's all-time greats. Instead, a moment of bad luck on the Ibrox field effectively destroyed his career and blighted the rest of his life. When he died at the age of 59, his goalscoring record set in that fateful season was still unbeaten, but he remained the forgotten victim of one of the saddest days in the history of Ibrox Park.

Despite Sam English's record tally of goals, Rangers were beaten to the League title by Motherwell – the Lanarkshire club's one and only Championship win. But it was a temporary blip, and they were soon back to winning ways, taking the flag for the next three seasons.

TWO GRAND SLAMS

Such was Rangers' dominance in that period that they twice won a clean sweep of all the major trophies on offer – the Scottish Cup, the League Championship, the Glasgow Cup and the Charity Cup. In the first of those Grand Slams in 1929–30, not only did the senior team sweep the board but the reserves also won their League and the Second XI Cup. The reserves were given their moment of glory for the home League game against Celtic in October. With seven first-team players ruled out due to international duty or injury, Rangers elected not to call for a postponement and pressed the second stringers into action instead. They responded by defeating Celtic 1–0, one of four victories Rangers recorded over their city rivals that season.

In 1933–34 the clean sweep was repeated, with players like goalkeeper Jerry Dawson, Dougie Gray, George Brown, Jimmy Simpson, Davie Meiklejohn, Sandy Archibald and Bob McPhail writing themselves into the Rangers hall of fame. Ibrox had become a fortress during that glorious period. A home defeat to Kilmarnock in December 1934 was the first in three years at the stadium, and the following season Celtic recorded their first League win at Ibrox for an astonishing 14 years.

FIRST FOREIGN VISITORS

In 1933 Rangers played host to the first continental club to visit Scotland. Rapid Vienna attracted a crowd of more than 40,000 to Ibrox on a bitterly cold January afternoon, far more than for any of the Scottish Cup ties being played on the same day. Although attendances were still buoyant, there was a feeling that fans were becoming slightly jaded with the domestic game, so the visit of the Austrians generated some much-needed interest.

After some pre-match comedy football from students in fancy dress, Rapid showed that they were more than capable of playing the game. Their quick, short passing drew applause from the appreciative Ibrox crowd, and it was no surprise when they took the lead with a well-worked goal from Bigan. A header from Bob McPhail put Rangers level and heralded a period of home dominance but, against the run of play, the Austrians again moved in front, this time with Ostermann beating Jerry Dawson. When Bigan scored a third, the Ibrox crowd reacted angrily and vociferously urged Rangers to get back into the game.

According to the *Evening Times*, 'some of the encouragement was in pithy language'. The paper also drew comparisons between the respective styles of the two teams. 'The visiting forwards were exceptionally good at short ground passing as a result of clever flicks and effortless touches. This was their most marked superiority and by comparison the Rangers were cumbersome in their methods.'

A reinvigorated Rangers fought their way back into the game in the second half and managed to pull level. Urged on by the Ibrox crowd, they might even have won the game, spurning a series of chances in the closing stages. The match finished 3–3 and the general consensus among players, officials and supporters alike was that it had been a successful experiment and one worth repeating.

LIDDELL TRAINS AT IBROX

As a former professional runner himself, Struth took a particular interest in athletics and the Rangers Sports meeting, which continued to attract some of the biggest names in the sport to Ibrox. Olympic gold medal-winning runner Eric Liddell, whose life story was later told in the film *Chariots of Fire*, was among them. In 1931 Struth learned that China-based Liddell was on a rare visit to Scotland and invited him to train at Ibrox – an offer that the athlete gladly accepted.

The Rangers players were in awe of Liddell and even Struth seemed on edge when he turned up at the ground for his session, ordering his team not to swear in front of the God-fearing runner. They need not have worried too much as Bob McPhail recalled in his autobiography. Liddell turned out to be quiet, polite, friendly and more than happy to mingle with the Rangers players. After a few visits, he started to take part in sprint training with them and was beaten by Rangers winger Sandy Archibald in a race over 440 yards on one occasion. According to McPhail, after the race Liddell 'smiled, said "Well done" and went to the referee's room to change'.

As well as big-name athletes, Rangers also fostered close links with local clubs. Clydesdale Harriers were among those who benefitted from their ties with the club, and Bellahouston Harriers were given their own key to Ibrox to allow their members to train on the track.

SWASTIKA OVER IBROX

An infamous black-and-white photograph taken 70 years ago shows the England football team standing in a line performing the Nazi salute. The occasion was an international match against Hitler's Germany at the Olympic Stadium in Berlin on 14 May 1938. In a misguided attempt at appeasing the fascist regime, the Foreign Office insisted that the players perform the salute. The result was outrage at home and a propaganda victory for the Fuhrer.

Two years earlier, Ibrox was the venue as the German national team took on Scotland. On this occasion the Scottish players declined the opportunity to raise their right arms in support of Hitler. But the Germans did achieve something of a propaganda coup by having two huge Swastika flags fly above the stadium during the match.

The German team and officials had arrived in Scotland on 12 October 1936 on a Lufthansa plane emblazoned with the Swastika. Their arrival from Cologne on the first-ever international flight into Renfrew Airport was met with a mixture of curiosity and outright hostility from the Scottish public.

After a night at the Central Hotel, the Germans trained at Ibrox in front of the local media. 'They are a fine looking body of men, strong physically and with the keenness of eye of the well-trained athlete, as all German youth hope to be,' one observer wrote. Despite that, it was widely believed that the Scots, with four Rangers men in their number, would be far too strong.

It would not be any exaggeration to say that the honour of an entire country was on the line at Ibrox that afternoon. It was only 18 years since Britain had been at war with Germany, and even in 1936 it looked increasingly likely that the countries were once again on a collision course. But the match was part of the Germans' attempts to portray themselves as friendly members of the international community, and the mood in the Scottish press was generally positive. 'Old Smith' in the *Daily Record* wrote 'The Germans come here as our friends. They must be welcomed as such. When the true spirit of sport is manifest, personal difference should be forgotten.'

Newspaper appeals were made, urging against any open demonstrations towards the German players during the game, and they seem to have been largely heeded by the 60,000 crowd. The only sign of dissent came from two young men, who were arrested after unfurling a red banner on the Ibrox terraces at half-time. In large white letters, the banner read 'Who murdered Jewish soldiers?'

With the Swastika flying alongside the Union Jack over the Ibrox stands, the Germans lined up on the pitch in their traditional white shirts, resplendent with a Nazi eagle symbol on each chest. In front of an army of photographers they raised their right arms in salute, before turning around to repeat the gesture towards the opposite stand. The salutes were performed twice more, during the playing of the two national anthems. In the stands, there were 500 German fans, who also joined in the saluting, much to the bemusement of the local supporters.

With the pre-match formalities finally out of the way, the match could get started. The Germans impressed with their fast passing and impressive ball control, and captain Fritz Szepan in particular caught the eye of the crowd, and not just for his flaxen hair. His contest with George Brown, the Rangers forward, was the highlight of the game. For the most part, Scotland were lumpen and predictable and had to rely on Rangers 'keeper Jerry Dawson to keep the Germans at bay more than once. As one reporter put it, 'Jerry beats Jerry'.

As the Germans flagged, the second half saw Scotland step up a gear, and two goals from Jimmy Delaney secured a hard-fought victory. On the final whistle, there were yet more salutes to the stands before the Germans finally left the field. A large crowd waited outside the Ibrox Main Stand for the players to leave, and afforded them a cheer and a friendly wave as they departed for the Highland-themed post-match meal at the St Enoch hotel. Given what had gone before and what was already quite clearly on the horizon, the reaction of the Scots was remarkable. The Germans were clearly delighted, if a little taken aback. Asked about the reception they had received from the Ibrox crowd, Szepan said 'We were pleasantly surprised.' The Schalke player continued 'I feel that games of this kind, in light of our experience today, should do much to promote a better understanding between the nations.' Similar sentiments were expressed by German FA representatives. Of course, any goodwill generated by the Ibrox match was forgotten three years later, as relations between Britain and Germany deteriorated and conflict seemed inevitable.

ANOTHER ROYAL VISIT

The 1937–38 season was Rangers' worst for more than a decade, finishing a distant third in the League and getting knocked out of the Scottish Cup in the semi-final by Kilmarnock. A Glasgow Cup victory was small consolation for a team used to picking up the big prizes. Crowds remained buoyant, though, and not just at Ibrox; inevitably, Rangers were the visitors when Celtic Park recorded its biggest-ever attendance of 83,500 on New Year's Day.

A crowd of 100,000 packed into Ibrox for the first time on 3 May 1938, but it was not a football match that attracted such vast numbers to the stadium. Instead it was a royal visit to mark the opening of the Empire Exhibition, which was taking place at nearby Bellahouston Park. During the depression of the 1920s and early 1930s, there were fears that the 'second city of the Empire' might be in a permanent slump due to the decline in heavy industry. The exhibition was intended to go some way towards re-energising the city, showcasing both its traditional and new industries to the world.

In fact, by the end of the decade, Glasgow was actually a city enjoying something of a resurgence in economic fortunes. This was largely due to the boost enjoyed by the

King George VI and Queen Elizabeth arrive at Ibrox for the official opening of the 1938 Empire Exhibition.

manufacturing industries as a result of the rearmament required to meet the growing threat from Nazi Germany. Nonetheless, the exhibition went ahead and proved to be a huge success, attracting more than 12 million visitors between May and December 1938.

King George VI and Queen Elizabeth (later known as the Queen Mother) performed the opening ceremony. It took place at Ibrox to allow as many people as possible to attend, and just like the investiture of 1917 the event was seen as a great honour for the club. On a sunny spring morning, Ibrox had never looked better. The entire stadium was decked out in colour, with the royal dais taking pride of place on the pitch in front of the north stand, draped in red and gold fabric. A red carpet swept across the green turf of the pitch from the south stand to the dais. Red bunting and flags from every nation of the empire adorned Leitch's Main Stand. And to top it all, music hall star Sir Harry Lauder, resplendent in kilt and blue bonnet, made a guest appearance.

The arrival of the king and queen was signalled by a fanfare from 12 trumpeters perched on a scaffold high above the west terracing, their brass helmets glistening in the sunshine. After a speech from the king, two squadrons of RAF planes dipped in salute over the stadium and then, to cheering and handkerchief waving from the crowd, the royal party departed the stadium for a four-hour visit to the exhibition.

Ibrox played host to numerous events during the exhibition. A national display of the Boys' Brigade was attended by tens of thousands of young men, many of whom took advantage of free admission to the exhibition across the road. A month later, 30,000 attended the national Boy Scouts' gathering and witnessed the release of white doves of peace. There was another royal visit when the Princess Royal, Princess Mary, inspected 2,000 members of the Scottish branch of the British Red Cross society, of which she was commandant-in-chief.

Football was not forgotten, though. A tournament was held at Ibrox to mark the exhibition, featuring Rangers, Celtic, Aberdeen and Hearts from Scotland, and Everton, Chelsea, Sunderland and Brentford representing England. Rangers were defeated in the first round by Everton, who were eventually beaten by Celtic in the Final. The trophy – a silver replica of the Exhibition's Tait Tower – remains at Parkhead to this day.

THE BIGGEST-EVER CROWD

As the war clouds gathered over Europe in 1939, it would be natural to assume that football would be the last thing on most people's minds, but that would be to ignore the astonishing public appetite for the game in Scotland during the decade. Attendances at the big matches had risen spectacularly during the 1930s, culminating in a world record crowd of 149,547 at Hampden to see Scotland beat England 3–1 in April 1937. That same season, Ibrox hosted its biggest attendance to date as almost 95,000 turned out for the Ne'erday derby against Celtic. But that figure was to be dwarfed when the old stadium next hosted the traditional festive season clash two years later.

By any standards, Monday 2 January 1939 was an exceptional day in the attendance stakes. The 10 First Division matches that afternoon were watched by a total of 268,000 people, including 45,061 at Tynecastle for the Edinburgh derby. Even Ayr United's middle-of-the table meeting with Queen of the South attracted a 12,200 gate, not far short of a record for the ground. But it was the turnout for the Old Firm match at Ibrox that made the headlines. Officially, there were 118,730 paying customers inside Ibrox – the biggest crowd for a League match the world had ever seen. In fact, it is likely that the true figure was even higher, as official attendance figures were often little more than educated guesses in those days. The number of fans who managed to sneak in without paying, combined with the youngsters who got a free lift over the turnstiles, would also swell the crowd by a few thousand. Just how many of the vast crowd would have actually seen the play on the field is another matter. It was estimated that thousands passed through the turnstiles but did not even manage to reach the rim of the huge Ibrox bowl. They had to rely on running commentaries of the action being passed down from fans who had managed to scramble far enough up the stairways to get a view.

Remarkably, pre-match predictions were for a crowd of around 60,000, which in itself would have been a tremendous attendance for any other match in Britain. But on a cold, dry day, the scenes in Glasgow city centre in the hours leading up to kick-off suggested that this was going to be something special. Southbound buses and trams crammed with supporters swept past packed stops, unable to take any more passengers. Huge queues snaked from the city centre underground stations, as thousands of supporters squeezed into trains heading south of the river towards Ibrox. Many decided the best option to get to the stadium was to travel the long way round the circular line. Others decided walking was the easiest option. The following day's *Daily Record* opined 'How everybody got to Ibrox is something of a mystery – and a miracle.'

Those who managed to reach the ground found themselves in yet more queues. Long before kick-off, the gates at the east end of the ground – the traditional 'Rangers End' – were closed, and mounted police shepherded the supporters to the other end of the stadium. Considering the numbers, the mood was good-humoured as the fans shuffled along to the opposite gates, but it wasn't long before these too were closed. An estimated 30,000 were turned away.

Inside the ground, barely an inch of space could be found. One report described the crowd as 'a seething, swaying mass of humanity, squeezing and manoeuvring for places from which they could glimpse the match spectacle which had set the throng roaring.' Some adventurous youths scaled the half-time scoreboard to get a view, others climbed drainpipes. Thousands more simply walked around for the duration of the game, unable to see anything other than the backs of those in the top row of the terracing.

Despite everything, the crowd was remarkably well behaved and there were very few injuries. Medics treated 80 supporters, mainly for crushing. Four needed treatment at the Victoria Infirmary, with one 61-year-old man detained for rib injuries. A girl collecting money for a local charity at half-time was also treated by ambulance men. She was left with a bloodied nose after being hit by a penny that was thrown towards her collection sheet.

The match itself was worthy of the massive crowd. The frenzy from the terraces seemed to be transmitted onto the pitch, and the game was played at a frantic pace. The home team started well, with two future managers (Scot Symon and Willie Waddell), a future assistant manager (Willie Thornton) and a future coach (Davie Kinnear) in their line up. Forward Alex Venters, who was always a thorn in Celtic's side, was a particular danger as Rangers' short-passing game flummoxed their opponents. Rangers opened the scoring in the first half through Kinnear, and Venters added a second before half-time. Celtic rallied in the second half and pulled a goal back but did not do enough to get the equaliser.

In the Blue Room after the game, Rangers chairman Jimmy Bowie was joined by various dignitaries, including his Celtic counterpart Tom White, Glasgow Lord Provost Patrick Dollan and Scottish League secretary William MacAndrew. During the post-match speeches Bowie predicted that the day's record crowd would soon be broken and that Rangers would be required to increase the capacity of Ibrox. In fact, he was wrong on both counts. World War Two was on the horizon, and this would be a high point as far as League crowds were concerned. Huge crowds, including several of more than 100,000, would still be seen after the war – and right up until the early 1970s – but the general trend would be downward.

The size of the crowd prompted immediate calls for the annual New Year meeting between Rangers and Celtic to be all-ticket, something that only applied to Scotland internationals at Hampden at the time. In a newspaper interview the day after the match, Bill Struth said such a move might be advisable if huge crowds were to become a regular occurrence. However, he was confident that Ibrox would easily be able to accommodate such attendances in the future. 'So far as Ibrox stadium is concerned, by the time the match comes around again, we will be able to take everybody who comes to it,' he said. 'We have alterations going on in the grounds just now that will give accommodation for 20,000 more. At present the accommodation is 136,000 if the spectators are properly packed.'

WAR AND PEACE

In September 1939 the inevitable happened and Britain declared war on Germany after Hitler's invasion of Poland. Football continued throughout the fighting, albeit in a limited form. The Scottish Cup was suspended and leagues were regionalised. Attendances were limited to 50 per cent of grounds' capacity, although there was an understandable drop in interest in the early years of the war. With the very real threat of air attack or invasion, suddenly football did not seem quite so important.

In January 1940 Ibrox hosted its first Old Firm derby since the outbreak of war. Following the record crowd of 1939, the decision was taken to make the match all-ticket. With a seat in the south stand costing five shillings, demand for tickets was less than overwhelming. A crowd of around 40,000 – a third of the attendance at the last Ibrox clash between the teams – turned out to see the rivals draw 1–1. Tickets were even being sold outside the ground by supporters who found themselves with too many, and it was realised that there would be no need for all-ticket matches while the country was at war, even between Rangers and Celtic.

For the third time, Ibrox received the royal seal of approval as the king and queen paid another visit in March 1941. In a show of strength aimed at keeping spirits up on the Home Front, the civil defence services put on a display in front of a large crowd mostly made up of schoolchildren and their teachers. The young audience cheered and waved handkerchiefs in appreciation as the royal couple emerged from the tunnel, before being introduced to the men and women of the ARP services. As they left the stadium, the king and queen were mobbed by crowds of young people on Edmiston Drive. The visit further reinforced the stadium's position at the heart of the community during the war.

HOME-FRONT HOSTILITIES

In September 1941 the world was in turmoil. In Leningrad, Russian troops were desperately fighting to keep the Germans out of their city. Off the coast of Iceland, a German U-boat was launching a torpedo at an American destroyer. In Washington, President Roosevelt was pondering whether to go to war with Japan. And in cities across Britain, tens of thousands of families were coming to terms with the fact that their homes had been reduced to rubble as a result of months of Luftwaffe bombing. But in Glasgow, it seems even the horrors of war took second place to the madness of the Old Firm. Apparently, the need for national unity against a common enemy was nothing compared to football fans' need to behave badly.

In front of a crowd of 60,000 at Ibrox, Rangers and Celtic met on 6 September in the Southern League. The Light Blues had enjoyed a good start to the campaign, winning their first four matches, and they raced into an early 2–0 lead. The match was being played in good atmosphere, until all hell broke loose four minutes before half-time. As he waited for a Celtic corner, Rangers goalkeeper Jerry Dawson shoved the opposing forward, Jimmy Delaney, to the ground in retaliation at being impeded.

A penalty was awarded, which the Scotland 'keeper duly saved. But the Celtic supporters massed on the western terrace, behind Dawson's goal, did not take the save well. Hundreds of beer and milk bottles were hurled from the Ibrox slopes in the general direction of the pitch, and fighting broke out behind the goal. On the orders of assistant chief constable Walter Docherty, a squad of police officers were dispatched into the heart of the disturbance, with truncheons drawn. Despite coming under attack from the Celtic supporters, the officers eventually managed to restore order but not before several fans were taken away on stretchers, mostly due to being hit by the flying bottles that filled the air.

The match eventually got under way again, and Rangers ran out 3–0 winners. But it was the scenes on the terracings that made all the headlines. The *Daily Record* described events as 'a ghastly travesty of sport' and 'a sickening spectacle for any decent minded man'. Glasgow Lord Provost Patrick Dollan threatened to ban Old Firm games for the duration of the war in an attempt to prevent further violence. In the end, just five arrests were made and four men escaped with small fines after appearing at Govan Police Court the following Monday. In handing down the sentences, Baillie Scanlon told the men 'If I thought it would stop such disgraceful scenes I would send you to prison.'

The behaviour of the Celtic fans that day would have provoked public outrage at the best of times, but during a time of national emergency it was seen as something approaching an act of treason by many. Men serving on the front line were furious to learn of the trouble. Two airmen who wrote to the *Sunday Mail* suggested that the way to deal with the problem was to force supporters from both teams to join the RAF and 'fight for something worthwhile'. Another letter from a 'disgusted' sailor based on a minesweeper on the south coast of England recommended a mine was dropped on the offending fans. He added, though, that this might be just a bit too quick for the 'rats' and that 'something slower and more painful might be better'.

The *Mail* columnist, 'Rex', condemned both clubs for failing to reduce the 'religious heat' that attracted such huge crowds to the derby matches. He wrote 'One would almost think they have encouraged it to ensure such crowds. The game itself seems now to be merely a thin cover for the "Billy or a Dan" challenge.'

It was the fourth time since war had broken out that Celtic supporters had been involved in violence on the terraces – the second at Ibrox – and when the SFA came to consider their punishment, they decided to come down hard. The association's War Emergency Committee shut down Parkhead for a month and banned the club from playing anywhere in Glasgow during that period. In a statement, the committee said it sympathised with Celtic for 'having a section of supporters of an undesirable type' but the only way they had of punishing the hooligans was by taking action against the club. The SFA also condemned the courts for failing to impose tougher sentences on the offenders. Rangers did not escape censure. The committee were unhappy at the way the home players showed dissent towards the match officials and ordered that referees would be removed from the list if they failed to deal with such behaviour from players in the future.

The war had some practical effect on Ibrox. The Rangers FC sign on the roof of the Main Stand was covered up, presumably in an attempt to confuse any passing German invaders. The stadium was also pressed into action towards the end of the war as a prisoner of war transit camp. Despite its proximity to the Clyde shipyards, the stadium avoided the attentions of German bombers and so was ready to return to full-time action when hostilities ceased in 1945.

THE IRON CURTAIN AT IBROX

In a 1946 speech about the post-war rise of the USSR and the Eastern Bloc, Winston Churchill popularised the phrase 'the Iron Curtain', relating to the division between communist eastern Europe and the West. 'From Stettin in the Baltic to Trieste in the Adriatic, an Iron Curtain has descended across the continent.' Rangers had their own version – a legendary defensive line that was even more difficult to get through than Checkpoint Charlie. In the post-war years, that defence would provide the foundation for another period of Rangers dominance.

Before the Kremlin pulled their own Iron Curtain tightly closed, Dynamo Moscow – the Soviet Union's leading team – visited Britain. Having come through matches with Chelsea, Arsenal and Cardiff undefeated, the Russians arrived in Glasgow in November 1945 for the climax of their tour – a match against Rangers at Ibrox. There was extraordinary interest in the game from the Scottish public, with unprecedented demand for tickets. In the days before European competition, visits from foreign teams were still a novelty and the aura of mystery surrounding the Soviets only added to the intrigue. In the run-up to the match, the newspapers were filled with stories of military-style training sessions and super-fit players, playing up the stereotype of machine-like Soviet athletes.

When tickets went on sale, queues stretched for miles, with some fans standing in line for up to 16 hours to get their hands on one. Unsurprisingly Ibrox quickly sold out, resulting in a black market that saw single tickets for the Main Stand being snapped up for a remarkable £30. This for a match that was to take place on a Wednesday afternoon.

There was a dramatic development on the eve of the match, when the Russians objected to Rangers playing Jimmy Caskie, who had recently been signed from Everton. After several hours of diplomatic jousting, which saw the Russians threaten to go home without playing the game, Rangers finally announced at midnight that they would not play Caskie. The crisis was averted, but the spat did little for relations between the two clubs ahead of the game.

By the time the game came around, Glasgow was at fever pitch. The Wednesday afternoon kick-off meant factories and offices across the city were empty, as thousands of workers took the day off to see the big game. For once, it lived up to the hype. The match would go down as one of the greatest in the history of Ibrox.

On a bright autumn day, the City of Glasgow Police pipe band entertained the 95,000 crowd before the kick-off. The two teams walked out of the Ibrox tunnel side by side, Dynamo in blue jerseys with a large white 'D' on the chest, Rangers in unusual blue and white hoops – a throwback to the colours they sported for three seasons in the early 1880s. The Russians presented Rangers with bouquets of flowers before the two teams stood to attention for the national anthems. Finally, after Glasgow's Lord Provost was presented to the players, the match could get under way.

Dynamo dazzled in the opening stages, with their fast, pin-point passing. A free-kick struck from 20 yards out by Kasev beat Jerry Dawson at his left-hand post, and Dynamo were one-up after only two minutes. Rangers hit back immediately and won a penalty four minutes later, only to see Willie Waddell's kick turned onto the crossbar by goalkeeper Tiger Khomich. The home team pressed for an equaliser but Dynamo soaked up the pressure and slowly got back into the game, with their intricate passing along the ground contrasting with Rangers' typically direct British approach. They doubled their lead in 24 minutes with a quality 20-yard shot from Karsev, after a brilliant passing move that left the Rangers defence chasing shadows.

For the first time in the game, the vast Ibrox crowd was silenced. It looked ominously as if Rangers could be on the receiving end of a heavy defeat, as they struggled to cope with the movement of the Russians. But the Scots refused to give up and were rewarded for their efforts with a goal from Jimmy Smith shortly before half-time. Encouraged by the goal, the Rangers fans urged the home team forward in search of an equaliser. The atmosphere was frenetic and it spilled over onto the pitch, with the Rangers players reacting angrily to the body-checking and jersey-pulling of the Russians, who were likewise riled by the tough tackling of the Scots. At one point, Dynamo brought on a substitute, as agreed before the game. But whether by accident or design, they failed to withdraw one of their players, and it was left to Rangers' Torry Gillick to point out to the referee that there were 12 opponents on the pitch.

Rangers laid siege to the Russian goal but found their defence impenetrable. Then, with only minutes to go, the linesman flagged for a penalty after spotting a foul by the Dynamo captain, Semichastny, that had been missed by the referee. This time George Young took responsibility and fired it past Khomich. A frantic last few minutes followed as Rangers charged forward for a winner, but it was not to be. The final whistle blew and honours were even.

The match had been a fascinating clash of cultures and styles, a precursor to the new European age that was just around the corner. With their never-say-die spirit, Rangers had matched the technical skills of the foreigners, but there were ominous signs that the British style of play might one day be overwhelmed by the continentals'. Unfortunately, no one paid heed to the warning signs and Rangers would pay the price for such short-sightedness on numerous occasions in the coming decades.

BULLDOG SPIRIT OF IBROX

If one figure from history personified Rangers' famed 'bulldog spirit', particularly in the post-war years, then it would have to be Churchill. So it was fitting that the wartime prime minister chose Ibrox as the venue for a huge gathering of Conservative Party supporters in May 1949. Despite Glasgow's reputation as a hotbed of socialism, the Tories were still popular among the city's working class at the time, particularly among the protestant community. It is likely, therefore, that many of the astonishing 22,000 who packed into the Main Stand and enclosure would have been Ibrox regulars on a Saturday.

With memories of his wartime leadership still fresh in the mind, Churchill was granted a hero's welcome by Glasgow. Crowds lined the streets and greeted his car with cheers as he made his way from the city centre to the southside. He arrived at the sun-drenched stadium with minutes to spare, walking down the players' tunnel to a huge ovation, before taking to the platform to deliver his speech. After four years as leader of the opposition, Churchill was plotting his return to Downing Street and used his address to pour scorn on the ruling Labour Party for what he felt was its failure to protect British interests and the encouragement it was giving to Scottish nationalism.

Churchill opened with a rallying call for unity and comradeship against socialism before bemoaning the fact that the use of the word 'British' was now frowned upon. If that was sure to be popular with the Glasgow audience, then his pledge that 'the people of Ulster shall not be forced out of the United Kingdom against their will' would have gone down even better. He went on 'We cannot forget, moreover, here in Glasgow of all places, that the people of Northern Ireland, by their loyalty to King and Empire, kept open our only outlet to the seas, by the Clyde and Mersey…while [Irish president] Mr de Valera and his Southern Irish government was quite ready to watch us, with perfect indifference, being enslaved by Hitler and sinking forever in the ocean of the past.'

Watching the old black-and-white Movietone footage of his Ibrox appearance, it is difficult to appreciate Churchill's power as an orator. Through 21st-century eyes, used to the slick presentation of the modern politician, his lisping delivery often comes across as awkward, stilted and somewhat laboured, and the content at times tedious. But it is clear from the film that Churchill had the audience firmly in the palm of his hand. An aside about his wife's Scottishness – 'she comes from Scotland you know' – is met with laughter and rapturous applause. Then, quite unexpectedly, as the speech meanders towards a close, there is a brief passage of classic Churchill that can raise the hairs on the back of one's neck, even today.

The voice rises to a passionate crescendo as he rails against the 'freezing and sterile fallacies of socialism' and urges the British people to free themselves 'from the bonds by which they are now cramped and restricted' and to bring back 'the prosperity and the enduring grandeur of the United Kingdom and of the British Empire and Commonwealth of Nations in all parts of the world.' The Ibrox crowd roared its appreciation just as if

Part of the huge crowd at Ibrox Park Stadium, Glasgow, listening to Mr. Winston Churchill.

THE
DAYS AHEAD

Speech by the
Rt. Hon. WINSTON CHURCHILL
O.M., C.H., M.P.
at the Ibrox Park Stadium, Glasgow
20th May, 1949

Brochure produced by the Scottish Conservatives as a memento of Winston Churchill's rally at Ibrox in 1949.

Willie Thornton had put the ball into the net. Two years later Churchill was back at No. 10, and he would remain prime minister until 1955. An onyx inkstand presented by the statesman to the club remains in the Ibrox trophy room today as a memento of his visit.

Watching intently from the stand that spring evening was a young American evangelical preacher named Billy Graham. He was impressed by what he had seen – and heard. One of Graham's colleagues, singer George Beverly Shea, recounted in a recent interview 'I never met him, but I heard Mr Churchill in Parliament and I also heard his speech in Ibrox Stadium, Glasgow, when he was running again for Parliament. He talked for 70 minutes. I was sitting beside Mr Graham and he was very impressed with Mr Churchill's oratory.'

Graham returned to Glasgow six years later, but this time he was the one taking centre stage as part of his worldwide crusade. A six-week run at the Kelvin Hall was followed by two spectacular closing rallies at Ibrox and Hampden Park. At Rangers' ground, 60,000 men, women and children crammed onto the terracings, enclosure and stand desperate to catch a glimpse of the evangelist and hear his words. Five hours before he began addressing the audience from a temporary platform on the pitch, hundreds were queueing up outside the ground, many without tickets.

Once the sermon got under way, more than 20 people had to be taken to the Southern General Hospital for treatment – the worst being a woman who suffered concussion after fainting and banging her head as she fell. At the climax of the service, thousands poured across wooden ramps onto the cinder track around the pitch to be 'saved' when Graham called for 'decisions'. It was verging on mass hysteria. The most remarkable thing was that this was an 'overflow' gathering – called at the last minute to meet the demand from those who could not get tickets for the next night's Hampden rally.

'MY MINCE WAS GETTING COLD'

Despite ailing health, Bill Struth continued to wield his influence over every facet of life at Ibrox well into the 1950s, and it was his enthusiasm that kept Rangers' Sports meeting at the forefront of British athletics in the decade. The event was vitally important to Rangers' finances in the post-war era, as the two-day event brought in up to £4,000 from the paying public.

Struth still had the influence to attract the biggest names in sport to perform at Ibrox – even when there were other conflicting demands. Scottish distance runner Ian Binnie accepted an invitation from Struth to compete, so had to turn down the chance to compete for Great Britain at an AAA event. A furious official called Binnie one evening to berate him for turning down the selection. 'England needs you,' he was told. In an interview with the *Herald* newspaper 40 years later, Binnie recalled 'I told him I was Scottish and that my mince was getting cold.'

After racing at Ibrox, Binnie was leaving the ground when he encountered Struth. The Rangers manager was so impressed by Binnie's decision to honour his promise that he presented the runner with a key to the ground. Binnie later said 'He said I could use the track any time, provided the players weren't training on it. It was the best track in Scotland then, and the greatest gift any athlete could have had.'

In April 1954, after a series of health setbacks, Struth finally resigned as Rangers manager at the age of 79, and he was replaced by Scot Symon. For the next two years Struth did his best to remain involved with club affairs as a director, but by the summer of 1956 his health had worsened to the extent that he was confined to bed. But with one final effort, Struth managed to summon the strength to make a final appearance at his beloved Ibrox Sports. In September 1956, on the eve of an Old Firm game, he died at his home in the southside of Glasgow. His passing left a gaping hole in Scottish football.

Like his predecessor, William Wilton, Struth had been a driving force in the development of Ibrox, so it was fitting that in 2006, 50 years after his death, the magnificent grandstand he had commissioned was renamed the Bill Struth Stand. His prediction in 1927 that it would still be standing 'long after the others have gone' has proved correct. Likewise, Struth's reputation as arguably the greatest football manager the world has ever seen stands just as strong.

THE CROWDS FLOCK BACK

If there were any fears that it would take time for Scottish football to recover from the effects of the war, then they were quickly dispelled. Rangers' opening League match of the 1946–47 season at Motherwell saw a crowd of 30,000, and 50,000 turned out at Ibrox for the visit of Hibernian the following week. The Edinburgh club won the game 2–1 and would go on to be Rangers' biggest rivals for the next seven years.

It was the start of a boom time for attendances, which was to last for two decades. Rangers' average home crowd for the season was 28,000, their highest-ever recorded and 5,000 more than the last official season before the war. During the next 20 years, the average Ibrox crowd reached as high as 45,000 and Rangers were consistently the best-supported club. Between 1946 and 1966, Rangers' average attendance was 34,000 compared to Celtic's average of 24,000. It was a less than successful period for the Parkhead club to say the least, and even their status as Scotland's second-biggest club was under threat, with both Hibs and Hearts regularly outscoring them in the attendance League tables, as well as on the field.

For those crammed onto the terracings, conditions were grim, especially at the big games. Toilet facilities were spartan and virtually impossible to access if you were parked somewhere near the front of the terrace. The solution was simple, if not exactly pleasant. Those with consideration for their fellow fans would utilise an empty beer bottle when nature called; the less respectful simply went where they stood, and if anyone was in their way then so be it. A more painful hazard came from above. Controversial incidents would invariably be met with howls of derision followed by a hail of bottles. Unfortunately, few

US athlete Tom Courtney (No. 3) wins the half-mile invitational race at the Ibrox Sports in August 1955. Note the large crowd on the terraces.

of the missiles made it much further than the lower levels of the terracing, meaning many a fan would leave the ground with blood streaming from a head wound.

Although Hibs were the greatest threat to Rangers' dominance, the Old Firm derbies remained the biggest draw and were still a powderkeg. In an attempt to lessen the chances of missiles being hurled between the rival sets of supporters, flags and bottles were banned. Notices went up around the terraces warning that 'Any persons found inside the ground in possession of flags, bottles or any other missiles will be removed from the premises and may be prosecuted.'

The Old Firm clashes have long been a source of salacious fascination for social commentators outside Scotland. Over the years dozens of eager feature writers and documentary makers have traipsed north to experience this most notorious of football matches first-hand. Of course it is not the action on the field that is the attraction but rather what is expected to take place on the terraces. In 1949 the *Picture Post* paper magazine sent one of its writers to dispatch a report from the front line of a match at Ibrox. Unfortunately for the author of the piece, the match passed off with barely a whimper, by Old Firm standards at least. He could barely disguise his disappointment: 'Not a banner has floated on bloodstained air. Not a bottle. Not a battle.'

The 64,000 crowd was lower than usual due to a boycott of the game, organised by the Celtic Supporters' Association over their perennial complaint that their team was discriminated against by referees. It was not the first Old Firm boycott – three years earlier, Rangers fans refused to visit Parkhead because of the prices being charged by the Celtic directors. This time it was estimated that around 35,000 Celtic fans boycotted the match, although that may be an exaggeration. The *Picture Post* reported 'The terraces at Ibrox's West End, where Celtic supporters traditionally gather, were half-heartedly empty a few minutes before the game began, whilst the East End terraces, the Rangers' spiritual home, seethed and heaved like a towering ant heap.' Celtic's appearance on the pitch was greeted with 'a noise between a coronach and a battle-cry of the clans in foray.'

Despite the smaller crowd, the policing of the match was as rigorous as ever. Ten mounted police and 150 on foot took their positions before the match, with a walkie-talkie squad co-ordinating the operation from the press box. The only message sent out over the airwaves throughout the afternoon was a half-time score update for the officers stationed outside the stadium. Rangers cruised to a 4–0 victory, with the Iron Curtain defence of goalkeeper Bobby Brown, Young, Jock 'Tiger' Shaw, Ian McColl, Willie Woodburn and Sammy Cox in typically imperious form.

The win helped propel Rangers towards their third League title in four years, although they were pushed all the way by Hibs and their swashbuckling forwards, known as the Famous Five. The previous season, the same Rangers defensive line had been almost ever present as the Ibrox men landed their first 'triple crown', winning the League Championship, the Scottish Cup and the recently created League Cup.

One Saturday in the summer of 1949 a young South African winger called Johnny Hubbard arrived in Scotland. Rangers' latest signing was met by Bill Struth at Renfrew Airport before being taken for tea at the St Enoch's Hotel in Glasgow city centre. The next day he visited Ibrox for the first time, meeting Ian McColl, who was in for treatment on an injury, and coach Jimmy Smith, who issued him with his training gear – a cotton shirt, a pair of dark trousers that stopped six inches below his knees and an old pair of boots. 'He gave me a ball and told me to go out and enjoy myself,' said Hubbard. 'I went out on the park and I couldn't believe what I was seeing.'

Growing up in Pretoria, Hubbard had never even heard of Rangers and had no idea what to expect from the stadium. He recalled:

I drew up outside the Main Stand in the taxi and thought to myself 'This is big!' Then I went inside and I saw the marble staircase, which was unbelievable, and then went into the dressing rooms and they were massive. As soon as I saw Ibrox for the first time, I thought 'This is unbelievable,' and from that day onwards I became a Rangers supporter...In South Africa I was used to playing in front of 4,000 maximum. My first game over here was in September 1949 and there was a crowd of 72,000. At a Celtic game you would get a crowd of 95,000 at Ibrox. All you heard was a constant noise; you couldn't make out any individual shouts, but that motivated you and got the adrenalin going. Mind you, just walking in the front door was enough to motivate you.

FLOODLIGHTS SWITCHED ON

Into the new decade, Rangers and Hibs continued to fight it out for dominance of the Scottish game, but there was a growing appetite among the fans to see the big European teams at Ibrox. The days of afternoon kick-offs were long gone, so the only way to stage these games was to install floodlights. With the stadium's close proximity to Renfrew Airport, the large pylon-style lights seen at most grounds were out of the question, so Rangers had to come up with a unique system located on the roof of the stands on both sides of the pitch. On the south stand side, the lights were located just under the edge of the roof, while on the north enclosure they were fixed to stanchions along the top of the barrel roof.

With Rangers having played in the match to inaugurate the Highbury floodlights in 1951, it was fitting that Arsenal should be invited north for the official switching on of the Ibrox lights on 9 December 1953. Floodlighting was nothing new. Rangers had of course trialled a system at the old Ibrox in 1888, and they had been used on various occasions by numerous other clubs over the years. But an irrational resistance from the football authorities – similar to their equally strident opposition to other 'dangerous innovations' like shirt numbers and substitutions – meant it was the 1950s before a ban on their use was lifted.

The Rangers supporters were clearly pleased at this development. The Arsenal match attracted a crowd of more than 70,000, which was the biggest attendance at a floodlit game in Britain at the time. However, the move was not universally welcomed. The lights, coupled with the smoke from thousands of cigarettes and the fog that seemed to permanently drift over Glasgow at the time, caused a haze that hung over the ground, making it difficult to see the the pitch. The lighting system brightly illuminated certain areas of the pitch but left other parts in the shade. Furthermore, faces could not be made out from the terraces, making identification of players virtually impossible.

As for the match, Rangers were dominant in the first half and took the lead through Willie McCulloch, who converted a cross from Willie Waddell. Arsenal took the honours in the second half and won the game with goals from Roper and Holton. To mark the occasion, at the end of the game the Arsenal players were each presented with a gift of a tea service. Willie Thornton, the stalwart Rangers forward, was also honoured by the fans on what was his final game for the club. All 75,000 of the fans stayed on after the final whistle to see him presented with a gift to mark his years of service.

Watching from the Main Stand with his dad that night was a promising winger from Edinburgh by the name of Ralph Brand. While the ceremonies took place on the pitch, the young man patiently waited for an audience with Bill Struth. It was certainly worth the wait: he marked his 17th birthday by signing professional terms with Rangers.

Brand was first spotted by Struth playing for Scotland Schoolboys against England at Wembley in 1952. The match had been shown live on television, and the Rangers manager had been tipped off by former Rangers player Bob McAulay, one of his network of scouts, to keep an eye on the young boy from Edinburgh. He was impressed by what he saw. 'When I got back home after the game I got a telegram from Mr Struth, which I still have, asking me to "phone him at Ibrox",' Brand said. 'In those days that was quite a thing for me because I never made phone calls! So I called him and he asked if I would like to go through and see him at Ibrox. So my father arranged with my Uncle Billy, who had a small Ford Prefect, to take us through to Glasgow and that was my introduction to Ibrox.'

As a promising schoolboy footballer, Brand had previously been courted by his home-town teams, Hearts and Hibs, and had visited their grounds, Tynecastle and Easter Road, on many occasions.

They were typical football stadiums of the day – they had a big stand and a main entrance, but it was just an ordinary door that you went in and then you'd go through the corridors or up wooden staircases with no lights to see the manager...That had been my introduction to football grounds – then we drew up on Edmiston Drive outside Ibrox. We went in the main entrance, where there was a commissionaire who ushered you in and sat you down. Then there was the marble staircase with the oak bannisters and the portrait of Alan Morton hanging on the wall...Going into Ibrox and going into Tynecastle and Easter Road was like night and day, and for a young boy this was really something else. In those days, to be allowed in that front door and especially to be allowed up that staircase, you had to be someone special. It was only those and such as those who were allowed up the stairs.

Having signed as an amateur, Brand spent the next year travelling through to Ibrox one night a week for training, before signing up as a professional at the Arsenal game in 1953. By then he had already made his first-team debut against Kilmarnock and was beginning to establish himself alongside his boyhood heroes like Young, McColl and Shaw. 'These guys were like grandfathers to me – they were so helpful and I really looked up to them,' Brand said.

In the last few years of Bill Struth's tenure, Rangers had begun to slip from their position of dominance. By the time Scot Symon took over in 1954 he knew he faced a major rebuilding task. Rangers were in turmoil, having endured one of their worst-ever seasons. Symon brought in youngsters like Bobby Shearer, Eric Caldow and Alex Scott to rub shoulders with great names from the days of Struth, including Young, McColl and Hubbard. The mix worked and Rangers were soon back at the top of the pile.

One of the highlights of that period was a 4–1 New Year's Day victory over Celtic at Ibrox in 1955. The star of the show was Johnny Hubbard. 'It is one of the games I remember most,' he recalled.

There was a huge crowd there as usual and Billy Simpson scored in the first half then Celtic equalised. Then with 14 minutes to go John Little gave me the ball at the edge of our box. I ran the full length of the field, beating four or five Celtic players, then the goalkeeper came out and I went round him and walked the ball into the net. It was the first goal of my hat-trick. Alex Ferguson, who had been in the crowd, later said that was the greatest goal he had ever seen. He said I was one of his favourites.

Remarkably, Hubbard's three goals that day were the last time a Rangers player scored a hat-trick against Celtic in the League. As he said, 'That is quite amazing when you think about it.' Later that year another South African made his mark for Rangers. In what was the first Scottish League game under floodlights, Don Kitchenbrand scored five goals in an emphatic 8–0 win over Queen of the South at Ibrox.

THE STARS AT NIGHT

The introduction of floodlights meant the way was now clear for a series of midweek glamour friendlies against English and foreign opposition. Over the next three seasons, Arsenal were regular visitors along with Manchester City, Rapid Vienna, Racing Club Paris, Dinamo Zagreb and the Argentinians, San Lorenzo. There was also a series of challenge matches against the British Army XI. For each match, Rangers produced a special edition of their match programme, which they billed as a Souvenir Floodlight Programme, adding to the sense of occasion. Results were mixed, but the games were well attended and, if nothing else, provided the club with some extra income and showed there was a definite appetite for regular competitive matches against continental teams.

Thanks to French journalist Gabriel Hanot that would soon become a reality. Hanot, the editor of the sports magazine *L'Équipe*, proposed the creation of a competition in a bid to settle arguments over who was the best team in Europe. After some negotiation with the sceptical leaders of European football's governing body UEFA, his competition finally got the official seal of approval. In September 1955 the first European Champion Clubs' Cup match took place between Portugal's Sporting Lisbon and Partizan, from Yugoslavia.

Hibernian, and not champions Aberdeen, were invited to represent Scotland in the inaugural competition and the Edinburgh club did well, reaching the semi-final stage. The following year, UEFA insisted that domestic League winners would qualify for the tournament, and thus Rangers, who had just won their 29th League title, became the first Scottish champions to take part.

FLYING THE FLAG IN EUROPE

Rangers were now flying the flag for Scotland in the European Cup, and the first night of European football at Ibrox in November 1956 brought a new and unique atmosphere to the old ground. The French champions OGC Nice were the visitors on a torrid night of rain and hailstones in the southside of Glasgow. A crowd of 65,000 braved the conditions to witness this clash of footballing cultures. Nice were typically continental, playing a rhythmic passing game, but were also guilty of persistent fouling, pushing, elbowing and obstruction. Rangers on the other hand persisted with the direct British approach of getting the ball down the wings and launching crosses towards a tall centre-forward. The Scots were no angels either but even their fouling was more straightforward than that of their foreign rivals.

Rangers dominated the early part of the game, but the French opened the scoring in the 23rd minute with a solo effort from outside-left Faivre. Five minutes before half-time, though, Max Murray scored Rangers' first-ever goal in European football. Shortly after half-time, referee Arthur Ellis called a conference of the two teams on the pitch and warned that he would 'stand no more nonsense'. When the match resumed, Rangers took control but could only add one more goal to their tally.

The match ended in chaotic scenes when the referee blew for full-time five minutes early. To the anger of the crowd, the players and officials disappeared from view up the tunnel. The mistake was eventually realised and the players had to be recalled to the pitch, with Rangers full-back Eric Caldow having to be retrieved from the bath.

Today, Caldow looks back with fondness at those massive Ibrox occasions. He said 'The atmosphere now for the big games is special but that's with crowds of 50,000. When I was playing in front of 80,000 the noise was out of this world. Playing in Europe for that first time was unforgettable. It was all about the thrill and excitement of such a new venture.'

Poor refereeing was a feature of European games, and former Rangers defender Harold Davis is of the view that many of them crumbled under pressure from the terraces. Their bad decisions created ill-feeling among the players and was a major contributory factor in the on-field trouble that was prevalent in the early game in Europe. 'The reason there were so many punch-ups and

In the event of the game to which this ticket admits being postponed for any reason, the ticket will be available on the postponed date. On no account will money be refunded.

EUROPEAN CLUB CHAMPIONS CUP

RANGERS v. O.G.C. NICE

IBROX STADIUM, GLASGOW

INCLUDING TAX
WEDNESDAY, 24th OCTOBER, 1956
KICK-OFF 7.15 p.m.

Section Q

Row O 176

Seat No.

THIS PORTION TO BE RETAINED BY HOLDER

A Main Stand ticket for Rangers' first-ever European Cup game against Nice in 1956.

so much bad feeling was the referees,' he said. 'In those days, 90 per cent of the referees were homers, and I suppose you can understand why. There were crowds of 80, 90 or 100,000, and they were all standing and were pretty volatile. Most referees in those days tended to go the home way and that led to bad feeling.'

Rangers lost the return leg in Nice and were knocked out following a Play-off defeat at the Parc des Princes in Paris. But the supporters and players now had a taste for European football, and there would be many more exciting nights of continental football under the Ibrox lights.

A NEW LOOK...

After 25 years in which the structure of Ibrox remained more or less untouched, there had been some significant changes by the time of the clash with Nice. The barrel roof over the north enclosure was woefully inadequate, covering only the rear of the terracing. In the summer of 1954 the width and depth of the cover was increased when a new pitched roof was built in front of the old structure and another section was added at the rear. The result was not particularly pleasing on the eye, but it increased the comfort for thousands of supporters. So popular was the new section that it became the haunt of some of the club's more 'hardcore' fans. Meanwhile, the floodlights that had previously been located on the old

A ticket for the football platform at Ibrox station. A single to Glasgow cost three and a half pence in old money.

Thousands of fans travelled to games by train and alighted at Ibrox railway station, seen here in 1957. It was closed in February 1967.

roof were removed and replaced with a line of lights along the underside of the new structure.

The other major stadium development during the 1950s took place behind the scenes in the Main Stand, with the opening of the Trophy Room. There was nothing like it in British football, and today the Ibrox Trophy Room remains a unique treasure trove of historic artefacts.

By the start of the 1960s Scot Symon had assembled one of the great Rangers teams of all time. The classic line up of the era is one that many old-time fans can still recite by heart: Billy Ritchie, Bobby Shearer, Eric Caldow, John Greig, Ronnie McKinnon, Jim Baxter, Willie Henderson, Ian McMillan, Jimmy Millar, Ralph Brand and Davie Wilson. Brand, who formed a prolific strike partnership with Millar and scored more than 200 goals during his 13-year Rangers career, looks back with great pride on those glorious Ibrox days: 'After I had got into the team in the early 1960s, when we had a really good side, being able to walk into the Ibrox dressing room before a game and knowing that the number-10 shirt hanging up in the corner was my shirt was really something else. You didn't have to look at the team sheet because the team practically picked itself in those days. It's difficult to explain those feelings – in fact the feeling is still here now when I think about it.'

Domestically, Rangers were back in what they considered to be their rightful place as the dominant force in Scottish football. In Europe, Rangers reached the European Cup semi-final in 1960, only to lose 12–4 on aggregate to Eintracht Frankfurt, including a humiliating 6–3 second-leg defeat in front of a huge crowd of 70,000 at Ibrox. The following season, the stadium played host to its first, and so far only, European Final. UEFA had introduced a second tournament alongside the European Cup, contested by the winners of national Cup competitions. Having defeated Ferencvaros, Borussia Mönchengladbach and Wolverhampton Wanderers, Rangers reached the two-legged Final of the new European Cup-Winners' Cup, where they faced Fiorentina. The Italians won the Final 4–2 on aggregate, having taken a 2–0 lead back to Florence from the first leg at Ibrox, which was a rowdy affair, marred by ruthless tactics on the part of Fiorentina at times. The Italians, coached by former Hungarian international Nandor Hidegkuti, were capable of playing intelligent, skilful football but, frustratingly, often fell back on the sort of cynical approach that is often associated with Italian teams. Unsurprisingly, the home fans in the 80,000-strong crowd were less than impressed.

Rangers, wearing blue and white stripes instead of their usual royal blue jerseys, struggled to break down the Fiorentina defence, and the Scots soon found themselves a goal behind as the Italians asserted themselves. A short pass back by Harold Davis was pounced on by Fiorentina, and Luigi Milan passed the ball into the empty net. Six minutes later the Austrian referee, Erich Steiner, gave the home team a penalty after Ian McMillan was fouled inside the penalty box. Fiorentina furiously protested that it had been a fair tackle, and the official was surrounded by wildly gesticulating Italian players. Amid chaotic scenes, assistant coach Beppe Chiapella raced onto the pitch to join the protests and had to be restrained by Swedish international winger Kurt Hamrin. It took several

A programme from the annual Rangers Sports meeting at Ibrox in 1958.

minutes to restore order before Rangers captain Eric Caldow was able to take the penalty. Goalkeeper Albertosi was more than six yards off his line when Caldow struck the kick past the post, but calls for a retake were rejected by the referee.

As Fiorentina increasingly resorted to rough-house tactics, the atmosphere inside Ibrox turned more and more ugly. One foul on Bobby Shearer sparked a torrent of beer cans and empty bottles onto the park. The mood turned even darker when Milan scored a second goal for the visitors a minute before the end. On the final whistle the Italian flag, which had been flying above the covered enclosure, was ripped down by frustrated fans. Police quickly moved into the crowd to rescue the flag as the Fiorentina players saluted all four sides of the ground.

The return leg was a far calmer affair, with the 500 travelling Rangers fans receiving a warm welcome in Florence. On the pitch, Rangers acquitted themselves well but went down 2–1. The first Final had ended in disappointment, but there was a feeling that it was only a matter of time before Rangers picked up a European trophy.

TALES FROM THE TERRACES

It is often said that it was a miracle that there have not been more deaths and serious injuries in Britain's football grounds. Anyone who has been carried 30 or 40ft on a packed, swaying terrace or who has been swept down a staircase, feet off the ground, by the sheer weight of numbers will understand that sentiment only too well. The feeling of panic and vulnerability that comes with the realisation that you are completely at the mercy of the crowd's movement is not easily forgotten.

It would be fair to say that the comfort and safety of fans was not exactly high on the list of priorities for club chairmen in the early 1960s. For the most part, their concerns began and ended with maximising the numbers they could squeeze into the ground. The new decade may have brought an exciting new team to the Ibrox pitch, but there was little sign of progress in improving the lot of the average fan. Indeed, the terraced areas had changed little since the redevelopment of the stadium after the disaster of 1902.

'Toilet facilities were little more than an open trench separated from the rest of the ground by a couple of brick walls,' recalled Ibrox regular Joe McCulloch. 'There wasn't even a roof. If you went in at the end of the match, the stench from the puddles of urine on the floor was unbearable. It was like something from the dark ages but that was how it was then. It summed up everything about the football ground experience at the time. The supporters didn't expect much and they weren't disappointed.'

At the west end of the ground – the so-called Celtic End, where away fans would gather on derby days – there was one large staircase that led to the exit gate at the Broomloan Road End of Edmiston Drive. The larger east terracing had two staircases – one in the south-east corner leading onto Edmiston Drive and one in the north-east corner that led fans onto Cairnlea Drive and eventually out onto Copland Road. The second stairway was the most popular, as it was the most convenient for access to the subway station and to the supporters' club buses that parked up in the area. At big games, perhaps 25,000 fans might have negotiated those stairs to leave the ground. The stairway, made out of compacted earth and railway sleepers, was split in two by a central wooden barrier, which ran from top to bottom. On both sides were wooden picket fences designed to keep the departing supporters on the staircase and stop them drifting onto the steep grass embankments at the sides.

For all the massive crowds seen at Ibrox over the years, the stadium had not witnessed a fatal accident since 1902. But on 16 September 1961 that changed. The day in question saw Rangers play Celtic in the first Old Firm League clash of the season. As these matches go, it was relatively uneventful both on and off the pitch. The *Daily Record* described the game as 'clean, sporting and wholesome, although no classic'. There was a dramatic finale, though, when Jim Baxter scored with a 25-yard drive with just two minutes to go, securing a 2–2 draw for the home team.

As the Celtic fans trooped home disappointed at missing out on the victory, the Rangers supporters streamed out of the ground on a high. Although they had dropped a point at home, the late goal made it feel like a win. But as they poured down the exit stairway, tragedy struck. In the middle of the crowd, two young men stumbled and fell. As the supporters behind them tried to hold themselves back to avoid trampling on them, the central barrier cracked under the pressure. Dozens more fans fell to the ground, and the fence running down the right-hand side of the stairway also collapsed under the pressure. Screams rang out as men, women and children were trampled underfoot.

Volunteer ambulancemen, who had been on duty for the game, rushed to the scene, and emergency crews descended on Ibrox from all over the city. There were heartbreaking scenes as medics fought to save the dying. One volunteer first-aider broke down in tears as he tried in vain to give the kiss-of-life to one victim. In the end, two men died in the accident and more than 40 fans were injured, with 22 needing hospital treatment. It could have been even worse had many of the supporters not managed to escape through the broken fence.

One of the victims, Thomas Thomson, from Gourock, had gone to the game with his brother, William. He was 30 and left a widow and two young children. The other man to lose his life was George Nelson from Penilee on the outskirts of Glasgow. He was just 22 and had met up with his 17-year-old brother, Roy, at the game.

Following the accident, the Scottish Football Association issued instructions to all its member clubs that they should carry out general safety improvements at their grounds. Rangers employed a firm of civil engineers to carry out alterations to Ibrox and spent £150,000 on ground improvements over the next few years, including the concreting over of the terracing. The wooden central barrier on the stairway was removed and replaced with six steel railings that divided the staircase into seven channels in an attempt to slow down the flow of supporters leaving the ground. The stairs were also concreted, and the wooden fencing that ran down each side of the stairway was replaced with heavy-duty barriers. This move was to have tragic consequences almost a decade later.

RIOT STOPS PLAY

Barely seven months after the accident, the Copland Road terracing at Ibrox was the scene of some of the worst crowd violence ever witnessed at a Scottish ground. The occasion was the Scottish Cup semi-final between Celtic and St Mirren. Midway through the second half, with the Paisley side leading 3–0, Celtic had a goal disallowed for offside. A disgruntled fan hurled a beer glass in the general direction of the pitch, but it landed among his fellow supporters, sending them scattering across the terracing. Police moved in to the crowd to apprehend the person responsible but as he was taken away a beer bottle flew through the air. This was the cue for hundreds of fans to leap out of the enclosure onto the cinder track.

Suddenly the air was thick with glasses and bottles, and hundreds more supporters charged onto the pitch. Police reinforcements were sent in from the Main Stand, but they

Fans young and old at Ibrox in 1960. Note the gentleman three rows from the front swigging from a bottle.

were swamped by the pitch invaders. Meanwhile, hundreds more Celtic fans swarmed onto the pitch at the other end of the ground.

Police wrestled with one pair who tried to rip the netting from the goal stanchions, while a group of youths charged into the centre circle, their arms aloft in mock triumph. As the fans battled with the police and among themselves, alarmed players from both teams cowered in the centre of the pitch before being herded through the rioters into the safety of the dressing rooms by police.

The *Daily Record* reported that at the height of the riot, rampaging fans pulled down Rangers' Championship flag from above the terracing and tried to burn it. Eye-witness James Gray told the paper 'They pulled the flag from the pole. Some of them took out matches and tried to set it alight.' Six mounted police moved in, and the trouble was eventually quelled as more officers arrived on the scene. The pitch was cleared and a ring of officers surrounded the part of the terracing where the worst offenders had congregated. In the final count, 20 fans were arrested, 30 were injured and eight required hospital treatment, including at least one who was knocked unconscious by a flying bottle.

After a 16-minute delay, the teams were able to return from the dressing rooms and the match was resumed. By this time thousands of fans had gone home, leaving the Ibrox terraces half empty. Amid this strange atmosphere, Celtic managed to pull back a goal but it was not enough to save the match. Their fans had done their best to have the tie abandoned but St Mirren marched on to the Final, where they met Rangers.

While the 1962 semi-final riot was at the extreme end of the scale, such terrace violence was hardly unusual in the 1960s. It may have been a coincidence, but attendances across Scotland were beginning to decline at the same time. For the first time since 1948, the average League crowd at Ibrox dropped below 30,000 in 1964–65, and while Rangers were by no means the worst affected by the attendance slump, the club believed that radical change was required to reverse the decline. They wanted a drastic League reconstruction that would have seen several of the country's tiniest clubs dropped altogether. The proposal was defeated, as was another attempt by the Scottish League, which would have seen the divisions streamlined from two to three smaller sections – based not on a footballing meritocracy but on attendances.

THE REAL DEAL

If there was declining interest in the bread-and-butter domestic matches at Ibrox, the same could not be said for the big games, particularly in Europe. Home attendances in the European Cup and the Cup-Winners' Cup rarely fell below 60,000 and regularly topped 80,000, as some of the biggest names on the continent visited Ibrox. The star-studded squads of AC Milan, Fiorentina, Standard Liege, Internazionale and Borussia Dortmund, as well as the English quartet of Leeds, Newcastle, Wolves, and Tottenham were all major attractions in the early years of European competition. Spurs and England forward Jimmy Greaves was overwhelmed by the atmosphere generated by the 80,000 crowd at their Cup-Winners' Cup tie in 1962. 'When the team took to the pitch the noise was deafening, the atmosphere intimidating in the extreme,' he recalled later.

Although the backing of such a massive crowd was undoubtedly a positive thing, it did have some drawbacks. Ralph Brand recalled:

It was just one constant noise from start to finish…But the noise meant the players couldn't hear ourselves shouting at each other during the game, something that is very important in football. Sometimes we would have to invent special signals to signify things…People often ask me how it felt to play in front of those capacity crowds and it was very thrilling. But I always say, on the other side of the coin, have you ever heard 60–70,000 people booing you off the park, because it happened like that. The supporters were very demonstrative. If the play didn't please them or the team maybe wasn't doing so well they weren't slow in letting you know. But that was all part and parcel of being a pro, of course, so you accepted it.

The visit of the magnificent Real Madrid team in 1963 really captured the supporters' imagination. The trio of Di Stefano, Puskas and Gento may have been nearing the end of their careers but they were still the superstars of European football. Among the 80,000

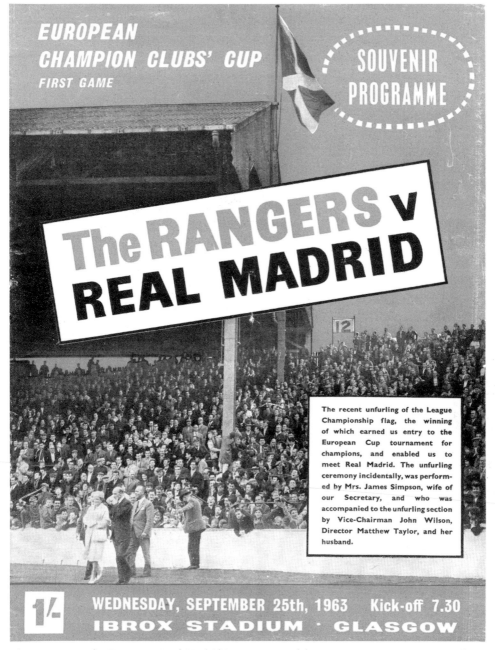

The recent unfurling of the League Championship flag, the winning of which earned us entry to the European Cup tournament for champions, and enabled us to meet Real Madrid. The unfurling ceremony incidentally, was performed by Mrs. James Simpson, wife of our Secretary, and who was accompanied to the unfurling section by Vice-Chairman John Wilson, Director Matthew Taylor, and her husband.

The programme for Rangers v Real Madrid in 1963, one of the great European occasions at Ibrox.

crowd was an 11-year-old lad called John Robertson. His first visit to Ibrox had been a 4–3 defeat to Clyde in the Glasgow Cup a couple of years earlier, but it was the visit of the white-shirted Real that has lived in the memory.

On a thrilling night, Rangers performed superbly as winger Willie Henderson caused the Spaniards problems with his close control and direct running. Defensively, Rangers snuffed out the threat of the Real forward line and looked to have done enough to secure a draw, at least. Then, with three minutes to go, Puskas swung his left boot and sent the ball flying into the Rangers net. It was a devastating blow, and it came too late for Rangers to respond.

Four decades later, the disappointment of the defeat remains with John Robertson, now a Member of Parliament and still an Ibrox regular. 'It was my first European game and the night will always be with me even though we lost 1–0,' he recalled. 'Rangers pressed all game but got caught out near the end to put a dampener on the evening. It was the quickest game I can remember and even though I was only 11 years old and 45 years have passed since, I can recollect the feelings if not the details of the actual game. The atmosphere was electric and made me want more of it. It remains a memory never to be forgotten.'

The second leg in Madrid was best forgotten, as an understrength team were torn apart 6–0 in the Santiago Bernabeu Stadium. But domestically Rangers were at their peak. It was the season that Scot Symon's team reached their potential. Led by 'Captain Cutlass' Bobby Shearer and inspired by the genius of Jim Baxter, they swept the board to claim a second treble. As they celebrated the achievement, no Rangers supporter could have predicted that it would be 11 years before they could celebrate another League title win.

ON THE RIGHT TRACK

For more than 70 years the Rangers Sports had been Scotland's leading track and field event, but with the death of Bill Struth the main driving force behind the annual meetings had gone. Declining crowds led to the event finally being scrapped. However, in the mid-1960s there was a slight return for athletics at the stadium. There was growing unease among the authorities at the level of trouble on Scottish terraces, especially at Old Firm games. In an attempt to ease the tension, they came up with various initiatives aimed at diverting the rival fans' attention away from each other. One such idea was to invite prominent athletes to take part in a series of half-time races on the cinder track round the pitch.

Hugh Barrow, a member of the Victoria Park athletics club, was one of the athletes invited to take part, running in a one-mile race on the Ibrox track at the 1965 Ne'erday match. It was a bizarre experience. 'On the day in question you were told to report to the primary school on Edmiston Drive where you changed,' he said. 'The athletes then warmed up on the training area under the Main Stand, sharing this arena with the City of Glasgow Police Mounted Division so you had to be careful.'

As soon as the half-time whistle blew, the athletes headed down the tunnel, while the players went in the opposite direction. 'When you took to the track, what an atmosphere! Not even an Olympic champion would experience this. You had been cautioned from wearing either blue or green vests in case you inflamed an already tense atmosphere – and that was a pity as my club, Victoria Park, wore blue/white hoops.' He went on:

Time was at a premium so you were on your marks immediately – the gun went – although you could hardly hear it – and you were off heading round the Copland Road bend. Then came the first surprise, the track was lined by police, sometimes actually on the track, so it became an obstacle race. Then suddenly, halfway up the back straight, a police snatch squad rushed out in front of you across the track, heading for the crowd. When you were on your next lap the snatch squad were on their way back across with a culprit so you had to swerve to avoid them for a second time...It wasn't exactly made for fast times; however, on this occasion I managed a win over my old rival, Ian McCafferty, who went on to greater things, including the Olympic 5,000 metres Final in Munich.

There was no prize money for the victor. 'For my endeavours I was presented with a transistor radio by Scot Symon and a cold wash back at the primary school.'

IBROX IN TURMOIL

After decades of stability, Rangers were plunged into crisis in the second half of the 1960s. Directors, who were so used to conducting business in private behind Ibrox's heavy wooden doors, found themselves having to justify their actions almost on a daily basis. The problems started on the field. Players like Ritchie, Shearer, Caldow, Millar, Brand and Wilson were moving towards the end of their Ibrox careers and, for the most part, their replacements failed to set the heather alight.

In 1965 Kilmarnock, managed by Ibrox legend Willie Waddell, won the League and, alarmingly for the Rangers fans, Scott Symon's team finished in a distant fifth place. The following season Celtic won their first title since 1954 under the leadership of Jock Stein, and the year after that they won the treble. Even more depressingly for the Ibrox faithful, Stein took Celtic to a European Cup triumph at the first time of asking in 1967. Symon found himself under increasing pressure, with unfavourable comparisons being made with his Celtic rival. Critics claimed his management style, similar to that of his predecessor, Bill Struth, was outdated and not suited to the modern game.

In January 1967 a humiliating Scottish Cup defeat to Second Division Berwick Rangers heaped further pressure on the manager. The scapegoats for the defeat were free-scoring young forwards George McLean and Jim Forrest, who never played competitively for Rangers

Manager Scot Symon gives his players some last-minute advice in this rare glimpse into the Ibrox dressing room before a 1960 match.

again. Rangers reached the European Cup-Winners' Cup Final in Nuremberg that season, but with no recognised strikers they failed to break down Bayern Munich and eventually lost 1–0 after extra-time. It was a brave effort but there was a sense of depression in the aftermath, as it came a week after Celtic had triumphed in the European Cup Final.

Six months later, with Rangers at the top of the League, Symon's 13-year tenure as manager was abruptly ended, as he was sacked in shameful circumstances. He was summoned to the home of chartered accountant Alex McBain, where he was requested to tender his resignation, as the board had decided he was no longer wanted as manager. Assistant manager Davie White, a young, modern 'tracksuit manager' with very little management experience, was appointed as Symon's successor in November 1967. He went agonisingly close to winning the League title at the end of the season, losing out on the final day to Celtic, but his reign as manager only lasted until March 1969, after a trophyless 16 months that ended with a shattering Cup-winners' Cup defeat to Polish team Gornik Zabrze.

During White's tenure, Rangers had two massive European matches against English opposition. In 1969 they lost 2–0 on aggregate to Newcastle United in the semi-final of the Fairs Cup. In the same competition, a year earlier, they lost by the same margin to

Leeds United. The second leg in Yorkshire was a sell-out, but back in Glasgow an astonishing crowd of more than 43,000 turned up at Ibrox to watch the game live on giant screens. The pioneering move was a huge success, and the idea would be resurrected by Rangers years later.

Until the shambolic Paul Le Guen era of 2006, White's reign was the shortest and most unsuccessful of any Rangers manager. He was unlucky in that he was inexperienced and was thrust into the role against Celtic's best-ever team. If nothing else, White brought striker Colin Stein and midfielder Alex MacDonald to the club. Both would become huge Ibrox favourites and would play key roles in the club's European Cup-Winners' Cup triumph in 1972. Willie Waddell, who had quit football management to move into journalism and was one of White's fiercest critics, was named as the new manager to almost universal acclaim. He immediately set about clearing out what he saw as deadwood and attempted to rebuild the Rangers team.

IBROX IN A NEW LIGHT

Ibrox underwent some more changes towards the end of the decade. A roof was built over the Copland Road terracing, and although it was hardly ideal in that it provided only

Rangers take on Eintracht Frankfurt at Ibrox. Light blue, disabled cars are parked along the touchline in front of the enclosure. The floodlights on the roof were installed in 1967 and were the third different type used by the club.

partial coverage, it meant that only the west terracing – the Celtic End – remained uncovered. The castellated trim on the press box also vanished. It had always been a somewhat ostentatious feature, but it was another feature of Leitch's Main Stand that marked Ibrox out from the crowd.

In February 1967 Rangers upgraded their floodlighting system at a cost of £25,000. Rather than the old system where the lights were fitted to the underside of the stand, the new lamps were on mini-pylons fixed to the roof of the Main Stand and the north enclosure. Bizarrely, it was the same system used to illuminate the Rock of Gibraltar. The lights were a vast improvement on the old system and cost much less to run – just £3 for a 90-minute game. After the lamps were put to the test for the first time, Willie Henderson, who was notoriously short-sighted, was asked his opinion. He replied 'I won't need my new specs now.'

The lights were first used for the 1966–67 European Cup-Winners' Cup match with Real Zaragoza, which Rangers won 2–0. It was played on a filthy March evening of heavy rain, driving sleet and high winds. It seemed that every European match of that era was played in stormy weather, and the conditions only added to the electric atmosphere created by the massive crowds.

WARNING SIGNS

WARNING. It is strictly forbidden to take alcohol into the stadium. Anyone ignoring this warning will be refused admission or if found with it after entry will be immediately evicted.

The singing of blasphemous songs or obscene chants will not be tolerated. Strong measures will also be taken against those who use irreligious words.

The Rangers Football Club appeal to all patrons to assist the police and stewards in every way.

(Signs erected at the Ibrox turnstiles in the late 1960s.)

The issue of crowd safety returned to the forefront again after two more incidents on the north-east stairway in the late 1960s. On 11 September 1967, after another Old Firm match, 11 fans were hurt in a pile-up on the stairs after one stumbled and fell.

Then, on 2 January 1969, in a near carbon copy of the 1961 fatal accident, there was another more serious incident. Rangers had won the game 1–0 through a John Greig penalty, and their fans had been in a jubilant mood. But the joy soon turned to terror as they surged down the stairway. Suddenly one supporter tripped and fell to the floor and others also lost their footing as his fellow fans tried to avoid trampling him underfoot. The pressure caused one of the new metal handrails to give way, resulting in more fans being thrown to the ground, leaving 24 needing hospital treatment, including two who were seriously hurt. As a police spokesman said at the time, 'It was a miracle no one was killed.'

Three accidents, two deaths and dozens of injuries in around seven years on the same stairway. It should have been warning enough that something needed to be done as a matter of urgency for the safety of supporters. Alas, the warning was not heeded.

TALES FROM THE TERRACES

British football terraces of the 1960s and 1970s were rowdy and often frightening places. The potential for harm came from everywhere. Of course, there was the obvious danger of injury posed by the design and maintenance of the terraces themselves. Minor injuries caused by crushing or falls were numerous, although rarely made the headlines. With no segregation between home and away fans, there was also the risk of getting caught up in fighting between rival gangs of hooligans. Even at Old Firm games there was little more than a thin line of policemen to separate the two sets of supporters. Furthermore, the threat of being knocked out by a flying bottle launched from the rear of the terracing was never far away. And even if you managed to avoid physical injury, getting caught in a downpour while exposed to the elements could cause minor illness.

Nonetheless, there remains a great amount of nostalgia for the terraces among Rangers supporters, and much of that is down to the camaraderie that existed among fans who stood shoulder to shoulder together on the Ibrox slopes. Many supporters also pine for the electric atmosphere generated by standing crowds, although there may be some selective memory at work there. The layout of the stadium meant the crowd was a great distance from the pitch, especially behind the goals, and even a decent 30,000 crowd could be lost in the vast bowl.

George Ritchie first stood on the Ibrox terraces as a 10-year-old in 1962 and has been a regular ever since. He recalled:

Yes, there was an amazing atmosphere in the old ground at big games like the Old Firm or European matches, but it wasn't always like that. Because most guys didn't have a season ticket you would pick and choose your games, and that meant there could be 80,000 at Ibrox for a derby match one week but less than a quarter of that at the next home appearance if it was a game against unappealing opposition. Although the official capacity was a bit less, the stadium was the same size as it was when there were crowds of more than 100,000, so you can imagine that if there were only 15,000 inside they would be rattling around a bit. On a freezing, foggy Saturday afternoon in December, a match against the likes of Queen of the South would struggle to raise any excitement at all. Having said that, when the old Ibrox was in full voice it was awe-inspiring.

THE DERRY END

During the 1960s, the younger and more headstrong element of the Rangers support gravitated towards an area of the ground that eventually became known as the Derry. Situated under the new 'cowshed' on the north enclosure, towards the Rangers End of the ground, it was from here that much of the singing emanated, especially at the more run-of-the-mill games.

Throughout the 1960s and 1970s, any crowd trouble within Ibrox was invariably not between Rangers fans and followers of opposition teams but rather between rival Glasgow gangs within the home support, usually on the Derry. Fan Derek Miller said:

> I suppose there were always gangs about at Ibrox, long before I was first taken as a five-year-old in 1966. But I remember in the period 1974, 1975 and 1976 there were always fights behind the Centenary Stand between various gangs. This was an entirely Glasgow thing, though. Even when the bottles and cans started flying, you knew if they were going across the terracing, that was the gangs at it. When they went towards the pitch, things were going against Rangers.

The fashion accessory of choice among the younger fans was the Rangers hard hat. These were bog-standard blue safety helmets, gaudily customised with Rangers stickers and photographs of players. As the missiles flew, they also came into their own as protective headgear.

CIGARETTES AND ALCOHOL

Not all of the youngsters in the crowd were fighting each other, though, as Derek Miller recalled. The spirit of entrepreneurship was alive and well:

> There were around 10 of us that used to go on the sadly now defunct Clarkston bus from Airdrie. We discovered by accident that if you went up to somebody offering 5p for a fag, he'd give you one and let you keep your money. So every other week you'd have the smokers among us going about the Copland Road terracing, gathering up as many fags as possible before the game started. Really, you could easily fill a 20 packet. Unfortunately, the big European and Celtic matches were harder as you couldn't move about the much larger crowds as easily.

In the days before alcohol was banned from Scottish football grounds, the terraces were awash with booze. A day at the football would not be complete without a carry-out. Typically this would consist of a half-bottle of whisky or perhaps a bottle of Eldorado fortified wine (El-D) and four cans of export, and it would usually be a top-up for a couple of hours worth of pre-match drinking in one of the pubs near the ground along Paisley Road West. No doubt all this alcohol helped improve the match-day atmosphere, but unquestionably it was the direct cause of most of the more unsavoury elements of life on the terraces. Fighting between supporters was usually the result of drunken bravado, as was the missile-throwing that marred many a game. The missiles themselves were usually empty bottles and cans.

Alcohol and its diuretic properties were also to blame for another of the hazards of the terraces. A few cans of beer would soon result in a full bladder, and rather than embark on a lengthy hike to the toilets, it was easier to go where you stood. The methods were varied, but the use of a can as a makeshift portapotty was the favourite. Unfortunately, technological progress made this more difficult, as John McMahon recalled:

One of the major problems on the terraces was the invention of the ring pull beer can. Before that a metal opener that punched a triangle shaped hole in the top was used. This meant you could punch out the top of a can with a series of holes. Despite the jagged edges, you could then – carefully – pish in the can, place it on the ground and tip it over allowing the contents to gently flow away. But you couldn't do that with the ring pull, unless you were a midget or not very well endowed. So guys would just pish and if you were in front of them you wouldn't notice until you felt the back of your trousers getting warm and wet and steam rising from them.

A passageway ran underneath the rear of the Derry that allowed supporters to change ends at half-time, but using it was fraught with danger from above. Fans who had filled their beer cans would pour the contents down the gap at the back of the enclosure, sending torrents of liquid pouring down onto the tunnel below.

Despite the unpleasantness, most Ibrox regulars in the 1960s and 1970s had their own favourite spot where they stood every game, and some veteran fans returned to the same location week after week for decades. George Ritchie said:

It was great to stand at the game with all your mates together in one spot. There was about a dozen of us from different parts of Lanarkshire and we stood in the same place at every game for about 10 years. The funny thing is, you would see the same people round about you every week who obviously did the exact same thing. You'd know their faces but not their names, but there was a bond there. You knew they were 'one of us' – Rangers men…Nowadays you meet up in the pub, walk to the stadium together then split off to different corners of the ground and sit beside someone you don't know. If you're lucky you get to know them over the years but it's just not the same as it used to be. I'm convinced that was a major factor in the atmosphere in those days and that is something I really miss. I used to love walking down Paisley Road West half an hour before kick-off, and you could already hear the Rangers End in full voice. Nowadays people stay in the pub for longer because they want to spend more time with their pals.

Derek Miller and his pals were also creatures of habit, 'We always stood at the top of the terracing – we just felt safer up there,' he said. 'When the crowd was 70,000 or 80,000, we sat on the crush barriers, and if the team scored we'd jump on to the passageway, as it really was mayhem on the Copland Road when Rangers scored in a big game. The worst thing about sitting on a crush barrier was that if nothing happened for a while, your bottom half went numb with pins and needles.'

LOVE AT FIRST SIGHT – David Watson

My love affair with the stadium began in March 1967 at the ripe old age of five and $^{11}\!/_{12}$ (those $^{11}\!/_{12}$ are very important when you're in your first year at school). Rangers was something my dad and brother spoke about, and the name was very familiar to me in my early years, but apart from a few posters on my brother's wall and some Rangers LPs, which were played regularly, I had very little to link me directly to the object of their desires.

That was about to change. My mum was a barmaid, my dad a long distance lorry driver and childcare was dealt with by instructing my sibling to 'look after your wee brother'. It must have been a chore for a 13-year-old to babysit, especially so on this occasion, as Rangers were at home to St Johnstone, which meant dragging me from our home in Cowcaddens all the way to Govan, which could have been on the moon for all I knew.

Undoubtedly, his mates gave him a good-hearted ribbing at having to play nanny, and I don't remember being overly happy at having to trek a few paces behind a group of adolescents who were speaking in the 'eggy language' common among Glasgow youngsters of the time. Bored, hungry and being unable to understand a word these teenagers said, I was unaware my life was shortly to change forever.

When we got off the smelly, red underground carriage that took us from St Enoch Square to Copland Road, I suddenly became mesmerised by the noise, the colour and the crowds. All of a sudden, there was something to interest this youngster, and when we reached the top of the stairs and into Copland Road itself, it seemed to me the whole population of Glasgow had descended on this one street.

We rounded the corner to what looked like a brick wall with a steep hill behind it. At the top of this hill were the brightest lights I'd ever seen, and I could see people climbing the stairs towards the light. I was too young to think this might be the bright light to which people say they are attracted when they have an out of body experience and imagine their time has come, but to me, this was heaven. I was more than a little disappointed when I heard my brother say 'We cannae take him in there. We'll go round the Celtic End.'

I'd heard the name 'Celtic' spoken in my house but usually in less than complimentary tones, and I felt I was somehow being treated to second-class treatment by going in that end. However, on rounding the corner onto Edmiston Drive, I was greeted by the sight of a building that was bigger than all the tenements in my street put together and was in awe at the enormity of what I was told was 'the stand, where all the toffs went'. This seemed to be true, as those waiting outside chatting looked as if they were dressed for church.

Anyway, I was gradually getting used to the noises of people shouting, some singing, others swigging from bottles, but what was to greet me when I entered this special place for the first time has stayed with me all my life. After the steep climb, during which I'd run three steps, stop to make sure I hadn't escaped my brother, then continue, I eventually reached the top. I looked first across the stadium at the bright lights, which dazzled my young eyes, then at the expanse of green in the middle of this vast bowl. Everything looked immaculate, from the men around me in their shirts and ties, to the red crush barriers, to the blue-and-white criss-cross of the Main Stand. I could not believe so many people could be gathered in one place, and all at once my nostrils were invaded by a new smell, one which I was later to become all too familiar with – a heady mix of stale beer, urine, tobacco smoke and Bovril. There was the fascinating sight of a man eating a pie which had so much grease dripping from it that the terracing step looked like someone had melted a candle on it, as it hardened in the spring air.

I found it hard to take in so many new experiences in such a short space of time, and the sight of cigarette smoke rising high into the night air, illuminated by the brilliance of the lights, was something I was to encounter on many future occasions. I would love to say I remember everything about the match itself but I don't. I only know from reading books that we won 4–3. However, I could not begin to count how many times I've been to Ibrox, and I have to thank my big brother for introducing me to something that has played an enormous part of my life – even if he was coerced.

GET YOUR MACAROON BARS!

One of the biggest grumbles of the modern-day football fan is the quality of the food sold from the concession stalls. Today's steak pies, pakora and cheeseburgers may not be quite Michelin-star standard, but there is no doubt that they are a significant step up from what was on offer in the 1960s. Ibrox had a smattering of snack bars selling pies and Bovril, but for the true Rangers catering experience you had to sample the fare of the macaroon man. He wandered the terraces selling foodstuffs of dubious quality and even more dubious nutritional value from a cardboard box. The sales pitch was loud and straightforward: 'Getyermacaroonbarsspearmintchewingum.' Needless to say, sickly sweet macaroon bars were a big seller, as was spearmint chewing gum. Another favourite was Chipmunk crisps, an obscure brand that only ever seemed to be sold in football grounds. These were all pre-packed, so you could be reasonably certain that what you were eating was safe. But only the truly brave or desperately drunk would go for the other option – the cheese roll. Sometimes these were so stale that they were inedible and only of any real use to the missile-throwing fraternity when they exhausted their supply of bottles and cans. On other occasions the rolls would be worryingly soggy. George Ritchie recalled 'If the guy was rummaging around in his pockets looking for change he would sometimes put the box down on the terraces. This was not a good sign. The concrete was usually soaking wet, even when it wasn't raining, and you don't need to be a genius to work out why. The box would just soak up the liquid and eventually it would soak through to whatever was inside. Just the thought of it 40 years on makes my stomach turn.'

On winter Saturdays, when the terraces were sparsely populated, the vendor's discarded boxes were put to good use. They made an excellent base for the mini bonfires that would spring up all over the slopes. Crumpled up copies of the *Evening Times* and *Evening Citizen* would be used as fuel to keep the flames alive, unless the colour spread was a poster of an Ibrox star, in which case it would be saved. Stewards were few and far between and rarely ventured onto the terracing, so supporters were essentially given a free rein to do whatever they liked.

Arguably the most iconic symbols of the old Ibrox were the light-blue invalid cars that lined the pitch at all games of the era. Old photographs show dozens of the three-wheeled vehicles parked up in front of the north enclosure, giving their drivers a ringside seat for the action on the pitch. For those stuck behind them on the terraces the view was not quite so perfect.

AMONG KINDRED SPIRITS – Gordon Semple

I was a Rangers supporter for several years before I finally saw Ibrox Stadium with my own eyes, and when I attended my first Rangers home game, from the outside at least, I was not impressed. Old buildings rarely impress small boys and I was no exception, but when I was on the inside, in the Main Stand, my admiration for the place grew.

The year was 1962, and at last my father had brought me to the place I longed to visit. It set in motion a habit that would become a key aspect of my life and even influence career decisions in the years to come. The stadium soon became a place where I felt at home, among kindred spirits, and it was a wonderful feeling anticipating my next visit to see Rangers playing there. My dad had little interest in football, but he somehow managed to take me to see Rangers on a fairly regular basis until I was old enough to go on my own.

I'm grateful to him for allowing my interest in the club to develop, and those early trips together across the River Clyde to Ibrox helped my involvement with Rangers to take root and grow. It was my dad again who opened another door for me when, at my insistence, he put my name down to become a Rangers ball boy. It took a few years before it happened, but in 1966, several years after applying, my dream was realised, and this allowed me to pass through the main door of the stadium, like the players, to become a very privileged person – an employee of Rangers FC.

The ball boys' dressing room was between the boot room and the home dressing room, and the three entrance doors were arranged close together at the end of a corridor to the right of the main hallway just inside the main door of the stadium. Our dressing room doubled as a warm-up area for the players and the late Kai Johansen was frequently the first player to come through, often with goalkeeper Norrie Martin. Eventually, others would follow, and I once had the misfortune to be in the way of a misplaced thunderbolt from Roger Hynd. My stomach inadvertently halted the ball in its skewed path. One doesn't forget moments like that!

One of the other ball boys, Craig Malloch, like me, was always early to arrive, and we would frequently have a kick-about with whatever we could find to use as a ball. We'd have a wander out on to the pitch too and once buried coins in the Rangers end penalty spot.

The table tennis room was near to the tunnel and Craig and I would enjoy a few games before the players arrived. The first player on the premises was always Dave Smith, a favourite player of mine even to this day, and he would play us at table tennis until the rest of the players assembled. If memory serves me correctly, it was at this point that Craig and I would put out the corner flags.

Being a Rangers ball boy was an enviable position to be in for a young lad in Glasgow, and although any Rangers supporter would have done the job for nothing, Rangers paid us a small sum for the service we provided. Reserve fixtures paid 1s (5p), ordinary first-team games rewarded us with 2s (10p) and European ties saw us receiving a not inconsiderable half-crown (2s 6d or 12½ pence). A small bottle of Schweppes lemonade was also supplied after the game.

In the 1960s the Ibrox pitch would rise in the middle slightly and gently, almost imperceptibly, slope towards the wings. My station as a ball boy was usually in front of the enclosure, but when I was on the opposite side of the pitch there was the added benefit of actually being on the field at the same time as the players, as we all ran out together before the start of the game.

During my year as a ball boy I saw most parts of the stadium but not quite all of them. It was many years later, around the early days of the Souness revolution, that I got my first look at the old press box above the Main Stand. The chap who was showing us around allowed us a glimpse into the area immediately above it, and I was astonished to see old League flags and an assortment of other bits and pieces that had effectively been left to rot up there. I still wonder what happened to this miscellany, as this area would have been cleared when the press box disappeared forever to make way for the new Club Deck.

I've been fortunate to see many changes to Ibrox over the years, and when I first witnessed the old place it had a grandstand, an enclosure, a covered terracing opposite the Main Stand and a completely open terracing at both ends. The first significant change I recall was the addition of the partial and inadequate cover at the Rangers End. I heard a story that the build for this actually started at the Celtic End and that it had to be aborted when the error was spotted. How true this is I cannot say, but perhaps there's still someone around who can confirm or deny.

Nowadays, the stadium has changed significantly, but it still feels like Ibrox always did, especially in the Main Stand and enclosure areas. There will be continued development of the ground in the years ahead, and hopefully the character of the place will remain unchanged, and when I look at the red-brick façade of Ibrox today, the term that springs to mind is 'cathedral'. Ibrox Cathedral – it has a nice ring to it.

'A VAST SEA OF RED, WHITE AND BLUE HUMANITY'

In 1969 the chief reporter of Charles Buchan's *Football Monthly* magazine was sent north to Glasgow to report on the unruly natives. His brief was to stand on the Rangers End at Ibrox during the new year derby. Just like the *Picture Post* man 20 years earlier, Peter Morris was part gripped and part appalled by the spectacle. He confessed to having been 'traumatised' by the experience but described the clash – which ended in a 1–0 victory for Rangers – as 'a passionate, exciting struggle for prestige'. Morris wrote:

Everywhere the half-bottles of whiskey (sic) were out, the beer cans, the pint glasses, smuggled in under coats, ready to be used as weapons if lunacy prevailed. 'Glas-gow Rangers! Glas-gow Rangers! We'll support you ever more!' At my end the Rangers following was massed – a vast sea of red, white and blue humanity, roaring out the old battle songs – some going back half a century – confident that THEIR TEAM, the beloved 'Gers, would triumph. Across the park behind the far goal, the Celtic hordes were banked in one vast defiant phalanx. Solid they were and by contrast, much quieter.

The author was disappointed at the attitude of the home support towards the away players, rather naively bemoaning the lack of praise for Jimmy Johnstone's dribbling or Billy McNeill's 'cool defensive work'. He noticed 'only vitriolic abuse delivered in thick Glaswegian accents, coarsened by alcohol and the continual roaring out of those awe-inspiring anthems. It must have been the same at the Celtic end.'

I TOOK A TRIP TO IBROX, MY FAVOURITE TEAM TO CHEER
Jim Loughran – dedicated to Sandy and the Carmichael family of Glasgow's southside

The Ulster links with Scotland are many and varied, and we have a shared history in religion, education, music, industry, commerce and, of course, sport. My own family tree, featuring such Scottish Lowland names as Hanna, McKee, Paterson, Lindsay, Boyd, Maxwell, Cochrane, Clydesdale, Wilson and Geddis, is testimony to our Scottish lineage.

Growing up in Belfast in the 1950s, football was the abiding passion of my generation, and the romantic sounding names of Scottish clubs The Rangers, Third Lanark, Heart of Midlothian and the biblical Queen of the South fascinated me. The Scots had been pioneers in bringing the game to Ulster. Rangers had been among the early Scottish visitors and played the Cliftonville club twice in 1886, winning 8–2 and 4–1. In the years before World War One, the Light Blues made regular trips to meet Linfield and Glentoran and also visited Dublin to play Bohemians.

William Wilton was often at local games in a scouting role, and in 1904 the Distillery club reported Rangers to the IFA for making approaches to their full-back, Willie McCracken. Evidently Mr Wilton didn't hold a grudge, for he brought Rangers over to play Distillery on 20 March 1911 in a benefit game on behalf of the Lord Mayor of Belfast's Municipal Milk Fund for Poor Children. In the 1920s Rangers, under William Struth, resumed their Ulster trips and had established close links with the Linfield club, whose traditions and colours were in the Rangers mould. There is an iconic photograph of Struth and the Rangers party laying a wreath at the cenotaph at Belfast City Hall. By then Rangers had several Ulstermen in the team, such as Manderson, McCandless, Hamilton and later Sam English.

Excursion trips were being made from Belfast by supporters to big matches like the Scottish Cup Final and Old Firm games, and these trips were advertised in the Belfast press of the period. Rangers and other Scottish clubs also regularly took part in five-a-side tournaments at Windsor Park. However, the outbreak of World War Two meant Rangers did not return to Belfast until 30 April 1946 when they played Everton at Windsor Park, and then on 10 May 1955 they took part in a match against Linfield in aid of the Sandy Row Orange Hall Extension Fund.

My uncle Willie often attended the Orange Demonstration each July in Glasgow and would return with copies of *The Rangers Supporters' Association Annuals*, with their match reports of games from the previous season and a souvenir colour picture of the team; names like Ritchie, Shearer, Caldow, Millar, Brand and Wilson rolled off the tongue easily, and I treasured these books. They remain among my favourite Ibrox memorabilia today.

By the early 1960s I was attending football games in Belfast, and the Scotland and Scottish League teams would contain many Rangers players. In 1961 Scotland beat Northern Ireland 6–1 at Windsor Park with five Rangers in the team and all six goals coming from Ibrox players. The first time I actually watched Rangers was on 31 Oct 1962, when they played Spurs (captained by East Belfast's Danny Blanchflower) in London in the European Cup-Winners' Cup, and edited highlights were shown on TV that night. By this stage I wanted to go to Glasgow to see the team but my father had died, aged just 37, and my mum was reluctant to allow me to go.

When the Rangers Supporters' Association was formed in the late 1940s it led to several branches being organised in Ulster, and our local club was the Lagan Village RSC in East Belfast, founded in 1963. In those days the Burns & Laird Company ran the Belfast to Glasgow overnight ferry service, and their ships rejoiced in the names of *Royal Ulsterman* and *Royal Scotsman*. It was Friday 19 March 1965 when I was finally allowed to make my first trip to Ibrox with Lagan Village RSC. We left The Primrose Bar on the Albertbridge Road to catch the 9pm sailing for Glasgow. The ship, which had both first and second-class lounges, was packed with supporters. Much drinking was involved, and the traditional Ibrox anthems were being sung with gusto. It was a very long night and I suffered from seasickness, as the North Channel could be a rough crossing; the Stranraer to Larne ferry, *Princess Victoria,* sank in a storm in 1953 with the loss of 135 lives – many of them workmates of my dad's from Short Bros Aircraft Factory. I awoke from a fitful sleep and went out on deck to see the ship move slowly up the Clyde in the darkness. As the light improved, the shipyard gantries and tall, grey tenement buildings of Glasgow began to emerge into view, and the ship docked at the Merklands in Partick to unload its cargo of cattle. It turned about and slowly reversed up river to its berth at the Broomielaw.

Lagan Village RSC had forged close bonds with the Hutchesontown/Gorbals RSC on Glasgow's southside, and they were on the quayside to greet us that morning. A coach was laid on to take us to Cumberland Street Orange Hall, where a welcome breakfast of sausage, egg and rolls awaited. I was amazed at the warmth and affection shown to us that day by complete strangers and formed life-long friendships with Tommy Carmichael and his wife, Margaret, from Aikenhead Road. Tommy and his older brother, Alex, were founder members of the Hutchie RSC.

I was taken up to Mount Florida to see historic old Hampden Park, the site of so many iconic Rangers triumphs. A year before, I'd listened on the radio as Rangers beat Dundee in the 1964 Scottish Cup Final, and the following year I would be part of the 127,000 attendance at the 1966 Final. On leaving Hampden, we went into town to Morrison's of Argyle Street – official suppliers of Rangers' scarves and souvenirs – where I bought a scarf. The shop was underneath Central Station Bridge, and the rumble of the overhead trains and superb Victorian architecture of the city made a lasting impression. To this day when I visit Glasgow with my wife we always go to Central Station, and the memories of that day in 1965 are evoked.

Walking back up Bridge Street to the hall, the bar was in full swing and I met the likes of the late Tommy Rodgers, who would later run Annie Miller's pub, and the late Willie Leckie. By now the coach was outside for the journey to Ibrox, and we made our way onto a packed bus. The Lagan Village RSC bannerette was placed on the window beside the driver.

Rangers' opponents that day were Kilmarnock, managed by Willie Waddell, who would eventually win the title from Hearts on goal average. We were without Jim Baxter – still sidelined with a broken leg. As we approached the stadium I could hardly contain my excitement as the huge red-brick façade of the Main Stand, with its Rangers FC in blue letters on a white background, loomed into view.

The place was a hubbub of noise, souvenir sellers, programme vendors and mounted police officers. Thousands of fans in Rangers colours surrounded the stadium as we entered the turnstiles to the right of the Main Stand, with its magnificent gold rampant lion on a blue shield on the gable. The huge stairways leading to the top of the Copland Road End were bordered by neatly trimmed hedges and fences.

The attendance for the game was given as 31,000 but seemed much larger to this Ibrox debutant as we took our places high up in the terracing to the left of the goalmouth. The Rangers team that far-off day was: Ritchie, Provan, Caldow, Greig, McKinnon, Wood, Brand, Millar, Forrest, Beck and Wilson. Due to the passage of time many of the match details are now forgotten, but the game finished 1–1, with a Ralph Brand penalty levelling the scores after Joe Mason had put Killie ahead. However, one abiding and lasting impression has stuck with me – never to be forgotten – and that was the first sight of the Rangers players emerging from the tunnel and running out onto the magnificent green sward of Ibrox. The players were immaculate in the most vivid of blue shirts with a simple white v-neck, pristine white shorts and above all those cherry red-topped black socks – the classic and quintessential Rangers look so beloved by Bluenoses of my generation. Sadly, today, along with many other factors in the downgrading of a once great institution, my match-day experience is spoiled by the ugly garish red names and numbers and the red panels and inserts that have ruined the simple and uncluttered Rangers strip in the name of commercialism.

Many more trips followed that of 1965. Later that same year the captain of the Glasgow to Belfast boat turned the vessel around due to trouble onboard prior to an Old Firm game on 18 September, and all passengers were ordered off on the quayside at Belfast. From those early days, when I was the first in our family to follow on, a whole dynasty has now followed me, with my own family – including nephews, nieces and maybe someday grandchildren – taking their own trips to Ibrox: our favourite place to cheer.

THE DARKEST HOUR

It was the night panic spread throughout Scotland. In thousands of homes across the country, mothers, wives and girlfriends fretted as news slowly emerged of a terrible accident on the stairway at Ibrox Park. In the days before mobile phones, they faced an agonising wait for confirmation that their sons, husbands and boyfriends were safe. For most, the anguish was short-lived, their fears allayed when their loved ones eventually walked – or in some cases, staggered – through the front door, oblivious to the events at the stadium. Tears of relief followed. But for the devastated families of 66 supporters, there was no relief and no emotional reunion. The tears did flow, but they were tears of grief. Their loved ones did not come through the front door. Instead they died in the most agonising way imaginable, with the life squeezed out of them on what became known as Stairway 13.

The date was 2 January 1971. Four decades later, the sense of loss and disbelief at how so many people lost their lives in such horrific circumstances remains. How could this possibly have happened? They just went to watch their favourite football team.

It had been a bitterly cold day in Glasgow. Temperatures never made it above zero, and a freezing fog lingered over the city for much of the day. On a frozen-hard pitch at Ibrox, the Rangers and Celtic players had battled with their usual level of intensity in front of 80,000 fans. In the 89th minute Jimmy Johnstone scored a goal that seemed to guarantee

A picture postcard view of Ibrox from the air in the early 1970s. The notorious Stairway 13 is in the top right-hand corner.

victory for Celtic. The away end erupted in joy, while many Rangers fans left as soon as the ball hit the net, assuming that the match was over. But, with the last kick of the match, Colin Stein scored a dramatic equaliser, shooting home after meeting a curling free-kick from Dave Smith. Now it was the Rangers fans who celebrated. Those who left early heard the roar and celebrated the goal as they left the ground.

Both sets of fans headed off into the cold evening, reasonably happy with their lot. As the players disappeared up the tunnel, PA announcer Kenneth MacFarlane made the usual safety announcement over the loudspeaker: 'Spectators are requested to exercise care in leaving the stadium.' But on the exit stairway leading from the east terracing onto Cairnlea Drive, a tragedy was unfolding that would claim the lives of so many supporters. They were crushed to death under the weight of thousands of fellow fans.

Plenty of theories have been put forward for the cause of the accident. The most commonly repeated is that departing fans, hearing the cheers for Stein's late goal, tried to return to the terraces and collided with supporters trying to get down the stairs. It is an account that was discounted by eye-witnesses, whose accounts showed the tragedy occurred several minutes after the final whistle. Due to the sheer weight of numbers, it would also have been physically impossible for anyone to have turned around and walked back into the solid wall of spectators leaving the ground. Yet, despite all the evidence to the contrary, the myth persists to this day and is regularly repeated in print.

The most likely theory is that someone stumbled on their way down the stairway – possibly a youth who had been on a friend's shoulders – causing the crowd to cave in. As more fans left the terraces, the crush intensified, resulting in the collapse of several steel barriers that ran up the centre of the stairway. Because there were so many people, there was simply no escape for those caught up in the crush.

In the end, 66 people lost their lives on the stairway. Each of the victims had their own poignant story. They ranged in age from nine to 43 and came from all walks of life and all parts of Scotland. More than a third were still in their teens. There was one female among the dead – 18-year-old Margaret Ferguson. Just days earlier she had made a doll as a Christmas present for the baby daughter of Colin Stein, delivering it personally to his home. Less than a week later Stein was attending her funeral. Five schoolboy friends from the same street in the Fife village of Markinch travelled to the game together and died together. Their funerals all took place on the same day, each attended by a Rangers player.

An estimated 145 fans were injured. Many received life-saving treatment as they lay on the stairway. Rangers manager Willie Waddell and his Parkhead counterpart, Jock Stein, helped the emergency services treat the injured as the dressing rooms were turned into makeshift casualty wards. Meanwhile, those who had perished were carried from the stairway back into the stadium, where they were laid out in a line on the playing field, their bodies covered with jackets and coats. It was a harrowing sight for all those who witnessed the scenes. The following are the stories of some of those whose lives were directly touched by the disaster…

The mangled railings on Stairway 13 the day after the 1971 disaster.   (courtesy PA Photos)

THE SURVIVOR – David Stirling. Evidence to the Fatal Accident Inquiry, Glasgow Sheriff Court

I watched the game from passageway 17. After the final whistle I stood for about three or four minutes and then moved to the exit. At the top of the stairs I saw some young men having a drink. A young chap had a bottle of whisky in his hand, and I said to him 'You're not going to drink all that yourself?' and he said 'Here you are mister, you can have it.' So I took it and took a mouth of it, then I gave it to my friend, Neilly Kelly, and he took a mouth of it and he handed it to my other friend, David Anderson. There was nothing out of the ordinary.

I saw another friend of mine, Ian Nicholson, about 15 steps in front of me. The next time I saw him he was turning round trying to wave the crowd back. I was just about at the first landing. He was walking down and then I saw him with his hands up. Someone had gone down – you could see the space where someone had fallen.

We were all trying to hold back. You could see the big chaps were trying to hold everyone back. There were kids all around us. The pressure of the crowd was just the usual coming out of a match; everyone squeezes up. But as we were all pressing down, you could feel yourself getting lifted off your feet by the people in front. Everyone was trying to hold back to ease the people in front out the road. I had my arm around three young lads, trying to protect them.

The next minute the pressure got so great that I felt as if I was going myself. I happened to get this left arm up and I got a breath of air. The next minute, there was a bang and the bannister burst and everyone flew forward. We were getting pressed together, and your body was getting lifted at an angle from the pressure behind, and the people in front were all falling. When the barrier went I seemed to fly through the air and landed on top of all the bodies. I started crawling and other bodies came on top of me, and they seemed to bridge me. I was at the bottom, lying half on top of others, and there were three young lads at my side.

About 30 or 40 minutes after that I got free. It took so long because there were bodies at the front of me and bodies at the back of me to be cleared away first. And bodies on top of me. There were some young boys to my left and to my right. I don't know if they were the same young boys I had been with before. There was a sandy-headed lad, I turned his head around and there was nothing.

THE AMBULANCEMAN – Jack Kirkland

After the final whistle at Ibrox that Saturday I went off home, unaware that anything unusual had happened, for I'd left from an exit far from the Copland Road End of the stadium and the stairway where the horror of Ibrox took place.

I was whistling when I arrived home, ready for my tea and a relaxing Saturday night in front of the television. My young daughter came running out to meet me and I held out my arms to her. Then I realised she wasn't smiling or laughing at me. She was breathless and shouting 'Daddy, Daddy! There's a man on the phone. He says you've to hurry.' I ran past her and into the house. It was the duty control officer who was calling. 'A barrier's collapsed at Ibrox, Jack. It looks bad. We have reports coming in all the time.' 'But I've just come from there…' and I thought, it can't be that bad. I would have known, surely? The officer told me 'It happened just after the final whistle. News of it is just beginning to come through. You'd better get back there, right now. There's a fleet of ambulances on its way now. I'm afraid the single-duty ambulance that's always there is sorely inadequate.'

When I arrived at Ibrox the scene was one of complete chaos. People were running about all over the place, shock etched on their faces. I had to fight my way through the crowd to reach the ambulance room in the main building. I just wasn't prepared for the sight that greeted me when I arrived there. There wasn't an unoccupied room in the building; patients were lying everywhere, on floors and in corridors, being treated by the St Andrew's Ambulance Volunteers in attendance. I saw two young nurses, only girls themselves, giving mouth-to-mouth resuscitation to men who lay dying, ribs crushed, faces smeared with blood. The air was filled with the cries of the dying and the injured. In the melee I managed to find my colleague, Robert Brown. We decided the best thing we could do was to return to the Main Stand and liaise with the senior police officer. We had to step over bodies that had been laid on the ground. Men were moaning in pain, their faces pain-weary. Police and ambulance men were giving the injured and unconscious oxygen or mouth-to-mouth resuscitation. Rescuers were taking many to the Main Stand for medical attention.

I checked in with ambulance control. No one hospital could cope with the number of injured we had here. Five hospitals were alerted to receive casualties. The Southern General was to take the majority of the injured. Others went to the Victoria, the Western, the Royal and the Royal Alexandria in Paisley. Paisley ambulance control, too, had been requested to assist and had dispatched three ambulances.

Off-duty ambulance officers and men had rushed from their homes to HQ to take up duty as soon as they heard the news of the disaster on radio or television. The officers had been sent to the hospitals receiving casualties and the police mortuary. Their task: to speed up the turnaround of ambulances and to make sure they were fully equipped before returning to the stadium.

Soon, processions of stretcher-bearers were carrying the injured to the waiting ambulances. No one spared themselves. Football officials from both teams worked as hard as anyone, the disbelief at the enormity of what had happened evident on all their faces. As soon as ambulances were loaded, they were heading for different hospitals. And then it was back for more stretchers and a seemingly unending stream of injured.

In all, 18 ambulances worked a shuttle service between the stadium and the hospitals. The ambulances had a difficult task. The heavy traffic congestion that happens after every football fixture would have badly hampered their progress but, thanks to the expert police assistance, they got through, with most of their patients being given oxygen therapy on the way.

Outside the ground, crowds of people, drawn by the news of the disaster on radio or television, stood silently, wondering if their loved ones were those in the ambulances – or worse – under one of those growing number of blankets on the ground inside. Once all the casualties were safely away, Robert Brown and I had the unenviable task of arranging for the transportation of the dead to the police mortuary.

The fatalities had been lined in rows inside, underneath the training tunnel, but when we tried to reverse our ambulances into the tunnel we realised that it was too low. The bodies would have to be brought out. With much reluctance we commandeered a groundsman's two-wheel trolley. The stretchers were loaded onto it and pushed through the tunnel to the ambulances. That is a sight that really shook me. The indignity of having to transport those bodies that way seemed just too much. It took the best part of an hour to complete this heartbreaking task. By the end there was hardly a face that wasn't streaked with tears.

When I checked in with ambulance control, I was told that Robert and I were to come to the Southern General Hospital to arrange for the transportation of further bodies to the police mortuary. The hospital was a hive of activity when we arrived there. Glasgow Corporation had offered to supply private cars for the transportation of the injured to their homes after treatment, and this offer had been gratefully taken up. Ambulances, taxis and cars zoomed in and out constantly. The ambulance crews were totally exhausted.

Robert and I had only just arrived and were talking with one of the crews when a taxi drew up and two men got out. They were supporting a third man, who was so shocked and white I thought at first he had been injured. One of the men came forward. 'It's his wee boy,' he indicated to the third man, who looked barely able to stand. 'He went to the match, and didn't come home. We've been to the stadium, the police sent us here. Said a few children had been taken to the hospital.' The man suddenly started to cry, 'Don't tell me he's deid. Please don't tell me he's deid.' One of the ambulance men went toward him and said, 'I brought in a boy not long ago. What was your boy's name?' The man whispered his boy's name in a sob. I think we all held our breath. We all prayed. The ambulance man clapped a hand on his shoulder. 'Aye, that's him,' he said. 'He's a casualty. All he's got is an injury to his ankle.' The man suddenly threw his arms around him and hugged him, with tears of joy streaming down his face. 'Aw thanks,' he kept saying. 'Aw God, thanks.' He was one of the lucky ones. Others, unfortunately, had sad news awaiting them.

In their endeavours to save lives, 3,240 gallons of oxygen were used. It may be that no lives were saved that way, that's something that we'll never know, but we like to think that there's somebody walking about out there today because of that oxygen.

Next day, Sunday, we were out again going round the various hospitals and the police mortuary to pick up our equipment. I was talking to a young policeman outside the mortuary when an old woman approached us. 'Son,' she said to me. 'I've lived in that building for over 40 years,' and with a blue-veined hand she indicated the tenement overlooking the mortuary. 'I've seen ambulances come and go, but I've never seen anything like what I saw last night. A long line of ambulances stretching as far as my old eyes could see. Down there…' She gazed along the road as if she could still see them now. 'I knew what was in those ambulances, and I just sat and cried. Do you know what I mean, son?' Her watery blue eyes filled up with tears. 'I just had to come out of the house to talk to somebody. Do you understand, son?' 'Aye,' I said. 'I understand fine.' She walked away, shaking her head and muttering 'It's a terrible thing. A terrible thing.'

'It's funny, for everyone there's something, just one thing, that makes tragedy sink in,' the young policeman said. I knew what he meant. I was thinking of bringing those bodies out through the training tunnel. 'Do you know what it was for me?' he went on. 'It was when I went into Govan Police Station, and there, lined up in pathetic wee bundles, were all the personal belongings of the dead. That's when it really hit me.'

All through that night the police were magnificent. They went to any lengths to help the public, and us. Whenever I hear people complaining about the police, I remember Ibrox and their tireless efforts to help everyone. They do a hazardous job to the best of their ability. It's a pity they're only appreciated when they're needed.

THE SON – Craig Smith, son of George Smith

My father was a kind and loving man who always had a smile on his face. In fact he was smiling the last time I saw him, on the day of the Old Firm game in January 1971. As he put his coat on to go to the game I asked if I could go with him. He laughed and told me I was 'too wee' (I was only four) but promised me that he would take me to another game instead.

My dad kissed us all goodbye and walked out the door. At about ten to five there was a newsflash on TV saying there had been an accident at Ibrox. There was no suggestion of the scale, just that some people had been injured. My mother looked worried but not concerned, but as the night wore on she started to get more anxious. They had arranged to go to the golf club dance, so she was concerned that Dad hadn't called. She started to call round friends and family but no one had heard anything. Then suddenly, the doorbell rang. My brother, Stephen, went to answer it, and I heard a scream from my mum. Stephen and my other brother, George, were standing with tears pouring down their faces.

He went to the game with his younger brother, John, brother-in-law Alex and two others. They all left together and headed for Stairway 13. As they got to the top they were separated from each other by the mass of supporters trying to leave the ground. My dad was forced round to the first stairway nearest the wooden fence. John and Alex were forced apart and down the next two stairways. John was unable to move and passed out. My dad was trapped, penned in, between bodies, dead and alive, against the wooden fence, the life being squeezed out of him.

John was passed over a sea of people and over the fence. As he came to, still groggy, he looked up to see his brother, my dad, standing upright, crushed to death, his face resting on the wooden fence.

I will never forget my mother's scream, the sound of people coming down the stairs of the house, my uncles hugging me and my brothers, saying 'Your daddy's dead son, your daddy's dead.' I remember thinking 'They must have got it all wrong, how can he be dead? He was at a football match – people don't die at football matches.'

After the disaster we received lots of support and comfort from friends and family. But the most touching thing that arrived was an envelope through the door. Inside was £30 and a simple note that read 'Sorry. I hope this can help. From a Tim.'

THE FRIEND – Shane Fenton

The morning of 2 January 1971 was like any other match-day morning for us young Old Firm fans from the south end of Markinch, with the usual mickey-taking, banter and side bets. Pete Lee, Joe Mitchell and myself – all Celtic fans – walked from Markinch along with Dougie Morrison, Peter Easton, Ron Paton, Mason Philip and Bryan Todd – all Rangers followers. We were headed for the CISWO Club in Glenrothes, where we would board the rival supporters' buses.

Despite supporting different teams we were all the best of mates, and most of us played for the Markinch United football team. Little did we know as we boarded our buses that it would be the last time we would see our pals.

The match itself was nothing out of the ordinary and looked to be heading for a no-scoring draw when Celtic scored in the last minute. We at the Celtic end decided to leave at this stage and were actually back on our bus for some 15 minutes before some of the older supporters arrived and told us that Rangers had equalised. At that time we knew nothing of the tragic events that were happening on Stairway 13. In fact, it wasn't until the bus made a stop in Kincardine on the way home that we heard something had happened at the Rangers end of Ibrox.

The older fans who had been at the pub for a refreshment had heard the news on the television. We never thought for a minute that Markinch boys had been involved. When I returned, many locals had already started to panic. My relatives, like those of the other boys who knew we were at the match, had already started enquiring to make sure we were all OK.

When the news eventually came through that Ron, Dougie, Bryan, Peter and Mason hadn't returned with the Rangers bus, all kinds of thoughts went through our heads. We hoped that they had just missed the bus and would arrive home later. We stayed out until late in the evening hoping they would appear on the last buses and trains into Markinch.

It was over the next couple of days when the devastating news that we feared became a reality. The entire village was in complete shock with the news that our five friends had been victims of the terrible disaster. The next few days Markinch, particularly Park View – the street where four of the boys lived – was awash with reporters, photographers and television news crews.

When it was time for the funerals, almost the entire town of Markinch – then a population of 2,344 – turned out to mourn the five local schoolboys. Three of the boys were buried side by side at Markinch Cemetery. The services of the other two were held at Kirkcaldy Crematorium. I can remember the cortège stretching back along the streets lined with mourners. Rangers' chairman, John Lawrence, attended the service at Markinch along with half a dozen players.

The boys may be gone, but 37 years on they are still remembered by the people of Markinch. Their names come up periodically when we recall schoolboy tales in our pub conversations. And there is a permanent reminder with the memorial plaque that is situated at the end of Park View.

The tragedy affected many people in different ways. For me, it put me off attending many more senior football matches. Before the disaster, I could count on one hand the amount of Celtic matches I had missed in the previous four years. Since it, I probably wouldn't need one hand to count the games I've been to.

THE EYEWITNESS – Maureen Oswell, 18 Cairnlea Drive.

Evidence to the Fatal Accident Inquiry, Glasgow Sheriff Court

I was in my sitting room watching the crowds entering and leaving the ground. My sister visited about 4.30pm and stood looking out the window. The gates had been opened to let people leave. My husband, who was listening to the game on the radio, told me that Celtic had scored. A short time later, he said Rangers had scored. After Celtic had scored, the stairs were absolutely packed. As far as they were concerned the game was over. The stairs can hold thousands and they were packed. Generally, as the game ends, they all line up at the top of the stairs and when the final whistle goes they all run down, but after Celtic scored they all just started moving.

The minute the fans realised Rangers had scored, naturally they stopped. No one could go up again, though, it would be like running into a brick wall. They all seemed to stop, started cheering and continued downstairs.

My husband said to me 'That is it, the game is over.' He switched off his wireless and started coming to the window. Everybody was happy. Just coming down the top of the first passage, I saw a boy was sitting on someone else's shoulders. He was naturally celebrating, and his whole body was swinging loose. He had his arms up in the air. I pointed him out to my sister, my husband and the children, and naturally we were all watching them because we had never seen this before. I said it was a stupid thing to do, and I did say 'something is going to happen'. I have seen men carrying their children like this, but their children's arms have been round their necks. With such a crowd, with him swinging loose like this – I had always warned my own wee boy about the stairs – I just felt something would happen. They were at a normal pace going downstairs, and they vanished. With the trees and what not, they do go out of view for a while and they come back into view, and I was watching for them. But I didn't see them again.

All of a sudden, it just seemed as if everything was going forward. The impression I got looking down on it was that it seemed to start further up and stop at this point on the landing. They all just seemed to be on the one side, falling in the way…it was like looking down on a lot of heads and they suddenly all started folding forwards. Everything seemed to stop at the landing second up from the bottom.

The movement was brought to a halt by the fans that were further down the stairs, stopping and turning round and starting telling the people from up top to go back. We couldn't really make out what was happening. The people at the bottom stopped, and the fans were trying to stop them right up at the top from going down, and they did stop them…I saw them all falling. It was as if a hole had appeared in the ground and people were just going. There were so many people that I didn't see any individual actually falling on the ground.

We saw one man running out with his head bleeding, and he immediately appeared with a policeman. That was the first thing we saw. We never thought for one minute that anybody had been killed or anything. Then we did see a few injured…I think the majority of them were inside, behind the turnstiles, so we didn't really see them. It was quite a while before we realised there were so many, because I think the majority were taken onto the park. The ones that were brought down that we saw outside or on the hill, they were more or less, what you would say, in their last stages…

ANOTHER EYEWITNESS – Robert Duncan, 16 Cairnlea Drive. Evidence to the Fatal Accident Inquiry, Glasgow Sheriff Court

I was looking down on the drive and I saw a walkie-talkie policeman going about. I noticed him move towards the big gate and go in. I wondered if perhaps there had been a fight or something in there, but it didn't turn out to be that way at all. He was going up the side of the fence. This is where all the trouble started, from halfway down the steps. There was a young man – he was carrying either a jacket or a raincoat – and whether that young man had lost his balance or whether he had been tripped I just couldn't say. He must have put his hand up to try and catch his balance.

They were coming down so fast that there were some men carried down there; I am sure their feet never touched one step all the way down. As a matter of fact, the rush was so much it was just like a river that burst its banks. For all the games I have watched people coming out of there, I think that was the worst time. The way they came down there, after that second goal was scored, it made all the people at the top of the stairway get so excited…they got what they wanted, a goal, and they turned to come down the stairway. On the stairway, walking down, they started to run and, of course, that is where people lost their balance.

One or two of the older men would turn round and put their hands out to try and stop the oncoming people, but it was no use, all in vain. That was when one was falling over the other…I thought to myself 'The pile of people is three to four feet deep.' They were bursting the side of the railings. It was just then that a policeman in front of my window asked if I had a telephone. I waved for him to come up. He said 'I must get an ambulance. There is a man down beside me and I am sure he is dead, and there might be another two.' I asked the man if there was anything I could do for him, such as giving them sheets or blankets, because we had to do that one time before, and he said 'I don't think so.'

There was so much going on by this time, because within a matter of minutes there were policemen arriving and I really don't know where they came from. They must have been coming from everywhere in the city. They were arriving there in motorcycles and squad cars. I don't know how they got through the people who had already left the stadium.

The people were staggering out, and I thought some of them at this time of the year had a drink in them but it wasn't drink. The one man who died in front of me looked round, and he just went down on his knees and that was it. I saw the ambulance arrive, and the driver and the other gentleman, who was in beside him, tried to give first aid to the man, and they worked exceedingly hard for a matter of five minutes or so, but they knew it was hopeless.

THE PLAYER – Sandy Jardine, Rangers' right-back

In an Old Firm game if you win or draw you're happy. If you are beaten it's a nightmare. So we were sitting in the dressing room, chatting about the game, unwinding with a bath. Somebody came in and said 'You'll have to get out the bath quickly', but did not explain why. There was no urgency. Then they came through and said 'There's been an accident, you'll need to get out really quick.'

We were in the process of getting changed into our clothes when they started bringing bodies in. I remember trying to find out some information before getting into the car to go home to Edinburgh. They said a barrier had collapsed and two people had died. By the time I left the stadium it had risen to 10, then 22 then 44. By the time I got to Edinburgh, it was 66.

There was a feeling of disbelief. You could not comprehend it. Even then, Ibrox was one of the most modern and safe grounds in Europe, by the standards of the day. I can remember being on the ground staff as a 15-year-old and part of my duties were to sweep the terraces. I remember sweeping the stairs, and the barriers were so solid you could not imagine them being twisted like that.

We were all told to come in on the Monday morning and we ceased to be a football club for three weeks. There are things I always remember. The first is the bodies being brought in. The second was seeing the people in the hospital and hearing them relate what had happened. How they had turned black because of the lack of oxygen and how they were lifted off their feet.

But the worst was attending the funerals of the young kids who had died. That was particularly traumatic.

THE POLITICIAN – Tam Dalyell, MP for West Lothian, speaking in the House of Commons, during the second reading of the Safety of Sports Grounds Bill, 18 January 1974

When I was a schoolteacher at Bo'ness Academy in West Lothian, along with teaching colleagues and the janitor I used to organise parties of 80 to 120 boys to visit evening European Cup matches at Ibrox Park, at a time in the late 1950s when Glasgow Rangers were having a successful run in international competitions. I confess to having had a certain sense of relief when the last pupil was back on the bus on the way home.

When I first heard about that terrible Ibrox disaster on that ghastly early January afternoon in 1971, my reaction was, frankly, one of 'There but for the grace of God went we.' The general point to be made is that it is no good allowing us to say 'Oh, but Ibrox was one in a million. If they had not scored a late goal, if the crowd had not turned back, if the goal had come a minute earlier or a minute later…', because any Scottish football fan can provide 40-odd 'ifs'. The truth is that, whereas the Ibrox disaster was the result of a culmination of unfortunate coincidences, the odds stacked against such an event were not all that long.

More than that, there may be other disasters that have been just avoided in the last 30 years. Nothing could have been worse than the aftermath of Ibrox. Welsh MPs of all parties, my right honourable friend, the Member for Huyton – Mr Harold Wilson – the prime minister and others have movingly described what they felt in the week of Aberfan. Ibrox was the Scottish Aberfan.

I shall never forget – many of my Scottish colleagues of both parties did the same – going to the funeral of a 16-year-old constituent in Broxburn, West Lothian, and being taken to his bedroom by his grief-stricken parents to see the lad's bed covered with flowers and the pictures of his Rangers heroes pinned around the wall. Nor do I forget the lasting distress of Colin Stein, whom I had taken abroad as a 13-year-old to play football from the Linlithgow Academy, who scored that vital last-minute goal.

Anyone in St Mungo's Cathedral, Glasgow, for the official memorial service must have taken a vow that day that a disaster of the order of Ibrox must never be allowed to happen again. This distressing human situation is much involved in the bill. For most honourable members, it is about that human tragedy and about families losing bread-winning fathers and teenage sons. When it comes to this kind of discussion, there are no grey areas.

The first principle is that football clubs are the only commercial venture providing entertainment that do not currently have to conform to legislation for safety. Would it be tolerated if theatre management were to say 'We are so squeezed for space that we cannot provide the safety element, which we ourselves know to be necessary, or guarantee the safety of our clients?' The answer is, of course not. Simply to articulate such a proposition shows its absurdity.

In this context of safety, football grounds are in the same category as theatres and cinemas. They, too, must be seen to be doing as much as possible for the safety of their clients. 'Clients' may be an unusual term to describe the regulars who go to Highbury, Anfield or Parkhead, but in terms of personal safety it is as clients to whom there are obligations that football supporters must be viewed.

If the money is not to be forthcoming, the question arises 'Do we have the bill or do we not?' If money is not to be found from government sources or from club sources, someone some time will say to us 'Be it on our own heads if there is another Burnden Park or another Ibrox Park.' Here, there is a feeling of responsibility.

THE AFTERMATH

As news of the disaster spread, Glasgow and the rest of Scotland were united in shock and sorrow. Messages of sympathy came from all over the world, along with promises of financial assistance for the families of the victims. US president Richard Nixon sent his condolences as did political leaders in New Zealand, Germany and elsewhere. The Pope also expressed his sympathies for the victims, one of many religious leaders to lend their voice to the tributes.

Within hours of the disaster, Glasgow's Lord Provost Sir Donald Liddle, who had been at the match, set up a fund to raise money for all those that would suffer financially. Rangers quickly announced they would donate £50,000 to the appeal. Celtic also made a contribution, and there were donations from many other clubs around the world. Offers of help also came from senior football figures in Brazil, Spain, West Germany, Portugal and Italy.

The day after the tragedy, Rangers made their first official public statement on the terrible events, praising the 'heroic efforts' of the emergency services, medical staff, employees of both Rangers and Celtic, and ordinary members of the public who had all done their best to help the victims. Manager Willie Waddell took responsibility as the public face of the club in the aftermath of the tragedy, issuing statements and generally taking control of what was an incredibly difficult situation for all at the club.

It was his decision that Rangers players should attend the funerals of the victims, and he also organised hospital visits for the squad to meet the injured. The players listened intently as the survivors told their harrowing stories of the horrors they suffered and witnessed on the stairway. At the Victoria Infirmary, 25-year-old Stewart McMillan told players Willie Johnston and Alfie Conn of his terrifying ordeal. 'The crowd were surging over the bodies like a tidal wave. I was caught by the crowd and jammed against a barrier. I am very lucky to be alive.'

Waddell later said that the players had been 'upset and moved' at what they had heard from the survivors. The emotional trauma would only get worse, as the players attended a succession of funerals for the victims later in the week. On one tragic day, more than 20 funerals took place in Glasgow alone. Heartbreaking scenes were repeated in towns and villages all over the country – a testament to the club's massive appeal out in the Glasgow boundaries. The most poignant scenes were in Markinch, where hundreds lined the streets to say farewell to five young pals who lost their lives. In the Stirlingshire town of Slamannan, two brothers, Richard and John McLeay, were laid to rest side by side in the same grave.

On Saturday 9 January a memorial service, attended by more than 3,000 mourners and watched by millions on television, took place at Glasgow Cathedral. Crowds gathered at the cathedral gates to hear the proceedings broadcast on loudspeakers. Rev Robert Bone, the parish minister for Ibrox, offered prayers for the 'ordinary man in the crowd' who put their own safety at risk in order to help others. He also praised the players who had done what they could to support the grieving. 'We remember with pride the determination of these young men to share in the grief of all the bereaved. They have seen in a week as much sorrow as many do in a lifetime.'

Two weeks after the tragedy, Rangers returned to footballing action. After the harrowing events of the last fortnight, it must have been something of a relief for the players to get back to what they knew best. Before the match with Dundee United, the Rangers team, officials and directors stood in silence for two minutes in tribute to the victims. A special edition of the match

The match programme for the first game at Ibrox after the disaster.

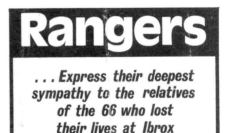

Rangers

. . . Express their deepest sympathy to the relatives of the 66 who lost their lives at Ibrox on January 2, 1971

. . . extend their good wishes for a speedy recovery to the 145 injured

AND

. . . offer their thanks to all those who worked so magnificently under tragic circumstances.

● Two minutes silence will be observed before today's match.

programme listed the names of all those who lost their lives, and the front page was devoted to a sombre black-bordered message from the club, which said 'Rangers express their deepest sympathy to the relatives of the 66 who lost their lives at Ibrox on 2 January 1971…extend their good wishes for a speedy recovery to the 145 injured and offer their thanks to all those who worked so magnificently under tragic circumstances.'

The atmosphere at the game was understandably muted, and many of the 27,776 crowd started to leave with 15 minutes to go. The stairway where so many lost their lives two weeks before remained boarded off at the top and bottom, with the mangled steel bannisters hidden from view.

THE INQUIRY

As grief consumed the nation, thoughts turned to how and why this disaster happened. The question on most people's lips was why had lessons not been learned from the two very similar accidents on the same stairway in 1961 and 1969? Prime Minister Edward Heath announced there would be two inquiries into the disaster – one would be a Fatal Accident Inquiry into what caused the 66 deaths, and the other would look at the more general issues of sports ground safety.

The weekly newspaper Inside Football *calls for new measures to make football grounds more safe.*

The FAI was to last seven days and began on 15 February at Pollokshaws Burgh Hall before Sheriff Allan Walker. A succession of witnesses gave their harrowing accounts of what had happened, including pathologist Professor Giles Forbes, who said that 60 of the victims had suffered asphyxiation and the other six suffocation caused by their airways being blocked. Fans who had survived the crush also gave their version of events, along with local residents who witnessed the tragedy unfolding from their homes.

Former Rangers manager Scot Symon told the court how improvements had been made to the stairway after the previous fatal accident in 1961, while he was in charge of the team. Rangers director David Hope and chairman John Lawrence were also called to tell the court what had been done by the club in the wake of the previous incidents.

After more than two hours of deliberations, the jury returned their verdict. Their written statement concluded that the accident had happened because one or more fans had fallen on their way down the stairs and that the pressure from the other departing supporters caused those at the front to fall over those who had collapsed first. The verdict ruled out the myth that the crush was caused by fans turning back after Colin Stein's goal, and also exonerated Rangers Football Club of direct blame.

A civil action taken later by widow Margaret Dougan was not so kind in its judgement of the club. Mrs Dougan, whose husband Charles died in the accident, was awarded more than £26,000 in damages, and her case prompted Sheriff J. Irvine Smith to issue a damning criticism of Rangers. Scathingly, he said little had been done to improve safety on the staircases after the previous incidents and found that the club appeared to have proceeded with the view that 'if the problem was ignored long enough, it would eventually disappear'.

THE SAFETY LEGACY

Meanwhile, the government appointed Lord Wheatley to carry out a detailed review of safety at all British football grounds. The inquiry recommended that football grounds should be licensed by local authorities in much the same way as a cinema or restaurant would be. Councils would be able to call on the expertise of fire brigades, building inspectors, engineers and surveyors, among others, who would have the knowledge required to decide whether a ground was in a suitable state to be used by the public. Lord Wheatley's reckoning was that Ibrox showed that a club could spend money on ground improvements, as Rangers had, but still not meet the standards of safety that were required.

The subsequent Safety of Sports Grounds Act of 1975 enshrined Wheatley's recommendations in law. If a club did not meet the standards, they would not be granted a safety certificate and therefore would not be allowed to use their ground. The certificate specified the total capacity of the ground, as well as the individual sections within, and insisted that entrances and exits met specific standards and were kept in a good state of maintenance. Areas considered unsafe had to be improved within a year and had to be completely closed down if they were beyond repair. Fines of up to £2,000 could be imposed for non-compliance.

Thirty years later, official documents were made public that revealed local authorities were prevented from taking control of safety at football grounds just six months before the disaster. The Scottish Office dismissed a direct request from councils to be given licensing powers over crowd safety at bigger grounds, saying that it would offer only 'marginal' benefits. In their written response, civil servants told the councils 'For the reasons given, (the Secretary of State) considers that the improvements which might follow the introduction of a licensing system would at best be marginal…and he therefore feels no step should be taken to introduce legislation to this end at the present time.'

The Ibrox disaster had demonstrated in the most tragic way imaginable that football had a responsibility for the well-being and safety of its supporters. While Willie Waddell set out to ensure that Rangers would never again find themselves mourning their supporters in such circumstances, other clubs were slow to react. It took the Bradford fire of 1985 and the Hillsborough disaster of 1989 to finally convince the rest of British football that the Victorian conditions endured by supporters were no longer acceptable.

A TIME FOR CHANGE

Barely six months after the Ibrox disaster, Rangers embarked on a European campaign that was to result in what was arguably their greatest achievement. While their League form was less than impressive, Rangers performed admirably in the European Cup-Winners' Cup, beating Rennes, Sporting Lisbon and Torino to reach the semi-final against old adversaries Bayern Munich. A superb 1–1 draw in Bayern's old Grunwalder Stadium set the scene for a momentous night at Ibrox – a night that many fans still consider to be the old stadium's finest.

The events of January 1971 had sent shockwaves throughout British football, and there was a distinct feeling of 'there but for the grace of God'. Exits at West Ham's Upton Park ground, for example, also had safety warnings installed in the early 1970s. The signs simply read 'Remember Ibrox.' Rangers had spent around £12,000 on improvements around the stairway, where the accident occurred. The main change was the building of 7ft-high concrete walls at the top of each stairway, aimed at filtering the departing fans and cutting down the numbers going onto the exit staircases at the same time. Large overhead signs were put up on gantries at the top of the stairway with the warning 'Caution – One step down.'

The proposals were the result of weeks of investigation by consultant engineers, including an aerial study of crowd movements at a Scottish Cup tie between Rangers and Aberdeen. Gordon Farquhar, of consultants W.A. Fairhurst, said at the time 'The use of aerial pictures was a great help. We found that one of the main reasons for the crush was a mass of people standing at the top of the stairway waiting for the final whistle. With a 7ft concrete wall there, they obviously will not be able to do this.'

The Ibrox improvements were passed by the Glasgow Dean of Guild in July 1971 and were successfully tested a month later at a pre-season friendly against Everton. It was the first time the tragedy stairway had been opened since the disaster.

BEHIND THE SCENES

The second leg of the semi-final in April 1972 was an 80,000 sell-out success. Demand for tickets had been enormous, meaning a busy time for ticket office boss Kenny MacFarlane, although thankfully he did not encounter the same sort of problems he faced the season before, when Rangers played Bayern in the Fairs Cup. He spent most of that match holed up in an office deep inside the Main Stand, counting out thousands of pennies and half-pennies, handed in by West German sailors in return for tickets.

MacFarlane, who had been on Rangers' books as a goalkeeper in the 1960s, was responsible for distributing more than half a million tickets a season, and that was in the days when all-ticket matches were few and far between. In a 1971 interview, he said 'I'm badgered a lot outside Ibrox when there is an all-ticket game in the offing. But you get to know your real friends – and also those pals who also crop up at certain times.'

A whole army worked behind the scenes at Ibrox on match days, and most came under the control of Jimmy Malloch. The first member of the Malloch family to work the Ibrox turnstiles started in 1890. Gavin Malloch initially worked at the old ground before moving with the club to the new stadium, where he rose to the post of head gate-checker and served the club until 1938. Several other members of the clan also took up jobs at the stadium. Under Gavin Malloch's guidance, they could clear a crowd of 100,000 in just 15 minutes.

Jimmy, who went by the title of turnstile superintendent, first started work in 1945 when Rangers played against Dynamo Moscow. He told the club newspaper in 1971 'Rangers have been the Malloch family's life. From my own point of view I can say that any money I get for my work at Ibrox is purely incidental. I grew up at Ibrox, as you might say, and my routine revolves around working at the stadium on Saturdays.'

Jimmy oversaw a team of 220 men – gate-checkers, stewards and car park attendants – on match days. So well regarded was he and his team that he would even send some of his squad to Hampden and Celtic Park to help out during big matches. Of the six Mallochs working at Ibrox in the early 1970s, Craig, the youngest, had the the most high-profile job, if not the most responsible. His role was to carry the board with the lucky programme number on it around the pitch at half-time.

Before each match, Jimmy would delegate a team of three to go round all the gates and check the number of times the turnstiles clicked shut at the match before. The gate men would then move into position and take cash from the paying punters before going round the gates again to record the new numbers. They got an accurate figure for the attendance by adding the sums up and deducting the number from the old number. The figures were then tallied with the takings before the cash was deposited at the bank. Incidentally, these figures did not include the hundreds, if not thousands, of youngsters who got into the match for nothing by persuading a paying customer to give him a 'lift over'. This was a tradition at Scottish grounds for decades and only really died out with the advent of all-seated stadia in the 1980s and 1990s.

VICTORY IN EUROPE

There are rare occasions in football when various factors come together to contrive a result that might otherwise be impossible. On the evening of 17 April 1972 the stars aligned themselves over Ibrox and allowed Rangers to topple the mighty West Germans. This was a team that had developed over five years since winning the Cup-winners' Cup in 1967 into one of the strongest on the continent. Ten days after the semi-final, six Bayern players starred in a West German team that destroyed England 3–1 in a European Championships qualifier at Wembley, and they featured heavily when the Germans won the tournament later that summer, followed by the 1974 World Cup. The same year, Bayern themselves won the first of three consecutive European Cups.

Rangers, on the other hand, were struggling domestically: once again they were out of contention in the League, were knocked out of the League Cup in the early stages and were soon to be eliminated from the Scottish Cup at the semi-final stage by Hibs. But Willie Waddell and his assistant, Jock Wallace, had done their homework on the Germans and identified their weaknesses. With the backing of a raucous home crowd, the players did everything that was asked of them. George Ritchie, who stood on the Rangers End, is in no doubt that the fans played a key role. He recalled:

It was one of those nights when the fans and the players fed off one another. They talk about the fans being a 12th man. Well I think we were a 12th and 13th man that night. I always loved European nights at the old Ibrox, but this was the one where it really came together. The noise was unbelievable when the teams came out, and it just seemed to be maintained throughout the whole game. I don't really remember much about the match at all apart from the goals but one thing that stuck in my mind was Rangers lining up to salute the fans before the game. They were wearing blue shirts and shorts, and I remember thinking how odd they looked, especially with red socks. The other thing that was weird was that all the advertising boards were for German products, obviously for the benefit of German TV. It all added up to make it a special occasion, different from the norm.

Sandy Jardine's goal in the second minute sent Rangers on their way, and the result was never in doubt after 18-year-old Derek Parlane, playing in just his fifth first-team game in place of injured captain John Greig, added a second goal after 23 minutes.

Frustrated at their inability to get the better of their supposedly inferior opponents, not to mention the muddy Ibrox pitch, the Germans lost their famed Teutonic cool. And as they argued among themselves, Rangers grew in strength. The final whistle was met with delirium both on the pitch and off it. The chant that rang around Ibrox was 'Barcelona Here We Come!'

On 24 May 1972 Rangers finally won a European Final, at the third attempt. More than 20,000 Rangers fans were in the Camp Nou to witness the historic 3–2 victory over Dynamo Moscow, and many of them made it to Ibrox the next day to welcome the players home, still wearing the sombreros they picked up in Spain. In all, more than 20,000 fans braved torrential rain to catch a glimpse of the trophy. A piper playing *Amazing Grace* welcomed the players into the stadium, and a full pipe band led the squad on a victory parade. The players made their way around the pitch on the back of a coal lorry festooned with red, white and blue bunting, with a Union Jack draped over the front. It made for a strange sight, and with the players in their Adidas tracksuits and huge sideburns, it was all very 1970s.

CHANGES AFOOT

Shortly after Barcelona, Jock Wallace became first-team manager as Willie Waddell stepped down and moved into a new administrative role as general manager. Waddell's first task was to successfully appeal against the two-year European ban imposed on Rangers due to crowd trouble after the Final. He succeeded in getting the ban halved, but he recognised the damage hooliganism was doing to the club's image. Waddell's belief was that if the supporters were treated well they would behave well. Furthermore, the 1971 disaster had demonstrated in the most horrific way imaginable just how unsafe every British football ground was. With these two ideas uppermost in his mind, Waddell devoted much of the next few years to turning Ibrox into the safest, most comfortable stadium in the UK, if not Europe. Within a decade, the old ground would be totally transformed.

The first major improvement was the installation of more than 9,000 seats in the north enclosure, creating the Centenary Stand at a cost of £70,000. The stand, used for the first time when Rangers played Celtic on 6 January 1973, was one of a number of measures announced by the club in 1972 to tackle crowd trouble.

Following a meeting with Glasgow's police chief constable, David McNee, Rangers declared that Ibrox would eventually be an all-seated stadium. The firm belief was that seating was a major factor in reducing crowd trouble. In the meantime, alcohol would be completely banned from the ground, and extra police and stewards would be drafted in to work inside and outside the ground on match days. Finally 'party songs' and obscene language would be outlawed. Waddell vowed the club would be 'ruthless' in ridding the terraces of 'hooligans who are besmirching the name of the club'.

Despite the directors' high hopes, the Centenary Stand was never particularly popular among the fans. Cruelly nicknamed the Cemetery Stand, its opening resulted in the Derry End crew shifting onto the Copland Road terracing, and while this removed what officials saw as an unruly element, the stand never quite managed to attract enough 'good' fans to take their place, except at big games.

The early 1970s saw attendances continue to slump in Scotland, and Rangers were not immune from the crisis. The final three League games of the 1971–72 season against Dunfermline, Hibs and Ayr United only managed to attract a total of 20,000 fans to Ibrox. For the Ayr match, the official attendance was given as 4,000, although even this dreadfully low figure was almost certainly an exaggeration, as it included all the club's season-ticket holders. In reality, it is highly doubtful that many of them would have been there to witness the 4–2 victory. The number of paying customers was probably fewer than 2,000. Surprising, considering it was the lead up to the European Cup-Winners' Cup Final.

In fairness these games were meaningless, as Rangers were already well out of the title race. However, as Rangers continued to struggle in the League in the early part of the decade, their average attendances continued to fall, plunging to a 35-year low of 22,000 in 1973–74. This was half the average of some seasons in the golden post-war era. Outwith the Old Firm derbies and the big European clashes, 30,000 was a good crowd and even this would get lost on the vast, open slopes that still had the potential to hold more than 100,000. The distance between the terraces and the pitch also added to the lack of atmosphere on all but the most special occasions. It was widely believed that the majestic old ground was far too large for the modern era.

The drop in attendances across Scotland was part of the reason for a major restructuring of the League system in time for the start of the 1975–76 season. Rangers had finally broken Celtic's nine-year stranglehold on the League title, winning the First Division by seven points from Hibs the previous season. In the first year of the new Premier League, they won the treble but actually saw their average Ibrox attendance drop by more than 2,000 to just over 30,000. However, the opening day of the season saw a milestone attendance of almost 69,600 for the derby with Celtic – no Scottish League crowd has bettered that figure since.

GERMAN INSPIRATION

In 1976 Willie Waddell began a Europe-wide search to find a model for the new-look Ibrox. The Westfalenstadion, deep in the heart of West Germany's Ruhr region, was exactly what he was looking for. The stadium, home of Borussia Dortmund, had been opened in 1974 in time for that year's World Cup Finals when it played host to Scotland, Brazil, Holland, Sweden and Zaire. The city had been contemplating building a new ground for the club for several years, but without state funding it would have been impossible. But when Cologne decided not to build a new stadium in 1970, Dortmund got the green light to be a host city four years later, paving the way for the new stadium.

The original plans would have seen a traditional oval ground but the costs were prohibitive, and a revised proposal of four single stands housing 54,000 fans was approved

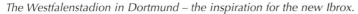

The Westfalenstadion in Dortmund – the inspiration for the new Ibrox.

instead. The design proved inspiring. The closeness of the stands to the pitch and the fact that all four sides were covered generated a tremendous atmosphere. Commentators nicknamed it the Scala of football; the Dortmund fans simply called it The Temple. Borussia Dortmund president Heinz Gunther was especially pleased. 'A roof over the head of the poor man,' was how he described it.

BLUEPRINT FOR A NEW IBROX

In December 1976 Rangers revealed their blueprint for the new Ibrox, and it was clear that the Westfalenstadion had been the inspiration. Like the German ground, Rangers' new stadium would consist of four separate stands, each with seated and standing accommodation, which would be built closer to the pitch to improve the atmosphere. Early plans suggested seating for 43,000 fans plus standing room for another 13,000. There was never any doubt that the historic Main Stand would remain, but it was decided that the Centenary Stand would be demolished, as would the east and west terraces behind each goal. The early artists' impressions showed open-sided stands, with open spaces underneath.

It was now six years since the disaster, and there was some frustration at the length of time it had taken to come up with firm plans for a new, safer stadium. Part of the reason for the delay was the introduction of new safety regulations, which came into force late in 1976. Rangers had been ready to go ahead with their plans two years earlier but feared their proposals could have been obsolete when the new legislation was introduced.

Waddell was convinced that the plans would meet the aims of improving safety and comfort for the supporters, while also tackling the ongoing problem of hooliganism. But at the same time, he recognised that it would be difficult to change football culture overnight. 'Our aim is to make the facilities the best possible for the fans,' he said. 'The best way ultimately to curb hooliganism is to have everyone seated. But we must accustom people to this position rather than force it on them. This is why we will still provide standing accommodation but this will, in the long term, all become seating.'

Glasgow District Council gave planning permission for the project in November 1977. Officials predicted the redevelopment of Ibrox would be of benefit to the city's recreational facilities and would lead to easier crowd control. Rangers also proposed to make use of the space below the three new stands to create 24,000sq ft of storage space, showroom and office accommodation. The railway cutting at the rear of the Centenary Stand was no longer in use and was to be built up to provide parking and more space for fans to move around. Rubble from the bulldozed terraces would be used to fill in the cutting.

Shortly after the plans for the new Ibrox were approved, the stadium received its first safety certificate under the Safety of Sports Grounds Act. Following an inspection, Strathclyde Regional Council imposed a crowd limit of 65,582 – around 5,000 fewer than the biggest attendance of recent years but considerably more than the new ground would

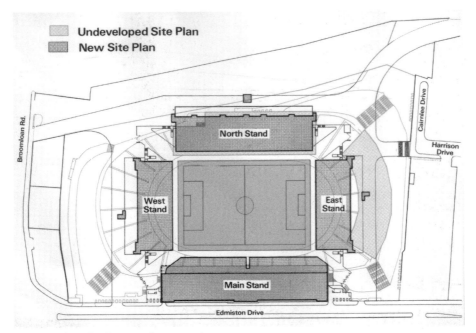

Architects' plans for the new Ibrox stands.

go on to hold. Rangers were satisfied by the limit but found themselves having to carry out various improvements. Damaged stairway treads on the south-east stairway leading to Edmiston Drive had to be replaced, and food kiosks behind the Copland Road terracing were ordered to be removed to allow better flow of supporters. The inspectors also wanted better facilities for the police, including a general office with a charge bar, two cells and a room where lost children could be accommodated, presumably while their fathers could watch the rest of the game.

FUNDING THE NEW IBROX

The cost of the redevelopment was originally predicted to be £6 million, although the final bill was eventually £10 million. The majority of the cost would be met from Rangers' hugely successful pools operation. Launched in the early 1960s, the scheme was the most successful of its kind in Britain and had been used to pay for much of the development work that had taken place at Ibrox over the previous two decades.

The pools scheme, run by retired Glasgow businessman David Hope, had also provided the £500,000 spent on Rangers' social club, which was opened at the rear of the Copland Road terracing in 1971. Hope modestly described his creation as 'the best in the world'. The club featured numerous lounges and dining rooms, all luxuriously fitted out in 1970s decor. A closed-circuit TV system transmitted the cabaret performances to every room in the building, and music was piped through no fewer than 47 speakers.

Three weeks after it opened, the club was closed down after being ravaged by fire. It took six months and another £250,000 to renovate it, but by the time it reopened with a performance by cabaret star Jan Douglas in September 1971, 10,000 fans had signed up for membership.

The club underwent numerous changes over the years and was always a popular haunt for fans, before eventually closing down in the early 2000s. The building, Edmiston House, is now the home for David Murray's call-centre business, Response Handling.

THE NEW IBROX

Rangers clinched their second League title in three years with a final-day victory over Motherwell at Ibrox in front of a crowd of 43,500. It was to be the last game of the Copland Road terracing, the traditional Rangers End. Bulldozers moved in soon after and began to raze the terracing to the ground. By the time the new season started, the huge embankment that had housed tens of thousands of fans at every home game for more than 70 years had been replaced with a building site. The stairway, where 68 supporters had died and hundreds been injured in a series of accidents the previous decade, was gone. Slowly the new Ibrox was taking shape.

The design and construction of the new-look stadium needed close co-operation between the club, architects TM Miller and Partners, consultant engineers Thorburn Associates and contractors Taylor Woodrow. The architects and engineers were first

Architects' plans for the new Ibrox stands.

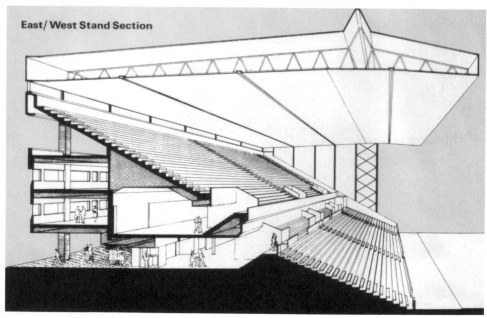

approached in 1976 to come up with a feasibility study based on a brief drawn up by Willie Waddell and his fellow directors. The brief required that:

- *All spectators would be comfortably seated, reasonably protected from bad weather and provided with a good view of the pitch.*
- *The seating decks should be free of columns.*
- *Fans should be as close as possible to the pitch.*
- *The roof should be clad internally and externally.*
- *The stadium should have a final capacity of around 40,000.*
- *Commercial office accommodation should be provided beneath the east and west stands.*
- *The existing terracing earthworks should be used to infill the disused railway cutting.*
- *The old boundary wall should be removed and modern, new turnstile units should be incorporated into the stands.*
- *The pitch should be maintained in its present good quality condition.*

The scale and shape of the new stands was largely determined by the fact that the existing Main Stand was to be retained. The design team decided to create three separate, rectangular stands rather than repeating the bowl shape of the old terracing. This meant the new structures could be built much closer to the pitch, resulting in the removal of the running track and the large grass semi-circular areas behind each goal. The plan would release large amounts of ground behind the east and west stands,

The Main Stand in 1978. (courtesy Farquhar Matheson)

which would be concreted over and used for car parking and as a concourse where fans could move freely round the stadium.

While the original proposals suggested standing areas at the front of each new stand, the final plans ruled this out. The three would be all-seated, leaving a standing area in the enclosure at the front of the Main Stand only. The obvious effect of this was to reduce the capacity even more, to a maximum of 44,000.

Another specification of the brief was that all fans had to sit within a radius of 90m of the centre spot, which meant that the corner areas between the stands could not be used, or at least not cost-effectively. The designers also decided to leave the corners open to allow growth of the grass. And in a stadium where there had been fatal accidents, safety was also a consideration. The open corners would allow easy access for the rescue services and, perhaps just as importantly, the designers felt that corners would give the fans the psychological reassurance that they would be able to evacuate the ground quickly and safely in the event of an emergency.

One of the biggest problems was how to ensure that the fans were protected from the elements but that the stand roofs did not block sunlight from reaching the playing surface at the same time. The closeness of the stands to the pitch made this a difficult task and one which would need to be revisited again years later when there was further redevelopment of the Main Stand.

The build would take place in three phases, starting with the tearing down of the east terracing and the building of the Copland Road Stand. Because the work was being carried out during the season, fans would be able to see how the development was progressing week by week. Only Old Firm games would be played away from Ibrox; for safety reasons the derbies would take place at Hampden because of the difficulties in segregating the rival supporters. Demolition work on the terracing began in the close season, and first to go were the red crush barriers, followed by the concrete banking. The front part of the compacted ash fill that formed the terrace embankment was retained to give a base for the lower seating section, but the rest was carried away to fill in the old railway cutting.

Building on the new stand started in late June. With off-duty construction workers picking up time-and-a-half to retrieve the ball from the building site during matches, the 1978–79 season got under way in August with a home defeat to St Mirren. During the close season, Jock Wallace had shocked supporters by resigning as manager after a fall out with Willie Waddell, and club captain John Greig was appointed to take his place. As the season progressed, the new structure gradually began to take place. First the steel-work skeleton was constructed, which allowed the stepped concrete slabs that would eventually support the seating to be installed.

By the new year the basic shape of the towering new structure was clear, but it was not until late February 1979 that the full scale of the stand would become apparent. Two huge cranes were brought onto the site to put the two end stanchions into place, before lifting the 65-ton, 250ft-long girder that spanned the two ends, 100ft high. It was a spectacular sight. Rangers' 82-year-old doorman, Bobby Moffat, told the *Evening Times* 'I have been here since 1919 and I have never seen anything like this.'

With the framework ready, the huge roof could now be put into place, followed quickly by the red brickwork around the steel. The walls were coated with graffiti-proof paint to keep maintenance costs to a minimum – an essential move in a city like Glasgow. Finally the multicoloured plastic seating was installed, with the red, yellow, blue, orange and brown sections giving the stand an even more distinctive look.

On the pitch Rangers were enjoying mixed fortunes under John Greig. He had gone straight from the dressing room to the historic manager's office after the shock resignation of Jock Wallace in the summer. Greig's team won the League Cup and the Scottish Cup and enjoyed two magnificent victories in the European Cup against Juventus and PSV Eindhoven before eventually being knocked out by Cologne. Despite an appalling start, they managed to take the League to a decider against Celtic in late May. Leading 1–0 at half-time against 10 men, they somehow managed to lose the match 4–2 and handed the League to their rivals. It was a defining moment for Greig. Had he secured the treble in his first season, his managerial career may well have turned out differently. Instead, his time in the manager's office is considered to be one of the most depressing in the club's history.

The new 7,500-capacity Copland Road Stand made its debut in the opening home game of the 1979–80 season. It just happened to be against Celtic. Fears that the match might not be allowed to go ahead were allayed when a safety certificate was granted by Strathclyde Regional Council on the eve of the match. With work already under way on the redevelopment of the west end of the ground, the attendance was limited to just 36,000 – one of the lowest for an Old Firm match in decades.

The Copland Road Stand takes the place of the 'Rangers End' terracing.   (courtesy Farquhar Matheson)

George Ritchie had stood on the terraces at countless Old Firm games but found himself in the Copland Road Stand on its opening day. 'In 20 years of going to games, this was the first time ever I had sat in a stand, which is quite amazing if you think about it,' he said.

It wasn't that I had some great objection to sitting, it just never crossed my mind to go anywhere but the terraces. The stand was for the toffs, and the terraces were where the plebs like me and my pals went. When they knocked down the Rangers End terracing we just moved round to the other end…For the Old Firm game we decided to try the new stand and it was quite an eye-opener. There were real toilets for a start! It was just so different to what we were used to. Everything was new and up to date, and I have to say I remember feeling a great sense of pride that day that our club was breaking new ground. I know a lot of people look back with nostalgia at the terraces, but my own view at the time was that that this was a huge step forward and, after the disaster, was needed. At the time, I don't think many people mourned the end of the terraces, whatever they might think now.

Despite the reduced capacity, the Rangers players were impressed by the noise generated from the new stand. Manager John Greig said afterwards 'The noise from that stand at the Celtic game was fantastic. The players were all commenting on it and we feel this could become our Ibrox equivalent of the Kop. It's always been the Rangers end but now the noise from the stand is magnified so much and the supporters are so much closer to the park, the noise can be frightening at times.'

It seemed to inspire the players as they powered into a two-goal lead shortly after half-time. With Roy Aitken sent off for Celtic, Rangers should have been comfortable winners but again they capitulated, losing two goals in the final six minutes.

Police figures after the game seemed to support the theory that the new all-seated ground would combat crowd trouble. Although there were 51 arrests inside Ibrox during the match – including one fan brandishing a 2ft machete – none were in the Copland Road Stand. In fact, Rangers chairman Rae Simpson announced at their 1980 AGM that there had been only one arrest in the stand in the first 16 months since it opened.

Rangers never recovered from blowing their two-goal lead in that Old Firm game, and the season would go on to be one of the Ibrox club's worst ever – they finished fifth in the League, were knocked out of the League Cup in the second round by Aberdeen and lost 1–0 to Celtic in the Scottish Cup Final. The Final ended in clashes between fans on the Hampden pitch, which were beamed live to the nation and later shown around the world. The rioting finally prompted the authorities to bring in new legislation to address the hooliganism problems that Rangers, and Willie Waddell in particular, had been attempting to tackle for much of the decade.

The most obvious impact of the new laws was the complete ban on alcohol from Scottish football grounds. Most clubs already had such a policy in place but it was rarely enforced, as the empty bottles and cans found strewn on the terraces after every match demonstrated. Now it was illegal to take drink to the game and could result in a fine or even a night in the police cells. Very soon, the tradition of taking a carry-out onto the terraces was a thing of the past.

It was another sign that the whole culture of football was changing and nowhere were these changes more apparent than at Ibrox. The Copland Road Stand was already proving popular, and in December 1979 Rangers announced plans to devote the entire 4,200-capacity upper deck to season-ticket holders. In the past, season tickets had largely been the domain of the privileged few but the new stands allowed the club to extend them to 'ordinary' fans. A season ticket for the Copland Road Stand would cost an affordable £40 and could be paid up in instalments. There were two main advantages of season tickets for the club – they ensured guaranteed income at the start of each season, and they made it possible to instantly identify any troublemakers and ban them from the ground if necessary. As John Greig said at the time 'It means that they always know who is sitting next to them. It means there will be no trouble.'

FIGHT NIGHT

The Broomloan Road Stand – identical to the Copland Stand – was officially opened with a pre-season friendly against Tottenham in August 1980, but the fact that one of the best-remembered events at Ibrox from the era was not a football match says much about how

The transformation of the west terracing into the Broomloan Road Stand. (courtesy Farquhar Matheson)

The programme from Jim Watt's world title fight against the American Howard Davis at Ibrox.

A seat in the Copland Road stand for the world title fight cost £20.

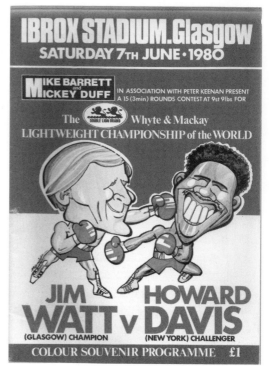

poor Rangers were on the pitch at that time. Two months earlier, Glasgow's Jim Watt retained his world lightweight boxing title on the Ibrox pitch. On a rainy night, American Howard Davis was the challenger in what was the first outdoor title fight in Scotland for 20 years.

The bad weather limited the crowd to around 15,000, leaving promoters Mickey Duff and Mike Barrett an estimated £100,000 out of pocket. But with tickets ranging from £5 to £40 and a live TV audience of millions in the USA, the fight was the most lucrative in British boxing history. Watt was reportedly paid £500,000, and he was made to earn his purse. Davis, a former Olympic gold medallist, took him to the full 15 rounds before the judges awarded the win to the home fighter, who had been roared on from the ringside by his wife, Margaret.

A poster advertising Watt's fight with Davis.

Watt was so much on top towards the end that the crowd was chanting 'easy, easy', and they stayed for almost an hour after the fight, cheering the champion. After the verdict, Watt grabbed the microphone and joined in with the fans, who were singing *Flower of Scotland*. Despite the lower than expected turnout, Davis was full of praise for the Ibrox crowd. 'The weather kept the crowd down and for that I am thankful. For what a noise they made every time their champion threw a punch. Some missed, some I blocked, but they still kept on roaring for their man.' Among those in the crowd that night were Andy McGrath and his pal. He recalled that it was not just a love of the sport that got the fans worked up for the fight. 'The pair of us, seasoned Rangers fans, took our seats in our regular place, the Centenary Stand. A half bottle of vodka and eight tins of McEwan's Export were laid out on the bench. All around us familiar faces, and some not so, also paraded their supplies for the duration. By the time Gentleman Jim came on we were all fired up. The fight went by in a flash, the USA's great hope completely out-boxed.'

THE TRANSFORMATION IS COMPLETE

The third and final phase of the Ibrox development got under way with the demolition of the Centenary Stand. In February 1981 construction work began on its replacement, the new 10,400-seat North Stand. It was essentially the same design as the two end stands but on a much larger scale. A £100,000 under-soil heating system, the only one in Scotland, was also installed to ensure the Ibrox pitch would remain playable, even on the coldest winter afternoons. Seven months later all the work was completed, bringing to an end the biggest and most dramatic football stadium development project Scotland had ever seen.

It was five years since Willie Waddell first appointed his design team to modernise Ibrox. Ten million pounds later, the job was done. The transformation was complete and

The Centenary Stand is replaced with the Govan Stand. (courtesy Farquhar Matheson)

The Rangers Shop was the first of its kind in Scotland when it opened in 1981.

total. From the huge, sprawling, grey bowl of 1976, the Ibrox of the 1980s was compact, bright and modern. It boasted facilities that the 1970s fan could not have predicted in their wildest imagination. Clean toilets, hot food, clear passageways and a seat for every supporter. The horrendous crushing on the terraces and exit stairways of years gone by had been eradicated. Not only was Ibrox Britain's most comfortable football stadium, it was also its safest. After the tragedies that had gone before, the most important thing was that fans felt safe in the new ground.

Rangers were also attempting to move forward on the commercial front. The first Rangers Shop was opened in April 1981 at No. 150 Copland Road, between the Ibrox subway station and the stadium. The shop, the first of its kind in Scotland, offered up a range of around 100 souvenirs and novelties, all featuring the Rangers crest. The usual

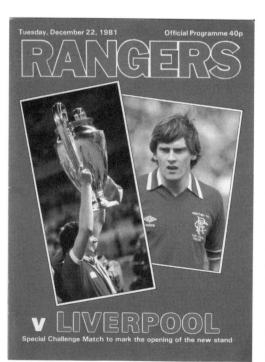

memorabilia was available, like strips, programmes, mugs, pens, pennants and scarves. But in addition, there was a range of more unusual, and sometimes frankly bizarre, items for sale. A baby's potty inscribed with 'I'm Potty About Rangers' or a bib bearing the legend 'I'm the Best Dribbler at Ibrox' is one thing; a pair of ladies' knickers emblazoned with the Rangers badge is quite another, even at the bargain price of £1.50.

On 21 September, the new-look Ibrox opened for business a month ahead of schedule with the visit of Celtic. Three months later, Liverpool were the visitors for the challenge match to mark the

Programme from the challenge match against Liverpool to officially open the Govan Stand.

A new pitch is laid at Ibrox in the 1980s. The multi-coloured seats in the stands were replaced in the mid-1990s.

official opening. Two-nil defeats in both matches painfully demonstrated to the fans that, while Ibrox was now the most modern stadium in Britain, the team on the pitch was woefully lacking in quality. Greig had inherited an ageing squad and as the veterans reached the twilight of their careers, the players brought in to replace them were underwhelming to say the least.

The mere mention of names like Davie McKinnon, Gregor Stevens, Ian Redford, Sandy Clark and Colin MacAdam is enough to send shivers down the spines of Rangers fans of a certain age. And it was not just Celtic that the Light Blues had to deal with now. The emergence of Aberdeen and Dundee United meant that Rangers were now floundering as Scottish football's fourth force, and the supporters voted with their feet, abandoning the gleaming new stadium in their droves. Although the average attendance was still the second-highest in the country, Ibrox was rarely more than half full. Even the European games, which had traditionally attracted bigger than usual crowds, held little appeal.

The only shining light during those dark days was Davie Cooper, the talented, if somewhat inconsistent, winger. For many fans in the early 1980s he was the only reason to attend Ibrox. 'I started going to the games with my dad in the late '70s and by the time the '80s came around it was starting to get really depressing,' recalled Duncan Stewart. He continued:

We lived about seven or eight miles from Ibrox and you could literally decide at two o'clock on Saturday afternoon to go to a game. We could drive to Ibrox, park on the street a couple of minutes away from the ground and walk up to the turnstiles with 15 minutes to go to kick-off. Once inside you could just about have your pick of any seat. We always used to go into the Govan Stand, which usually meant Cooper was playing in front of us in the second half. There were weeks when he really looked as if he couldn't be bothered but there were always, always one or two moments of magic in every game. If you were really lucky you would be there for one of the games where he was really up for it, and these were special. The fact that there were often very few people there to witness it made it even better in some ways...I remember one freezing cold night in 1984 when we played the Australia international team in a friendly for some reason. There must have only been about 4,000 inside Ibrox but Cooper was brilliant. He scored both goals and tormented the Aussies. You really did feel privileged to have been there to see it.

A ticket for the event to celebrate the 100th anniversary of the Boys' Brigade at Ibrox in 1983.

THE BOYS' BRIGADE

CENTENARY SALUTE

IBROX STADIUM, GLASGOW
(BY COURTESY OF RANGERS F.C. PLC)

SATURDAY 27th AUGUST 1983
2.15 p.m. £3

COPLAND ROAD STAND – ORANGE SECTION

FRONT

ENTER BY TURNSTILES 5-14

Row V Seat No. 9

THIS PORTION TO BE RETAINED BY THE HOLDER.

But despite Cooper's best efforts, season after season in the early 1980s ended in failure, each one seemingly worse than the last. There were few highlights for the hardcore who turned out at Ibrox week after week. Greig bowed to fan pressure after a poor start to the 1983–84 season and resigned. After first failing to lure Aberdeen boss Alex Ferguson and then Dundee United's Jim McLean to take his place, Rangers appointed Jock Wallace to the post for the second time. After a bright start, he too suffered from a lack of quality players, and the Rangers slump continued.

A GLIMMER OF HOPE

One of the few bright spots of the era was a UEFA Cup match against Inter Milan in 1984, which briefly resurrected memories of the great European nights of the past. Having lost the first leg 3–0 in Italy, few gave Rangers much hope in the return game at Ibrox. And when they lined up with Northern Ireland centre-back John McLelland playing as a makeshift forward, expectations were lowered even further. But roared on by a raucous 30,000 crowd, Rangers got off to a whirlwind start, and the place erupted in the fifth minute when Australian international Dave Mitchell headed the opening goal. Ten minutes later Altobelli equalised and that should have been that, but Rangers refused to give up and quickly went back in front through a magnificent long-range strike by Iain Ferguson. Early in the second half he headed in another goal to set up a tremendous last half-hour.

Urged forward by the crowd, Rangers threw everything at the Italians but the goal would not come. In the end the 3–1 victory wasn't enough to progress, but it is a match that lingers in the memory of fans and players alike. Rangers midfielder Robert Prytz, a Swedish international, recalled 'I have never experienced an atmosphere like there was in the stadium that night. You felt that they were going to lift you off the pitch – it was incredible. We played exceptional football that night and you could see how scared they were. A lot of that was down to the crowd. The fans were unbelievable.'

The drama of the Inter game was a false dawn. As the decade progressed, results got worse. The 1985–86 season started well, with five wins and a draw at Celtic Park. But in late September, Dundee came to Ibrox and left with a 1–0 victory. The following week, Aberdeen visited the stadium – a match that saw the first significant crowd incident inside Ibrox since the new stadium had been opened. Duncan Stewart watched events unfold from the Govan Stand.

We had started the season quite well, so everyone was well up for the game and there was a big crowd inside Ibrox, maybe about 40,000. In those days Aberdeen brought a big travelling support – they took the top tier of the Broomloan. They were notorious for having a big 'casual' element in their support and I always remember how the police would walk them from Ibrox to Queen Street Station in the city centre to stop them causing bother. It was the same with Hibs in that era…So the atmosphere was quite tasty from the start and this seemed to translate onto the pitch. Early on the game degenerated into a bit of a kicking match and the referee clearly lost control. Quite honestly, any number of players from both teams could have been sent off, but in the end it was Hugh Burns, the Rangers right-back, who was the unlucky one. He brought down a player, John Hewitt I think it was, right in front of where I was sitting with my dad. It actually wasn't that bad a tackle but the player made the most of it and he got a straight red. We were shocked and to make it even worse, Aberdeen scored straight from the free-kick. Craig Paterson got himself sent off for a crazy body-check, and then they scored again. It was an absolute nightmare… In the second half Rangers did OK but we were never going to pull the game back with nine men. We were on the break towards the Aberdeen goal when suddenly hundreds of fans spilled onto the pitch from the east enclosure. There was no aggression but it didn't look like anyone was planning on leaving the pitch any time soon. The players all got taken off, and Jock Wallace came out to calm the fans down. It was chaos, though, and folk were getting taken away on stretchers. To this day I've no idea what caused it, but I just remember watching from the Govan Stand thinking this was probably the worst thing I had ever seen in football. Two Rangers players sent off, getting gubbed 2–0 and now a riot! I'd never seen any sort of crowd trouble close up before so I was a bit concerned about where it was all going. Eventually they did get the game restarted, and inevitably we lost another goal. And that was pretty much that for the season. It was downhill all the way from then on.

It was clear that something dramatic needed to be done to provide a team fit to play in the magnificent new stadium. In the spring of 1986 an announcement was made that was to reinvigorate the club and send shockwaves through Scottish football.

IBROX REVOLUTION

In the dark depths of the second Jock Wallace era, Rangers and Celtic fought out a dramatic 4–4 draw at Ibrox. It was a classic game, the initiative swinging back and forth between each team. There was not much in the way of silky football played but there was plenty of graft as Rangers fought back from 3–2 down to take a 4–3 lead, only to lose a late equaliser.

Celtic were on their way to the League title, so it was hardly surprising that the draw had been celebrated at Ibrox like a title win, given the mess the Rangers team were in at the time. Among those said to be unimpressed by the scenes of elation was David Holmes, the new Rangers chief executive.

Holmes had been appointed to the post by the John Lawrence construction group, which now had a controlling interest in the club, with the aim of stopping the rot and reversing what seemed to be a terminal decline in fortunes. The story goes that the reaction to the 4–4 draw made him decide there and then that urgent action was needed. There may be some truth in the story, but it would be a surprise if Holmes had not already recognised that something needed to be done to breathe new life into the club. Ibrox was arguably the best stadium in Britain, but the fare offered on the park was simply not good enough. Fifth place in the League, no trophies and plummeting attendances told their own story.

Dramatic changes were needed and they came on 7 April 1986. Wallace was removed as manager, and to the shock of the football world, Graeme Souness was named as the new player-manager. With ex-Dundee United assistant manager Walter Smith as his number two, Souness set about creating a team that did the magnificent stadium justice. Armed with the Lawrence group's chequebook, he lured two of the biggest names in English football to Ibrox – goalkeeper Chris Woods and centre-half Terry Butcher.

A wave of optimism swept over the long-suffering Rangers support as the new season got under way. It was only slightly dented by a shambolic opening day at Easter Road, when Souness was sent off and Rangers lost 2–1 to Hibs. Four days later, in front of a crowd of more than 27,000, Ally McCoist scored the only goal of the match to claim the first win of the Souness revolution, against Falkirk. It was a stuttering start to the season, though, and it was not until the Old Firm game at Ibrox at the end of August that the new team showed signs that they had what was required to reclaim what the fans considered to be their rightful place at the top of Scottish football.

The 1–0 victory was secured with a fine goal by Ian Durrant, set up by a piece of sublime skill by Davie Cooper. Terry Butcher was stunned by the atmosphere inside the ground. 'It was more intense than anything I have ever experienced before and the noise was unbelievable,' he said at the time. The match was significant, as it was the first Scottish League game to be broadcast live on television, and it was also sponsored by drinks firm Guinness. Gate receipts, TV rights and sponsorship money topped up the Ibrox bank balance by almost £250,000 – a sure sign that the box-office appeal of the new Rangers was paying dividends.

The new professional approach on the field was being mirrored in the club's off-field activities. Years after the concept was embraced in England, Rangers finally set about cashing in on corporate clients. A new executive lounge was opened in the Main Stand, with a restaurant that could provide match-day meals for up to 240 clients. Local companies were targeted and urged to take out tables capable of entertaining up to 10 guests for the season. Supporter Duncan Stewart recalled:

It was just such an exciting period. Not just because we had Souness and Butcher and Woods – although that was nice – but the whole club seemed to be on the up. We got a real DJ in to play the pre-match music, electronic scoreboards were put up on the stands behind each goal, even the match programme seemed more professional. It just seemed that someone somewhere had suddenly realised that this was the late 1980s, not the early 1970s, and that we needed to catch up with the rest of the world. We had such a modern stadium, but before the Souness era everything else about the club was just so old-fashioned. Or at least that's how it seemed to 14-year-old me.

FEEL-GOOD FACTOR

For the first time in almost a decade, there was a feel-good factor about Ibrox. Crowds were booming, with the average attendance for the first half of the season topping 34,000. The 500,000th customer of the season went through the turnstiles two days after Christmas, when 42,165 turned out for new signing Graham Roberts's debut. Roberts was signed from Tottenham, and his purchase proved to be the final piece in the jigsaw.

Rangers went on a 19-game unbeaten run in the League between October and April, which took them to within touching distance of the title. Proof of the huge turnaround from the previous season came at Ibrox on 10 January, when Rangers hammered Clydebank 5–0 with a hat-trick from Robert Fleck and a double from Ally McCoist. But it was not the scoreline that highlighted the dramatic changes at Rangers. Almost exactly 12 months earlier – on 11 January to be precise – just 12,000 watched the same two teams battle it out at Ibrox. This time the crowd was an astonishing 36,400. Duncan Stewart recalled:

I was there for both games and it was amazing how things had changed. A year earlier the team was made up of the likes of Nicky Walker, Hugh Burns and Bobby Williamson. No disrespect to those guys, but you needed to be a die-hard or a masochist to drag yourself along to Ibrox on a freezing January afternoon for a dour battle with Clydebank. Now we were playing some brilliant football. We had big-star names like Butcher and Souness, and home-grown guys like Davie Cooper, McCoist and Fleck were on fire. You didn't care who the opposition were, you just wanted to see this team play.

In the midst of all the positivity came a scoreline that was such a shock that it could have derailed the entire season. Twenty years had passed since Berwick stunned the world by knocking Rangers out of the Scottish Cup and for all the lows the Ibrox club had endured in the years that followed, they had not suffered another defeat to match it. No one could have predicted that this season would throw up a result that would run it close for shock value.

With Graeme Souness's multi-million pound squad sweeping all before them, Premier League strugglers Hamilton Academical were hardly expected to put up much of a challenge when they met in the third round of the Cup at Ibrox. For 70 minutes the match went as expected, with Rangers bombarding the Hamilton goal, where they found goalkeeper Dave McKellar in inspired form. For all their pressure Rangers could not find a way through. Not that anyone expected Accies to breach the Ibrox defences. At the other end, Chris Woods was so under-employed that he could take the plaudits of the 36,000 crowd when it was announced over the PA system during the game that he had broken the British shut-out record. Woods went on to reach 1,196 consecutive minutes without conceding a goal, but his record-breaking run was to come to a sudden and surprising end.

Adrian Sprott was the man who silenced the Ibrox crowd just as the clock hit 70 minutes. A long ball aimed towards the Rangers penalty area looked harmless enough, but a momentary lapse by defender Dave McPherson saw the ball squirm under his studs and into Sprott's path. He made no mistake with his finish, and somehow Hamilton were ahead. Even then, most of Ibrox – including the visiting support – assumed that Rangers would get back into it, but as time ran out, the goal did not come. The home team resorted to launching high balls into the penalty area, but nothing they could do could break down the Accies' defence.

When the final whistle sounded, there was a sense of disbelief around the stadium. The powerful new Rangers had been knocked out of the Cup by the paupers of the Premier League. This was not how it was supposed to be in the brave new world. It was the biggest shock since Berwick, but this time there would be no repeat of the knee-jerk reaction in 1967 that arguably cost Rangers the League and a European trophy. Instead the defeat seemed to focus the minds of the players and management team, and drove them on towards the Championship.

February and March were crucial months and Rangers came through them with flying colours. The humiliation by Hamilton was quickly consigned to the past, as the victories kept coming – along with the crowds. The millionth customer of the season was among the sell-out crowd when Hearts visited Ibrox on 25 April. An Ally McCoist hat-trick gave Rangers a 3–0 victory that put them on the verge of the title.

The only downside of this unprecedented box-office success story was the difficulty in coping with the demand. Run-of-the mill matches were now being designated as all-ticket, resulting in massive queues every week at the ticket office. But the inconvenience was a small price to pay for supporters who had been starved of success for almost a decade.

The following week, the barren years officially came to an end. At Pittodrie, Terry Butcher scored in a 1–1 draw against Aberdeen, while Celtic suffered a shock 2–1 defeat at home to Falkirk. After nine years, Rangers were finally champions again and the final whistle sparked incredible scenes, as thousands of fans swarmed onto the Pittodrie pitch to celebrate with their heroes.

PARTY TIME

Seven days later, the official party took place on a beautiful sunny day at Ibrox. And after so long in the doldrums, the Rangers fans were desperate to make the most of it. Fancy dress was the order of the day, and the stands were filled with all manner of teddy bears. Rather more difficult to comprehend was the presence of the Pink Panther and Father Christmas.

The pre-match entertainment started with a match between the club's schoolboy signings, which was followed by the Under-21s parading the League Cup and the trophy they had won themselves at a high-profile tournament in France. Then came the main attraction, the triumphant team. Led by captain Terry Butcher, the players took to the field to a deafening roar and a standing ovation. They returned the complement by lining up in the centre circle to salute the fans – a move met with rapturous applause. Opponents St Mirren got a slightly less euphoric reception when they decided that they too would take a bow in the middle of the pitch.

George Ritchie, a regular throughout the dark days, said 'This was the kind of day some of us thought we might never see again.' He continued:

In the early 1980s when we were sometimes getting crowds of 10,000 and the team was finishing fourth or fifth in the League, you just couldn't imagine any way it was going to improve. We had this magnificent stadium that was never full, and some weeks you just felt like giving up. But through it all there was a sense of unity – the guys who were turning up to endure this dross every week were in it together. That's what kept you going really...And as we got closer to the climax of Souness's first season, those of us who had been there for the horrible times felt that we were getting our reward. It was magnificent to see the stadium full every week. Finally it was operating the way it was supposed to, and finally it really felt like home...At that last game of the season against St Mirren, I felt so emotional just seeing all the young bears in the stands who had never seen Rangers win the League in their lifetime. It wasn't much of a game but it will always be my favourite Ibrox day.

The League trophy was to be presented at the end of the 90 minutes but most of the 44,000 crowd could have happily skipped the actual match and gone straight to the presentation and celebrations. The game itself was a forgettable 1–0 home win, but the scenes after the match were memorable. Ritchie remembered:

As the game came to an end, Ibrox was awash with colour and noise. It was like all those years of misery had built up and there was finally this huge release of emotion. Everyone seemed to be waving a scarf or a flag above their head so it was a sea of red, white and blue. When the final whistle blew, hundreds of youngsters piled onto the pitch. They were probably copying what they'd seen at Pittodrie the week before and more than likely thought they'd get a big cheer, but instead they got absolute pelters from the rest of the crowd. There had been warnings that the presentation wouldn't take place if there was an invasion, so everyone was booing them and chanting 'Off, Off, Off'. It was nothing too serious though, and the players were back on the pitch pretty quickly.

The lap of honour came after the trophy presentation. Butcher, Woods and Roberts led the celebrations on the pitch to a soundtrack of the season's unofficial anthems, *Championi* and *We Are The Champions*. The captain took off his Rangers top to reveal a T-shirt bearing the legend 'MacButcher – English Connection'. Needless to say, Woods and Roberts each had their own version. The imports lapped up the adulation from the stands, but it was even more special for the Scottish players, especially those like Davie Cooper and Ally McCoist; Rangers supporters through and through who had suffered through the last decade as much as the fans in the stands.

It was not just the players and fans who were enjoying the success. Behind the scenes there were many who had given years of loyal service to the club. Veteran kit man George 'Doddie' Soutar was one of them, and he found himself on the Ibrox pitch alongside the players as they celebrated the title. Commissionaire Stan Holloway had the honour of 'standing guard' at the front entrance of Ibrox for many years. He rarely got to see the team play at home, being on duty on match days, but he got to know the players better than most.

Finally, Rangers had a team that lived up to the splendid surroundings of Ibrox Stadium. On and off the field, the club had been transformed, and the support that had gone into hibernation for nine years had been reawakened. Graeme Souness and David Holmes had dragged Rangers and the rest of Scottish football out of the dark ages and into the modern era. The game north of the border would never be the same again.

At Ibrox, the new big-name players had brought with them a new breed of supporter. Not everyone was pleased at the arrival of the Camel Coat Brigade – well-off businessmen who snapped up the best and most expensive seats in the house. Many fans saw them as bandwagon-jumpers who were only at Ibrox to bask in the reflected glory of stars like Souness and Butcher, but it would be churlish to dismiss these well-heeled followers as not being 'real fans'. Obviously there were some glory hunters among their number, but many had supported Rangers for years and were happy to spend their cash on their passion. An overcoat and collar and tie did not necessarily make them any less of a fan than a Copland Road season-ticket holder. David Holmes insisted at the time 'There are no plans to shut the doors and let a select few in. There will always be a place for those who want to pay their money on the day.'

It was an undeniable fact that times were changing, though, and the first evidence of that came in the closing days of 1986–87, when Rangers announced a new VIP ticketing initiative. Members of the Premier Club would have their own spot in the rear of the Govan Stand for each home game and would be given the right to buy a ticket for a seat at European and domestic Cup ties. But it came with a hefty price tag, the cost of some seats rising from £60 a season to £160; even with the option of paying it up at £15 a month, many supporters felt they were being priced out of the game. It would be a complaint heard time and time again in the years ahead.

GLORY DAYS

The arrival of Graeme Souness and the return of the glory days saw the crowds flock back to Ibrox, and even the failure to retain the League title in the second season of the revolution failed to impact on demand for tickets both domestically and in Europe.

The Championship win took Rangers back into the European Cup for the first time since 1978–79, when they had beaten two of the tournament favourites, PSV Eindhoven and Juventus, on their way to the quarter-final. Nine years later they again had to face one of Europe's leading lights – champions of the USSR, Dynamo Kiev. The first leg in Ukraine was watched by a 100,000 crowd in the stadium – and another 12,000 on big screens at Ibrox. It was the first time since the Fairs Cup match against Leeds in 1968 that the club had put on such an event, and it was an impressive turnout considering it was a daytime kick-off in the middle of the week.

Kiev won the first game with a dubious penalty, won and converted by Alexei Mikhailichenko. But with a large, noisy crowd behind them in Glasgow, Rangers were confident that they could turn the tie around. The Soviets certainly knew what to expect, with one club official warning that Ibrox would be a 'cauldron'. The spokesman told the *Izvestia* newspaper 'We will have to contend with a particularly fanatical and hostile crowd.' What Kiev did not predict was a classic piece of gamesmanship by Graeme Souness. The first thing the visitors noticed when they arrived at Ibrox was that the pitch had been narrowed by two yards on each touchline. Despite protests from furious Kiev officials, Rangers had done nothing illegal, and Souness had succeeded in his aim of unsettling his opponents.

Ibrox was a 44,000 sell-out and, just as predicted, the stadium was a cauldron of noise at kick-off. Once the game was under way, the Rangers players did everything they could to put further pressure on Dynamo, and in the 23rd minute it all seemed to pay off. After collecting the ball safely following a Rangers attack, Kiev goalkeeper Victor Chanov attempted to bowl the ball out. Somehow he contrived to throw it straight at the backside of defender Sergei Baltacha. The ball broke to a disbelieving Ally McCoist, who laid it off for Mark Falco to roll it into the empty net.

The winning goal came five minutes into the second half, when McCoist headed home from close range. Ibrox erupted again, and the frenzied noise levels barely dipped for the remaining 40 minutes of the game. For many, the atmosphere generated that night was the loudest the stadium had ever known. Kiev were well beaten, and the crowd had played a massive part in driving Rangers to victory. Gornik Zabrze were comprehensively beaten in the next round, but Rangers were beaten 3–2 on aggregate by the Romanians Steaua Bucharest in the quarter-finals.

A third-place finish in the League was deeply disappointing but it was to be the last time for almost a decade that Rangers would not win the title. The following season was the start of a period of domination that would eventually result in nine consecutive Championships.

FOOD FOR THOUGHT

Ibrox continued to undergo a few minor changes, the most obvious being the introduction of an extendible players' tunnel – the first of its kind in Scotland. New club sponsors McEwan's Lager had their logo emblazoned over the tunnel, making it resemble a giant can of lager when it was fully extended. Another innovation was the launch of a new range of fast food on sale in the stands.

The days of cold pies, macaroon bars and spearmint chewing gum were now a distant memory. In their place had arrived pakora, hot dogs and charcoal burgers, all given a Rangers-themed name.

Price list:

Bears Pakora	*£1.10*
Blue Nose Burger	*£1.10*
Loyal Charcoal Burger	*£1.10*
Champions Hot Dog	*£1.10*
Premier Pies	*£0.50*

Crisps	
Aye Ready Salted	*£0.30*
The True Blues	*£0.30*
Ibrox Hot Shots	*£0.30*

The new menu captured the fans' imaginations and generated yet more publicity for the club. Although it was hardly haute cuisine, it was decidedly more exotic than what had been offered before, and it showed an acumen in marketing that had been missing in the past.

As Rangers continued to rack up success on and off the field, outside investors began to look enviously at what was happening at Ibrox. In late 1988 Edinburgh-based steel magnate David Murray dramatically took control of the club from the Lawrence organisation. Murray was a friend of Souness, who has been credited with bringing him to Ibrox after Murray failed in an attempt to buy his home-town team Ayr United.

With the continued success of the team, it became apparent that Ibrox was simply not big enough to cope with demand. The 44,000 capacity, specified when the new stadium was designed, reflected the prevailing mood of the time – an era when attendances were falling throughout the footballing world. Indeed, for the first few years of its existence, the new Ibrox was embarrassingly oversized for most matches. Few pundits in the mid-1970s would have predicted the game's sudden return to popularity a decade later, but Ibrox was close to selling out for every game as the 1980s drew to a close. The average attendance in 1988–89 was just under 40,000, compared to the post-war low of 16,400 in 1981–82. The most startling thing about the latter figure is that it was still the second-highest average in the Premier League – a clear indication that the rest of Scottish football was still far behind the Old Firm in terms of the size of their support and therefore the ability to generate income.

If Rangers, at their lowest ebb, still attracted a bigger box office than Aberdeen, Dundee United, Hearts and Hibs, what chance did these teams have of keeping up when the Govan club got its act together? As would be proved in the years to come, the answer was, simply, none.

IBROX EXPANDS

The new Rangers owner, David Murray, was keen to increase the size of Ibrox and complete the transformation to a fully-seated stadium. The Hillsborough disaster of April 1989, when 95 Liverpool fans lost their lives in a terracing crush during an FA Cup semi-final, added new impetus to the proposals. The report on the tragedy by Lord Justice Taylor was published in January 1990 and called for radical changes to the design and construction of football grounds.

Having acted unilaterally after their own tragedy, Rangers were light years ahead of every other club in Scotland when it came to meeting the terms of the Taylor report. Nevertheless, proposals for a major redevelopment of Archibald Leitch's Main Stand had already been drawn up before Lord Taylor made his recommendations, although they remained under wraps for some time before being made public.

Replacement of the stand was not an option, not least because the fascia had been given B-listed status on 15 May 1987, preventing its demolition or any major change to

The Main Stand was granted listed building status in 1987. Four years later, a third tier was added to the stand but the historic red-brick fascia was retained.

its character. The listing did not include the terraces, seats or roof, and the radical solution was to build a new seating deck on top of the existing stand. The Club Deck, as it would become known, would provide 6,000 more seats and executive boxes and dining for up to 600 corporate guests. Access to the top level came via two striking glass-walled towers, one at each end of the stand.

Architect Gareth Hutchison was commissioned by Rangers to come up with the design. His brief was to create a new deck, free of columns, that allowed the retention of the seating and structure below. An 'elegance and economy of structural form' was also required, and the new roof was to extend far enough to give cover to the enclosure.

Various options were considered for the design of the roof. A cantilever roof was ruled out because of the depth required, and the size of the towers that would have been needed for a cable support meant that was also dismissed. The scheme eventually adopted a huge single girder, spanning the entire 145m length of the stand. As well as being the most appropriate option for the new structure, it was in keeping with the design of the other three stands.

The project needed around 2,700 tonnes of steel – supplied by David Murray's company – of which 350 tons were in the main roof girder alone. The existing corrugated roof of the Main Stand was removed, along with the old press box, in the summer of 1990 and a temporary roof was immediately put in place to allow the stand to remain open throughout the construction work. Foundation work began in August that year and was completed the following January, allowing the start of steelwork erection. On 12 June 1991 the main roof girder was lifted into place by two enormous cranes, said to be the biggest in the world, which had to be specially shipped in from South America. The girder was the largest single-length span ever lifted in Britain and possibly Europe. It was the equivalent of lifting the Blackpool Tower and laying it on its side.

The Main Stand's old wooden tip-up seats, which had been in place since the grandstand opened in 1929, were replaced with blue plastic seats, which detracted somewhat from the character of the stand but provided far more comfort for the supporters, as well as a consistent look.

After a complex 18-month construction, the new and improved £20 million stand was opened for business in December 1991 against Dundee United. It increased the Ibrox seating capacity to 38,000 and helped generate even more match-day income for the club through the £75,000-a-season private boxes on the executive deck. The majority of the seats in the Club Deck itself were allocated to debenture holders, whose investment raised almost half the total cost of the stand development.

Controversially, Rangers secretary Campbell Ogilvie also confirmed that the enclosure – the final non-seated area of Ibrox – would eventually be replaced with seats by August 1994. The plans to get rid of the enclosure had first leaked out in the autumn of 1989 when Liverpool chief executive Peter Robinson revealed to a newspaper that he was talking to Rangers about their plans to create an all-seated stadium. This set alarm bells ringing among elements of the support, who were hostile to the plan, and this became full-blown anger when the proposal was eventually confirmed by the club.

The fanzine *Follow, Follow* launched a campaign to save the standing area. An editorial in the magazine read 'The secrecy in which the plans to remove the enclosure were prepared is an unforgivable disgrace. It is contemptible that we were not consulted in any way before the blueprints were drawn up, nor even given a choice between alternatives. I prefer to sit, but I want everyone to have the choice. I want at least one part of the ground to be affordable on a regular basis to the young, the old and the less well-off.'

The point about the cost of attending matches was particularly pertinent. In 1991 Campbell Ogilvie pointed out 'In 1986 we had less than 3,000 season-ticket holders. That has risen to 27,000 and within the next few weeks, sales will top the 30,000 figure. That is substantial in anyone's language.' With so many seats now going to season-ticket holders, it could be extremely difficult for non-holders to get to a game. Furthermore, the tickets that were sold on a match-by-match basis were all full price, meaning children, OAPs, students and the unemployed all had to do without a discount if they wanted to watch their team. As the Rangers success story continued, the ordinary fan was seemingly being priced out of the game.

Despite the protests, the proposal to scrap the enclosure went ahead as planned, eventually providing Ibrox with seating for 48,500. The enclosure's final match became a carnival occasion as its regulars said farewell to the stadium's last link with the past.

DOMINANT RANGERS

The late 1980s and early 1990s saw Rangers go from strength to strength on the field. The League was regained in 1989, during a season that had seen two magnificent Ibrox victories over Celtic. The 5–1 thrashing in August featured a stunning volleyed goal from Ray Wilkins – one of the best seen at the stadium. Rangers were so far ahead that many supporters still see that game as a missed opportunity to avenge the 7–1 League Cup Final defeat. Mark Walters was the star in January when Rangers again destroyed Celtic, this time 4–1.

The following season saw a second successive title collected with some ease, with Rangers finishing seven points ahead of nearest challengers Aberdeen. Not for the first time in recent years, the club had stunned the footballing world in the close season. On 10 July 1989 Graeme Souness introduced his latest signing – Scotland international Maurice Johnston. The news, announced in the Blue Room at Ibrox, was a sensation. Not only was Johnston a Roman Catholic and a former Celtic player, he had been paraded at Parkhead wearing the green-and-white hoops only days earlier, having apparently pledged to return to 'the only club he ever wanted to play for'. But the deal stalled and Rangers pounced, delivering an astonishing blow to their rivals. Celtic, possibly still reeling from the shock of losing their star signing, finished the season in fifth place, 17 points behind the champions and just 10 above bottom-placed Dundee.

In the closing stages of 1990–91 Rangers were locked in a battle with Aberdeen to win what would be their third Championship in a row, when Graeme Souness abruptly left to become the new manager of Liverpool. Walter Smith stepped up to take his place and found himself facing a final-day showdown against Aberdeen at Ibrox, with a team crippled by injury and suspension. Anything less than a win would have handed the title to the Dons. But in an electric atmosphere, a makeshift Rangers swept Aberdeen aside, winning 2–0, with both goals scored by England international Mark Hateley.

For Rangers fan Stevie Tyrie the game is one of the most memorable he has attended at the stadium. He recalled:

One of the most dramatic days ever witnessed at Ibrox was the 1991 title clincher against Aberdeen. I've got so many memories of that day, including ones specifically about the stadium. Ibrox can be a wonderfully intimidating place when the crowd are pumped up. What I remember about the stadium prior to kick-off is that there was a palpable noise going round the stands as the anticipation of the support grew. Because the crowd is right on top of the players at Ibrox I'm convinced that played a huge part in unnerving the Aberdeen players, as you could see a few of them were seriously rattled by the noise that was being created...I've also seldom seen the stadium so awash with colour. It was a throwback to older times, with virtually everybody wearing at least one bit of Rangers regalia, and I remember thinking it created a wonderful scene. The stadium has witnessed some sights over the years and that day I can't help but think we were destined to win because the game was being played on our home turf. There's a presence at Ibrox that's hard to describe; it's as if, because it's the spiritual home of Rangers fans all over the world, it envelops their feelings for the club, as well as those of supporters and players and management who have since passed on...Every time I go into Ibrox I consider it a privilege but occasionally you get a real sense of destiny, of knowing things are going to happen for us and that day was one of those times. All the emotions and triumphs that have been witnessed at Ibrox over the decades are reborn, expressed again by the support who happen to be in the stadium on any given day, and that was how entering Ibrox felt that day in May 1991. Because of what Ibrox means to so many people, that represented itself in a magnificent display of support that just wouldn't have been possible to recreate anywhere else in the world.

BATTLE OF BRITAIN

While Rangers were continuing to dominate domestic football in Scotland, they struggled to make much of an impact in Europe, much to the frustration of the fans, who felt the club should be capable of stepping up to the next level. The late 1980s and early 1990s saw numerous failures in the early stages of European competition, but there was one season that stood out from the rest. In 1993 Rangers went within just one game of reaching the Final of the inaugural Champions League before falling at the penultimate hurdle.

The qualifying rounds started with a relatively comfortable victory over Danish champions Lyngby. But it was the next round that captured the public's imagination, as Rangers took on Leeds United in what was immediately dubbed the Battle of Britain. A place in the lucrative group stages of the competition was at stake. Leeds were instantly installed as favourites, with the English media predictably dismissing Rangers' chances because of the poor quality of the Scottish League. This simplistic analysis failed to take into account the quality of players that Walter Smith had at his disposal. The likes of Mark Hateley, Richard Gough, Stuart McCall, Gary Stevens, Trevor Steven, Andy Goram, Ally McCoist and Ian Durrant would have walked into any team in the English top division.

The hype in the run-up to the first leg at Ibrox ensured that the stadium would witness yet another special European night. The stage was set for a classic, and the players did not disappoint. Amid fears of crowd trouble, away fans were banned from both legs but that had little effect on the atmosphere. The players emerged from the tunnel to a wall of sound from the 44,000 Rangers fans, and the noise continued as Leeds kicked-off. Less than a minute later the crowd was silenced, when Gary McAllister hit a brilliant volley into the top-left-hand corner. As Rangers centre-half Dave McPherson recalled, 'It was one of the best atmospheres I had ever played in and Gary McAllister silenced it pretty quickly.'

For a few moments Ibrox was eerily quiet. Within seconds, the sound levels had reached a crescendo again, and the players reacted just as positively. Leeds fans and neutral observers may have expected the early goal to knock the spirit out of Rangers, but it had entirely the opposite effect. The players knew they had another 89 minutes to turn the game around, and with the backing of the Ibrox crowd, they set about their task.

In the 20th minute, the equaliser came in bizarre fashion when Leeds goalkeeper John Lukic flapped at an Ian Durrant corner and somehow managed to punch the ball into his own net. Ally McCoist added a second before half-time, but despite waves of Rangers pressure, Leeds managed to hold them at bay and there was no more scoring. It was a narrow lead, but the players and fans were satisfied after the nightmare start.

Duncan Stewart had been living in England at the time and travelled home to be at the game with a sense of trepidation:

Everything I had read in the papers in the run-up to the match had been negative towards Rangers. By the time it came around I had started to believe what I was reading and feared the worst. But right from the beginning the atmosphere inside Ibrox was unbelievable and I knew that, whatever happened in the second leg, that we were going to win. Even when we went behind I never doubted it. The fans and the players were magnificent that night. It was Ibrox at its best.

Just as in the Ibrox game, the second leg at Elland Road saw the visitors get off to a dream start through a superb Mark Hateley strike in the opening minutes. But unlike the first leg, the home team failed to respond and never really looked likely to recover. Rangers soaked up the pressure and sealed victory on the hour with a goal on the counter-attack by Ally McCoist. Eric Cantona's goal for Leeds was too little, too late. Rangers had reached the promised land of the Champions League, ensuring Ibrox would see another three great European occasions.

SO CLOSE…

The group stages started with an exciting 2–2 draw with the brilliant French champions, Marseille, on a night of torrential rain in Glasgow. Marseille had been 2–0 ahead with 10 minutes to go and were convinced they were going to win the match. But defender Basile Boli, who signed for Rangers two years later, recalled in a 2006 interview 'That was without accounting for the Rangers fans. They made such a hullabaloo, such a huge wall of noise, that Rangers were spurred on and came back to draw 2–2.'

After a win away to CSKA Moscow and a draw at FC Bruges, Rangers were back at Ibrox for the visit of the Belgians. A 2–1 win, thanks to a freak goal by defender Scott Nisbet, set up a virtual European Cup semi-final against Marseille in the south of France. The winners of the match would have been guaranteed a place in the Final, but the game ended 1–1. As a result, the finalists would not be known until after the final group games. Rangers were playing host to CSKA, while Marseille were in Belgium. Because Marseille had the better head-to-head record, the Scots knew they had to go one better than the French champions.

On an emotional night at Ibrox, Rangers failed to break down the Russians, despite incessant pressure. A combination of poor finishing and brilliant goalkeeping meant the game ended 0–0. But in any event, with Marseille winning 1–0 against Bruges, the result in Glasgow was immaterial. Tears flowed as the scoreline in Belgium filtered through to Ibrox. The capacity crowd stayed to the end to hail their heroes, and the players were given a huge ovation as they took a final bow.

Rangers were out, and the European dream was over for another year, but the run had given the players and fans a taste of club football at the highest level. Ibrox was a natural home for the Champions League. Under the floodlights, with the stands packed to the rafters, the stadium looked magnificent emblazoned with the special UEFA branding. And ever since that first campaign, the pseudo-classical strains of the official Champions League theme have been synonymous with the ground.

But the competition was not exactly a happy hunting ground for Rangers. Under Walter Smith, the club took part in two more Champions League campaigns and came bottom of their group on both occasions, managing just one win in 12 games.

END OF A GOLDEN ERA

Domestically, though, Rangers were unstoppable as the League titles kept coming and truly world-class players were recruited. For many supporters, brilliant Danish winger Brian Laudrup, signed in the summer of 1994, was the best player ever to grace the Ibrox pitch in a light-blue jersey. His close control, vision and pace were simply too much for Scottish defenders to cope with, and in his first season he helped propel Rangers to their seventh title in a row, finishing 15 points ahead of second-placed Motherwell. The summer of 1995 saw remarkable scenes outside Ibrox, as thousands turned out to greet the next superstar signing – Paul Gascoigne. Gazza also proved his worth, scoring an Ibrox hat-trick on the final day of the season against Aberdeen to secure the eighth consecutive title.

The growing status of Ibrox looked set to be recognised by UEFA in 1996, with the awarding of a showpiece European Final. The ground was proposed as the venue for the European Cup-Winners' Cup Final, and it would have been the first staged in Glasgow since Hampden hosted Bayern Munich and St Etienne, 20 years earlier. It would also have been the first European Final at Ibrox since the 1961 Cup-Winners' Cup clash between Rangers and Fiorentina.

UEFA's executive committee met in Birmingham on 15 December 1995 and were expected to rubber-stamp a proposal from the club competitions committee. It would

Seats and a video screen were installed in the corner between the Broomloan Road and Govan Stands in the mid-90s. The same work was carried out at the Copland Road End.

have been another high-profile coup for the club, not to mention a highly profitable one. But instead of going to Ibrox, the governing body awarded the Final to the King Baudouin Stadium in Brussels. It transpired that a cardiologists' conference in Glasgow clashed with the date of the Final, meaning there were not enough hotel beds available in the city.

Curiously, despite coming so close in 1996, Ibrox has never been proposed as a Final venue by the Scottish Football Association since, even though it holds a UEFA five-star rating. Hampden, on the other hand, has been nominated twice by the SFA and was granted the 2002 Champions League Final.

In the summer of 1996 the Ibrox capacity was increased again, when the corners between the Copland and Broomloan stands and the Govan were filled in with another 2,500 seats. By now the multi-coloured seats in the three new stands had been replaced with an all-blue colour scheme. Thanks to a UEFA scheme to help developing nations, around 6,000 of the old seats eventually turned up at the Zalgiris Stadium in Lithuania. Another 400 were bought by Highland League club Wick Academy. Enterprising committee members contacted the club when they heard the seats at Ibrox were being replaced and, after a guided tour of the stadium and a meeting with Walter Smith, they returned North with the seats in the back of a refrigerated lorry. The seats now take pride of place in the stand at their Harmsworth Park ground.

Two giant video screens were also installed, which would allow pre-match entertainment to be shown to fans and live action to be broadcast during the game. The screens also gave Rangers the option of screening away games to a paying crowd at Ibrox. One such game came at the end of the 1997–98 season. Having equalled Celtic's record of nine consecutive League titles the previous season, Rangers were attempting to win their 10th in a row, with their Glasgow rivals doing their best to stop them. The League race went all the way to the final day, when Celtic were at home to St Johnstone and Rangers were away to Dundee United.

Demand for tickets for Tannadice far exceeded demand, and Rangers decided to show the game on the big screens to give as many fans as possible the chance to watch the game. An astonishing 29,000 supporters turned out at Ibrox to watch the game. Rangers had to beat United and hope that St Johnstone could take something from their visit to Parkhead. Although the game was being played 80 miles away, the atmosphere at Ibrox was as electric as for any match on the hallowed turf. Even an early goal by Henrik Larsson at Celtic Park could not stifle the noise, and when news of a St Johnstone equaliser spread round the stadium, there was a cheer that could have been heard at Parkhead. Unfortunately for the Rangers fans, it turned out to be a false alarm. Someone listening in on their radio had got it wrong and Celtic were still in the lead. The cheers were soon for real when Brian Laudrup scored, followed by a goal from Jorg Albertz. For a while it seemed that the 10-in-a-row dream might just become a reality for the Ibrox faithful, but their hopes were killed when Celtic scored a second goal. The songs continued defiantly to the end, but the reality finally sank in when the final whistle went. After nine years of invincibility, Rangers had relinquished their crown.

There was a sense of disbelief in the stands that a golden era was over. Walter Smith had already announced that he was standing down, and many of his team would also be leaving Ibrox in the close season. Dutchman Dick Advocaat was the new manager, and he was given almost unlimited funds to create his own team.

HAPPY BIRTHDAY, IBROX

In his first two seasons, Advocaat's squad produced some of the best football the old stadium had ever seen from any team. In Europe in particular, Rangers were becoming a force to be reckoned with. After the dismal days of the mid-1990s, when Champions League appearances were often an embarrassment, the fans could enjoy their European nights again.

There were swashbuckling victories over Bayer Leverkusen, Parma and PSV Eindhoven. Bayern Munich somehow escaped from Ibrox with a draw after being pummelled for 90 minutes, while Austrian champions Sturm Graz were destroyed 5–0 in one of Rangers' best-ever European performances. The exciting, attacking football produced by Advocaat's team inspired the Rangers support, and there was a tremendous atmosphere at all the Champions League games. Visiting players spoke in awe of the noise generated from the

Ibrox stands, most notably Monaco's Croatian striker Dado Prso. So impressed was he by what he heard during a 2000 group game that it was a major factor in him signing for Rangers a few years later.

In December 1999 Rangers celebrated Ibrox's 100th birthday by inviting a galaxy of stars from throughout the decades to take a bow on the pitch. Fittingly, the anniversary coincided with a match against Hearts – the team who visited the stadium when it opened almost exactly a century before. At half-time, on a cold, wet night, three days before Christmas, comedian Andy Cameron took to the field and introduced a host of legends from the past. A seemingly endless list of heroes trooped out into the semi-circle to take the adulation of the 50,000 crowd. They included Jimmy Smith, Jock 'Tiger' Shaw, Jim Baxter, John Greig and Terry Butcher. The last out was Brian Laudrup, by now playing in Holland for Ajax, who received a deafening reception.

In his programme notes for the game, Dick Advocaat told how Ibrox had made a huge impression on him when, as Dutch national team manager, he had visited the stadium to watch some of his Scottish-based players in action. He wrote:

I will always remember the marble hallway at the entrance and, even to this day, the one thing that stuck in my mind was Stan the commissionaire. He was proudly standing there in his uniform ready to take me up for my cup of tea and show me where I could meet the Dutch players after the match. For me, that was class. You don't have that sort of thing in Holland. I love all those unique things about Rangers – they have a charm that gives the club a character of its own.

Ibrox had changed beyond recognition since it opened in 1899; indeed nothing of the original ground remained. In its place stood a modern, safe, state-of-the-art stadium, one that was steeped in history and tradition.

A FITTING MEMORIAL

Before the Old Firm game of 2 January 1991, Rangers unveiled a memorial to the victims of the Ibrox disaster to mark the 20th anniversary of the tragedy. Sadly, the minute's silence that preceded the match was shamefully interrupted by jeers from the Celtic fans, whose actions flew in the face of the united sense of grief that had engulfed Glasgow at the time of the tragedy.

The memorial itself – a small plaque – was considered inadequate by many, and as the 30th anniversary approached, moves were initiated to create a more fitting tribute to those who lost their lives. Sculptor Andy Scott was approached by Senga Murray, the artist responsible for the murals painted in the Blue Room at Ibrox, which honour the club's managers, captains and chairmen. Scott came up with a series of proposals, and in the end it was decided to proceed with his suggestion of a statue of former captain John Greig

A statue of former Rangers captain John Greig was erected outside the Main Stand in 2001 to mark the 30th anniversary of the Ibrox disaster.

Some of Rangers' legendary captains feature on a mural painted by artist Senga Murray on the wall of the Blue Room.

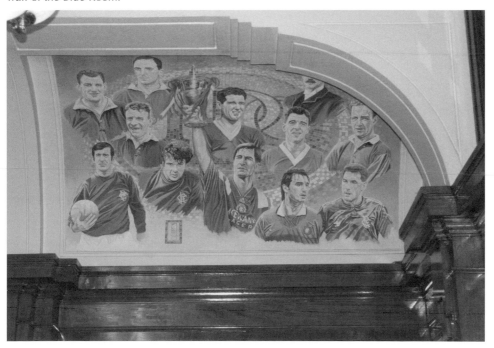

Senga Murray's depiction of the Ibrox pavilion.

– voted the greatest-ever Ranger by fans. Greig was seen as a figurehead for the club and was the captain at the time of the disaster. The sculpture is mounted on a red-brick plinth that features a plaque bearing the names of all 66 who lost their lives in the 1971 tragedy. The victims of the 1902 disaster and the accident in 1961 were not forgotten, with their names listed on another plaque alongside.

The statue was unveiled at a sombre service at Ibrox on 2 January 2001 – 30 years to the day after the disaster – and 471 relatives gathered outside the stadium to watch the ceremony take place. Inside Ibrox, more than 5,000 supporters gathered to watch the emotional service on giant video screens. Scarves and flowers from both Rangers and Celtic fans were laid at the statue.

The ceremony was an emotional occasion for the grieving families, who had waited a long time for their loss to be marked by the club. During the service conducted by Rev Stuart MacQuarrie, relatives sobbed in silent prayer as they laid wreaths at the foot of the bronze statue. For many it was worth the long wait simply to see their relative's name on the plaque. Margaret Malcolm, who was now 86 years old, lost her 16-year-old son, Russell, in the crush. She said afterwards 'Russell had his whole life ahead of him. It has been worth the wait. I just needed to see Russell's name up on that plaque.'

MY IBROX

ABSENCE MAKES THE HEART GROW FONDER – Paul Dunnachie

My first memory of being at Ibrox was the Scottish Cup third-round tie against Hamilton in 1987, yes – that match. I was 11, and as a birthday present to a friend of mine, his father took us to the game. Looking back, I was quite inspired by the place: the noise, the colours and the number of people. As the team was announced over the loudspeaker prior to the match, a massive cheer went up for each player as their name was read out; there were also fans having their names read out by the announcer. It was decided – I wanted to come back every week, this was where the team played and the crowd got involved.

As we were sat in the Govan Stand, I was fascinated by the enclosure under the Main Stand. It was obvious that this was where the singing was starting and that's where I wanted to be. Over the next dozen years or so, until I moved from Glasgow, the east enclosure is exactly where I watched virtually all of my football.

As I grew up, I became a Rangers nut, plain and simple. One of my friends and I absorbed as much about the club as we could – the history of the players, the trophies and the ground itself. We spent many a school holiday standing outside the main door to get the autographs of the players as they reported for and then left training. I was even one of a lucky few that managed to sneak into the west enclosure one summer morning when someone left one of the exit doors open. We all ran on to the terrace and stared at the newly laid pitch for five minutes or so until the commissionaire, a gentleman I seem to recall was named Stan Holloway, chased us back out on to Edmiston Drive.

To this day, I love the front façade of the stadium; the red brick, the blue window frames and the glimpse that you can get into the Blue Room, Trophy Room and manager's office. I had a friend from down South come up to watch a Rangers v Aberdeen match in March 2007 – it was to be his first match at Ibrox. A friend of mine picked us up from Glasgow Airport, and a silent arrangement was made that we would drive past Ibrox Stadium on the way – it was a clear, crisp night and there was a stunned silence in the back of the car as the Ibrox virgin first saw the Main Stand. 'Is that really a football ground?' was all he could say – an understandable question from someone whose match experience had been at the modern-day Meccano grounds thrown up in the last decade or so.

I always make a point of driving over to Ibrox when I travel back to Glasgow – not on a match day but

The Rangers Hall of Fame on display above the Ibrox marble staircase.

The manager's office has barely changed since Bill Struth's day. Present-day managers conduct their daily business in an office at Rangers' training complex.

just for a quick 15-minute stop-off, when I get out of the car and take a wander up to the enclosure entrance, the statue of John Greig, the Davie Cooper gates between the Main Stand and the Copland Road End and to the plaque commemorating the Ibrox disaster, close to the site of the original stairway. Absence might have made the heart grow fonder since I moved away from Glasgow, but I really enjoy taking a short time to remember all the good times at the stadium. It's strange to have such an emotional attachment to a building, and I just can't imagine making the time to visit an old school or place of work in the same way.

In the late 1980s–early 1990s, leaving the ground at the end of the match from the east enclosure when it was standing could be one of the highlights of the weekend. If the match had been exciting or important then it would be likely that there would be a lot of singing as the throng made its way to the alleyway at the top of the enclosure and along to the exit at the east of the ground. My most vivid memory is of people banging the wooden wall that ran along the back of the enclosure in time to the singing and it making an enormous noise by the time you got a few people doing it. Add to that the now traditional *Bouncy* song that started up in the late 1980s and even leaving after the game could be an event. It was quite common for our friends who sat in the Govan and Main Stands to be left outside waiting for us for a long time until the enclosure guys appeared.

I'm not sure when I started it, but I always double-tap the exit whenever I leave Ibrox (well, any football ground now). I must have seen people doing it when I was

younger and picked it up from there. It's one of those strange habits that you pick up. I suppose it's like saying 'until the next time' as you leave the stadium. It's definitely a less widespread practice than 20-odd years ago, but you still see people doing it and you know that they are usually of the same era as you.

The Blue Room at Ibrox today, where VIPs are entertained before and after matches.

I remember Davie Cooper's return to Ibrox in the autumn of 1989 and the east enclosure singing 'There's only one Davie Cooper', which was followed by 'There's only one Bobby Russell' – another ex-Ranger also playing that day. The tributes to past heroes continued with songs for Jock Wallace, Graham Roberts and some others. It was a day when I realised as a teenager that the adage 'once a Ranger, always a Ranger' was very much a heartfelt sentiment.

I've been at matches when opposition players were dealt some treatment. Chic Charnley, Roy Aitken and Peter Grant were particular targets but always gave a bit back and were relatively good-natured. However, I've never seen one person subjected to such a sustained barrage of abuse as Bradley Kerr, the evening he appeared as a substitute for Arbroath in the League Cup. Bradley was about 6ft 4in, had long hair and was built like a toothpick, and the poor guy had everything thrown at him that night: 'Bradley's got a boyfriend', 'Bradley, Bradley blow us a kiss', 'We love you Bradley we do', 'Bradley for Rangers', 'Bradley for Celtic'. I think the poor guy had to retrieve the ball from in front of the enclosure to take a throw-in at one point, and you could see his face just burning up at the pounding he was taking – all in good fun.

In May 2007 I was able to fulfil a boyhood dream and play a match on the pitch at Ibrox through the Football Aid charity. I paid up to get 45 minutes as a right-back – but in the end, I got to play another 25 minutes or so of the second half as a centre-half defending the Copland Road End. Pinch myself? You bet I did!

On the day, we were to report in at the main entrance, through the swing doors and into the famous marble hallway and up the staircase, past the bust of Bill Struth and up to the top of the stairs and the doorways to the manager's office, Blue Room and Trophy Room. The representative of the charity bounded up the stairs and was halfway up before I'd taken more than a few steps. 'You'll understand if I take me time?' I asked. And he did.

After a tour of the Blue Room and Trophy Room, we went to get changed for the warm-up and match in the dressing rooms, and seeing a jersey with your name on the back of it hanging on one of the pegs in the panelled dressing room was definitely one of those never-to-be-forgotten moments. To run out on to the pitch for the warm-up and the game itself was unforgettable. To have family and friends in the stand watching my attempts to grace the turf just made it all the more special. The fact that my team won 10–2 and I was off the pitch by the time the two goals were conceded also means that I technically have a clean sheet!

I have got a bit angry when I've visited Ibrox in the last couple of years. The place generally needs a bit of a scrub and a lick of paint in places. It doesn't seem much to ask that Rangers invest a bit of time and money once or twice a year to clean the place. I'm sure that the youth players would have done this in the past – maybe this just isn't seen as something that is the done thing any more?

Generally, the catering facilities are a joke and the stewarding and policing is over the top – the concept of going along to the football and being able to blow off a bit of steam seems to have been lost somewhere along the line. I'm glad that I went to Ibrox in the late 1980s and through the 1990s; today, it seems to have lost a bit of the magic. Maybe it's me getting older, or maybe things really have changed on match day. Either way, the memories are better than the current state of affairs, and to me that is sad.

FINAL RESTING PLACE – Stevie Mochrie

My uncle, Ronnie Low, emigrated from the Springburn district of Glasgow to Hamilton, Ontario, Canada, in the late 1950s. He followed Rangers even though he lived across the big pond, and like most ex-pats he joined the local Rangers supporters' club, the Hamilton Exiles RSC. Unfortunately in the 1990s, my uncle Ronnie took ill with cancer and passed away. His last wish was for his ashes to be scattered at Ibrox – a place he still held dear even after all those years. Unfortunately, Rangers didn't agree to such requests, as thousands of people would have been requesting it. Well I don't know how it happened – John Greig certainly had something to do with it – but Ronnie's family were told his ashes could be buried at the side of the park next to the Govan Stand.

The day arrived, and my father and I and some guests from Canada assembled in the Ibrox main foyer, before being taken round the park where a small hole, just big enough for Ronnie's ashes, had been dug. My dad and I were told we could say a small prayer and recital before the strains of the pipes rang round the empty stands. One of the Canadian guests was a young lad who played in the Kingston Ontario pipe band, and he played *Amazing Grace* and a slowed-down version of *Follow, Follow*. There was not a dry eye in the house. Workers doing maintenance work stopped and stood silent for those few poignant moments, and injured player Seb Rozental, who was getting his fitness up by running up and down the rows of seats, was another silent witness.

After laying uncle Ronnie's ashes, we all returned to the Main Stand, where we talked about Ronnie at last being able to watch his beloved Rangers once more. A very emotional day for all who were there. A note on this event was that at the next home game we attended in the Govan Stand, we looked down to where Ronnie's ashes were buried and, to our horror, saw that an advertisement board now stood there. We burst out laughing at

the thought of Ronnie bemoaning the fact that, after at last being back home at Ibrox, they go and put an advertisement board on top of him.

The ashes of ex-pat Rangers fan Ronnie Low are buried at the edge of the Ibrox pitch during a poignant ceremony attended by his family.

BATTLE OF BRITAIN – Murdo Fraser, Conservative MSP for Mid Scotland and Fife

Of all the matches I have attended at Ibrox over the years, the one that sticks in the memory the most was the famous Battle of Britain clash between Rangers and English champions Leeds in 1992 in the Champions League qualifier.

Nowadays we have become accustomed to the Old Firm being the equal of top Premiership sides, but back then Scottish football was very much regarded as the poor relation of the English version. Despite the Souness revolution, pundits from south of the border were widely predicting a comfortable Leeds victory over two legs. With the first match at Ibrox, the home team had a lot to prove.

Despite the absence of away supporters due to a concern about violence, the atmosphere in the ground was electric and the fans in fine voice. The singing came to an abrupt halt after only the first minute, when McAllister scored for the visitors. But Rangers came back strongly and were rewarded with a Lukic own-goal 20 minutes later. The irrepressible Ally McCoist put the home side into the lead before half-time. With no more goals in the second half, that was how it ended, Rangers winning 2–1. Predictably, there were massive celebrations in the stands for the home team, and no one wanted to leave the ground.

Those few brave souls who made the trip south for the second leg, defying the travel ban in the process, were not disappointed, as Rangers won that 2–1 too (including a superb Hateley strike after only three minutes) – a comprehensive victory over the English champions. It would be a long time before we would hear lazy assumptions about the poor quality of Scottish football from the southern media again.

THERE BUT FOR THE GRACE OF GOD – Revd Stuart MacQuarrie, chaplain of the University of Glasgow

Rangers FC is one of the great institutions of Scotland. Love the club or loathe it, Rangers represent much of the great of the past and much of the hopes and aspirations for the future. Ibrox Stadium epitomises the club spirit. Solid. Substantial. The marble hallway and staircase in an art deco style hint at modernity. Muted blues in the detail and the famous RFC crest etched in the lampshades express a tasteful reminder that this is no ordinary stadium. No ordinary club.

On the 30th anniversary of the Ibrox disaster of 1971, at the stadium, I conducted a service in memory of those 66 people who died. Lives full of hope, aspiration, promise, and which were crushed as a result of a combination of freak circumstances. I thought then and still think of those 66 lives, and there but for the grace of God was I, who had also been at the game that day. The unveiling of the memorial and the service remind us that these lives will never be forgotten. They are part of the Rangers story. They as Rangers supporters are our people. We are their people.

CHANGED DAYS – Derek Miller

In my view, there was a much, much better atmosphere at the old Ibrox. I personally miss the old stadium, and I know that people have drifted away from the football because of the all-seated stadiums. I no longer attend the matches, because I honestly believe that Rangers FC don't want my type of support any more. For example, me and my cousin went to a Rangers v Hearts match last season. We were in the Broomloan Road Stand, right beside all the police at the enclosure side. Rangers won 2–0, but the match for us was terrible. We were constantly watched. On the other hand, the old Ibrox had heart, an atmosphere second to none. A full Copland Road terracing in full voice was unbeatable.

BORN TO BE A RANGER – Iain MacLeod

I have been going to see Rangers since primary school. My second primary school was Ibrox Primary, just across the road from the Copland Stand, where I now sit in the rear section. I have been a season ticket-holder for over 30 years now, having just reached my 50th birthday, but every time I enter the ground I always think about my first-ever visit. My mother was pregnant with me and attended a summer sports meeting held at Ibrox in 1957. I arrived shortly afterwards in October. My mother is now in her 70s but remembers going to the meeting because the runner Chris Chataway was appearing and demonstrating the four-minute mile. My mother remembers the sports event being well attended and recalls an announcement being made that Chris Chataway's wife had given birth to a daughter. When my pals talk about their first visit I take great pride in telling them I was there even before birth.

THE TROPHY ROOM

In a former billiard room at the end of a long, narrow corridor in the Ibrox Main Stand is a room that many consider to be the very heart of the stadium. The unassuming wooden entrance door states it is the Trophy Room but it is so much more than that. There is plenty of silverware, of course – it could hardly be otherwise for the world's most successful football club. But what makes the Rangers Trophy Room so special is the myriad other priceless pieces that have accumulated over the last 135 years. Virtually every surface in the room is covered with mementos and gifts, each one telling part of the Rangers story. There are contributions from the biggest names in the world of football – Real Madrid, Manchester United, Barcelona, Bayern Munich, Liverpool – alongside items gifted by some of the game's lesser lights. They are all given equal prominence.

Until the 1950s, the many trophies amassed by the club over the decades were housed in the boardroom, while other items gathered on their travels were kept in the manager's office. But the introduction of floodlit friendlies in the early 1950s followed by competitive European football saw the club start to accumulate a vast amount of memorabilia from around the world. It soon became apparent that the existing arrangements just would not suffice. Inspired by a visit to Real Madrid's stadium, manager Scot Symon came up with the idea of creating a room within the stadium to showcase the club's treasures.

The Trophy Room was housed in what had been a games room for the players. Three large glass cases filled with glittering silver Cups, cut-glass vases and medals dominated the room. On the far wall hung a huge and imposing portrait of Bill Struth – presented on his retirement as manager – surrounded by miniature versions of every League flag won by the club. Pennants from past opponents lined the other walls alongside framed photos of legendary players from the past. It was an instant hit, attracting thousands of visitors.

Many Rangers supporters would love to see a club museum opened in or near to Ibrox, and it is surprising that a club with such a rich history has not yet gone down that road. However, there is a belief within the club that the Main Stand itself is a museum and that the Trophy Room is the jewel in the crown.

Fifty years on, the Trophy Room continues to be a major attraction for Rangers fans, and Struth's painting still dominates the room, still surrounded by League flags, now numbering more than 50. There are now twice as many cabinets and countless more things to see, all with their own story.

One of the most intriguing items on display is the Loving Cup. For the last 70 years, a ceremony has taken place within the Blue Room at Ibrox that has become part of the club's folklore. To mark the coronation of King George VI in 1937, industrialist and Stoke City president Sir Francis Joseph had 30 pottery cups cast from an original mould, which was later destroyed. He presented one to each of the English first division clubs and to the two teams promoted from Division Two. The others he gave to the king himself, the Football League, the FA and the British Museum. The last one he kept for himself, until

The Trophy Room is packed with silverware and mementos dating back to the earliest days of the club's existence.

Rangers played Stoke in a benefit match to raise money for relatives of the victims of the Holditch colliery disaster.

As a thank you for taking part in the fund-raiser, the Cup was presented to Rangers. It was a condition of the gift that at the first home game of every year, the recipients should fill the Cup with champagne and toast the health of the monarch, and that tradition continues at Ibrox to this day. Every year Rangers invite the chairman of their first visitors of the new year to take part in the ceremony. Of course, traditionally the Old Firm played each other on New Year's Day, so on many occasions the Rangers chairman of the day was joined in the Blue Room by his Parkhead counterpart. Celtic supporters, who are often heard to be singing obscene and abusive songs about the Queen, may be surprised to learn that their senior club officials have been happy to raise a Cup in Her Majesty's honour for many years.

In the days before European competition, Rangers regularly played challenge matches against top European clubs, both at Ibrox and overseas. These games were far more competitive than the tame friendlies we see today, as the famous clash with Dynamo Moscow in 1945 demonstrated. Three years later, the Light Blues escaped from the Scottish winter and embarked on an 11-hour trip to Lisbon to face the Portuguese champions, Benfica.

The club was presented with an ornate caravel that is now on display in the Trophy Room as a memento of the match, which they won 3–0. But before the game there was another gift that was rather less gratefully received. The Rangers players were presented with a pig that captain Jock Shaw was supposed to lead out onto the pitch as a mascot. Not surprisingly, he was less than enthusiastic at the prospect of taking to the field with a farm animal and could not be persuaded to go through with it. The fate of the animal after this cruel snub is not recorded. As a footnote to the story, on the flight home Rangers winger Willie Waddell got talking to one of the air hostesses. They obviously hit it off because they eventually ended up getting married.

European opponents have provided many of the items in the Trophy Room, some more interesting than others. While some clubs obviously do not put a huge amount of thought into their gifts – Stuttgart's uninspiring plaque for the 2003 Champions League games springs to mind – others are remarkable in their intricacy. One of the most striking items is a black vase presented by Polish club GKS Katowice after a 1988 UEFA Cup tie, which Rangers won 5–2 on aggregate. Virtually every visitor to the stadium asks where it came from. The 17-inch tall piece was carved out of a single lump of coal and features intricate patterns and a carving of a helmet-wearing miner.

A portrait of Bill Struth surrounded by every league flag won by the club takes pride of place in the Ibrox Trophy Room. The bike was a gift from the French club St Etienne.

Another unusual piece of memorabilia is a racing bike donated by French champions St Etienne before their European Cup tie in 1957. The cycle, a state-of-the-art model, was made by a local manufacturer and it was presented as a symbol of the club's home town. It was put in storage until the Trophy Room was opened two years later and has been a fixture ever since. It sits, somewhat incongruously, propped up against the wall below the huge portrait of Struth. St Etienne seemed to specialise in unusual gifts; for their European Cup meeting in 1975 they presented Rangers with a genuine French miners' lamp.

Other notable gifts from European opponents include a spectacular jewel-encrusted trophy presented by Turkish team Ankaragucu, an elegant clock tower from Borussia Mönchengladbach and a silver samovar tea urn presented by Dynamo Kiev in 1987. Norwegian club Lillestrom gifted a traditional hunting horn to mark the European Cup-Winners' Cup tie in 1979, while Dutch giants Ajax presented a wooden clock in 1973, which still hangs proudly on the Trophy Room wall. The gift was a memento of the very first European Super Cup, which was played in 1973 between the European Cup winners (Ajax) and the European Cup-Winners' Cup holders (Rangers) as part of Rangers' centenary celebrations.

Some of the items that adorn the Trophy Room have come from closer to home. One of the most impressive is a stag's head that looks down sombrely from the wall. It has been his home since 1959, when he was presented by Inverness Caledonian. The occasion was the inauguration of the new floodlights at the Highland club's old Telford Street ground, when the locals took on an Old Firm select made up of members of the Rangers and Celtic first-team squads. A crowd of more than 6,000 packed into the ground to see this historic coming together of two bitter rivals. It has often been said that Rangers 'don't do friendlies' and with quality players like Jimmy Millar, Johnny Hubbard, Bill Paterson and Sammy Baird representing the blue half of Glasgow, it was clear that this also applied even when they only made up part of the team. Baird scored a hat-trick in a 4–2 win. Bizarrely, the records show Rangers also contributed one player called King to the XI...and another called Queen!

So grateful were the Caley officials for the appearance of the Rangers players that they had the stag sent to Ibrox, much to the consternation of the staff at the stadium, who had no idea why a decapitated animal's head had been dropped off at the front door unannounced. Had it been a few years later they might even have feared it was some kind of Godfather-style threat from the McMafia. It also begs the question: if the stag's head was sent to Rangers for their involvement in the game, what part of the poor animal's anatomy was presented to Celtic?

But while many of the items in the trophy room have interesting stories attached to them, ultimately it is the footballing honours that are the most meaningful. At the time of writing, Rangers are the holders of the two Scottish domestic Cup competitions, and both the CIS League Cup and the Scottish Cup have pride of place in the main trophy cabinet. Alongside them stands the Scottish Victory Cup – a trophy played for in 1946 to celebrate the end of World War Two. The tournament marked the return of national football to Scotland after the enforced regionalisation during hostilities, and it was a prestigious competition, as the Scottish Cup had not yet been resurrected. Rangers were presented with the trophy after winning the Final in front of a crowd of more than 100,000 on 15 June, beating Hibs 3–1.

The League flags that cover the back wall of the Trophy Room are a striking illustration of Rangers' dominance of Scottish football for much of the last 130 years, as are two stunning collections of medals from legendary stars of the past – Richard Gough and Bob McPhail.

To many supporters, nine-in-a-row captain Gough is the epitome of what it means to be a great Ranger. Fearless, inspirational and fiercely competitive, he was a rock in the centre of the Rangers defence throughout the historic run. He was one of only three players to be at the club for the entire duration of the nine-in-a-row success and the only one to pick up a medal every season. Ally McCoist and Ian Ferguson, the other two, both had gaps in their collection because they missed games due to injury. Gough's nine Championship medals are currently on loan to the club and are on display in the Trophy Room.

In the cabinet opposite sits what is undoubtedly the greatest collection of football medals to be found anywhere in Scotland. In the unlikely event that it was ever to be sold on the open market, the 36 badges won by Bob McPhail would fetch tens of thousands

The unique collection of medals won by Bob McPhail is on display in the main trophy cabinet. It is pictured in front of the CIS League Cup.

of pounds. McPhail joined Rangers in 1927 and spent a glorious 14 years at Ibrox, playing 466 games and scoring 281 goals. His goals and all-round play helped Rangers to one of their most successful periods of all time and brought him nine Championships, six Scottish Cups (a club record), five Glasgow Cups and six Charity Cups. His talents also saw him capped 13 times for Scotland in an era when there were far fewer international games. He was also picked on numerous occasions to represent the Scottish League. By any standards it was a spectacular career.

The medals of McPhail on show at Ibrox cover a 20-year period, stretching from a Schoolboy international appearance in 1919 to the Scottish League win of 1938–39. As well as his Rangers honours, there are also medals from his days as a juvenile with Ashvale and in the junior ranks with Pollok. His professional career began with Airdrie, and the Trophy Room houses winners' medals from the Scottish Cup and the Lanarkshire Cup, which he won while at Broomfield. But it is for his glorious time at Rangers that McPhail will forever be remembered, and he was a regular visitor to Ibrox until he died in August 2000 at the age of 94. His autobiography, first published in 1988, provides a fascinating insight into a bygone era of football and is recommended reading for anyone with an interest in the history of the game, whether a Rangers supporter or not.

Another individual prize given a home in the Trophy Room is Ally McCoist's Golden Boot for finishing the 1991–92 season as Europe's top scorer. His 41 goals helped Rangers to a fourth consecutive League title and won him the title of Scotland's Player of the Year. Signed from Sunderland in 1983, McCoist endured a difficult start to his Rangers career, but he fought to establish himself and soon became a massive crowd favourite, thanks in equal measure to his prolific goalscoring ability and his infectious personality. He went on to score 355 goals in a career that spanned 15 years, and he returned to the club as assistant manager to Walter Smith in 2007.

Gough, McCoist and McPhail have all played hugely significant parts in the Rangers story, but without the commitment of Moses McNeil and the other founders of the club, they may never have been given the opportunity to take centre stage. So it is fitting that Moses is given a prominent place among the countless items in the Trophy Room.

In the showcase, alongside Bob McPhail's medals, the Victory Cup and the latest silverware won by the first team, sits an eight-inch tall silver Cup. At first glance you could be forgiven for missing it, such is its relative insignificance in stature. But on closer inspection, the inscription 'Won By Moses McNeil. Rangers Football Club' can be read, and instantly its true significance becomes apparent. The trophy was not actually for football; it was won by McNeil at a local athletics meeting.

At the age of 16, Moses McNeil, his brothers and some friends formed what would go on to become one of the world's biggest, best-known and most successful sporting institutions. None of the founding fathers could possibly have predicted what Rangers would become, but they laid the foundations that ensured that the club would have every chance of success in the future.

THE POWER OF IBROX

There is no question that when the crowd is giving the team 100 per cent backing at Ibrox, the players react accordingly. Average players find themselves able to lift their performance to another level, while good players are capable of something a little extra-special. Games that should be lost on paper can be drawn or even won. The concept of the crowd as the 12th man is nothing new, but there is no doubt that the fans can play their part at Ibrox on a big occasion.

Since the advent of European competition in the late 1950s, most of the continent's best players have performed at Ibrox. Many of them have been blown away by the experience. Old Trafford, the Bernabeu and even Celtic Park may be bigger, but Ibrox on a big European night generates a unique atmosphere.

The design of the stadium amplifies the noise from the fans, and the sound can be frightening when all four stands are in full flow. The fact that the stands are so close to the pitch means that the noise on the pitch is deafening. The Champions League theme is drowned out by the fans. Players standing just a few yards apart can find it impossible to hear each other speak. Some of the biggest names in football have spoken in glowing terms of the European experience at Ibrox.

Thierry Henry (Barcelona/France) after Rangers v Barcelona, Champions League, November 2007:

> I know the atmosphere that's generated here and that makes it tough for any team. I thought the fans were unbelievable again. They were not swearing or shouting stupid things, they pushed their team forward and that's great to see...They were just trying to get behind their team and push their players. They did not concentrate on having a go at the opposition...It is the first time I have played at Ibrox and it was great. It was a special atmosphere.

A wall of noise and a spectacular card display greeted the players of Rangers and Barcelona as they took to the pitch for this Champions League group-stage match. The words 'More Than A Club' were emblazoned across the Govan Stand – a nod towards Barcelona's motto and the feelings Rangers' fans have for their own club.

The Broomloan and Copland Stands had card tributes to Rangers' European Cup-Winners' Cup triumph 35 years earlier, which took place in Barcelona. Henry was just one of many superstars in the Barca line up alongside Thuram, Puyol, Xavi, Iniesta, Ronaldinho and Messi. But against the odds, Rangers managed to snuff out the threat from Barca's superstars and held out for a 0–0 draw.

After picking up seven points out of nine with a tremendous start to the Champions League campaign, Rangers went on to be eliminated at the group stages. But they dropped into the UEFA Cup and went on to reach the final in Manchester, only to lose 2–0 to Zenit St Petersburg.

Ruud Van Nistelrooy (Real Madrid/Holland) ahead of Rangers v Villarreal, Champions League, February 2006:
I'll never forget that night we (Manchester United) played there. The atmosphere was unbelievable, very hostile. We managed to score an early goal but that only quietened the crowd for a little while. Villarreal will think they've experienced a lot of good atmospheres but I really think the Rangers support could startle them. If that happens, Rangers have to take advantage. I really believe they should just go for it in the first 20 minutes.

Van Nistelrooy was playing for Real Madrid when Rangers and Villarreal drew 2–2 in a thrilling Champions League last 16 match at Ibrox. He had twice appeared at Ibrox in the Champions League. In the 2003 competition he was with Manchester United when they won 1–0 at Ibrox and 3–0 at Old Trafford. Four years earlier he had appeared for PSV Eindhoven, when Dick Advocaat's Rangers overwhelmed them 4–1 at Ibrox. Van Nistelrooy scored from the penalty spot, but his contribution was overshadowed by the performance of fellow countryman Michael Mols for Rangers.

Dado Prso (Rangers/Croatia) after Rangers v Porto, Champions League, September 2005:
The atmosphere and build-up is fantastic here. I know a lot of players all over Europe and they say that the atmosphere at Ibrox on a Champions League night is the best they've experienced. I know it because I was a Monaco player who played here against Rangers, remember. The players raise their game for this tournament, but I believe the Rangers fans raise their game too.

Thomas Buffel (Rangers/Belgium) after Rangers v Porto, Champions League, September 2005:
The atmosphere was fantastic and the tempo was very high throughout. I played Champions League before with Feyenoord but this was a great game. The crowd was fantastic and I couldn't even hear the Champions League hymn before kick-off because they were singing so loudly.

Porto had won the Champions League two seasons earlier under Jose Mourinho, and while they had lost their coach and several of their star players they were still expected to progress from a group also containing Inter Milan and Artmedia Bratislava. In an exciting game, Danish striker Peter Lovenkrands gave Rangers a first-half lead, which was cancelled out just after the break. Porto piled on the pressure but it was Rangers who went in front again through Dado Prso.

With 20 minutes to go, Porto equalised again with almost a carbon copy of their first goal, and they looked most likely to win at that stage. But spurred on by a noisy crowd, Rangers showed great determination to get back into the game, and Ibrox erupted when Sotirios Kyrgiakos headed home a cross from Barry Ferguson to secure the points in the closing minutes.

The computerised turnstiles are quiet on a non-match day but if Rangers are playing at home the area is packed with fans.

Rangers went on to qualify for the last 16 – the first Scottish club to make it into the knock-out stages of the competition since it was reorganised in the mid-1990s.

Gio Van Bronckhorst (Barcelona/Holland) ahead of Rangers v Manchester United, Champions League, October 2003:

I don't think any stadium in the Premiership can compare with Ibrox. It's not untrue to say that players can suffer from it. I know from Ruud when we played PSV at Rangers that he thought it was one of the most atmospheric games he'd experienced. He thought it was very frightening. So now he has to face it again. For him to go there again, it will be the same experience. OK, United players play all the biggest games in full stadiums, but I think that most of them will find a really different atmosphere.

Former Rangers midfielder Van Bronckhorst, by now playing for Barcelona in Spain, warned that his countryman Van Nistelrooy and his Manchester United teammates might struggle to cope with the Ibrox atmosphere. Van Bronckhorst had played against PSV in 1999 during Rangers' 4–1 win in Glasgow.

Gary Neville (Manchester United/England) after Rangers v Manchester United, Champions League, October 2003:

This was the loudest atmosphere that I have known, compared to any English ground away from home. There have been certain nights at Old Trafford in European games – the ones against Juventus come to mind – when the atmosphere was incredible. But this was definitely up there with the best. It was fantastic. When we came out at the start I was looking around me and I saw people in the directors' box jumping up singing, and I was wondering what was happening. It is not usually like that. The crowd beating us was never going to happen but thank goodness they didn't score.

John O'Shea (Manchester United/Republic of Ireland) after Rangers v Manchester United, Champions League, October 2003:

It was a fantastic atmosphere at Rangers, and their supporters gave their players an extra lift, without a doubt. It was incredible playing out there and we were saying 'if only we could get that every week' in the dressing room afterwards.

The massive amount of hype that preceded Sir Alex Ferguson's first competitive return to Ibrox since his Aberdeen days ensured that Ibrox was a cauldron of noise. Fans were each issued with a blue card to create a 'Blue Sea of Ibrox' as the teams emerged, and an old song of that name was reintroduced as part of the pre-match repertoire. The din was deafening as the game got under way, but Phil Neville silenced the crowd in the opening minutes when he scored an unlikely goal. Rangers and their fans recovered from the shock and deserved at least a draw from the game, but it was not to be and Fergie headed back south with a smile on his face.

The rest of the campaign was a shambles for Rangers, and they ended up bottom of their group after losing their remaining three games to United, Stuttgart and Panathinaikos.

Paolo Vanoli (Rangers) ahead of Rangers v Stuttgart, Champions League, September 2003:

I was at Ibrox twice in the space of a year with Parma, and these two games will always stick in my mind. The atmosphere was incredible. I couldn't believe the fans were singing right up until the last minute, and the players seemed to be responding to the noise. In the Champions League qualifying tie we lost 2–0 and I always remember the fans singing that Simply The Best *song by Tina Turner. The noise was incredible. I played in lots of different stadiums when I was in Italy but for some reason I always remember these nights in Glasgow. In Italy you don't get that kind of atmosphere at matches. The supporters at Ibrox seemed to help the team win the game. It's not easy for the away team to get a victory in an atmosphere like that.*

Vanoli had been part of the highly talented Parma team that was defeated by Rangers in 1999. Many fans consider the atmosphere at Ibrox in the first leg, which Rangers won 2–0, to have been the best at the stadium in modern times. The ground shook after Tony Vidmar and Claudio Reyna beat the Italian 'keeper, Gianluigi Buffon. Rangers were beaten 1–0 in the second leg but progressed to the Champions League.

Henning Berg (Rangers/Norway) after Rangers v Stuttgart, Champions League, September 2003:

That was better than Old Trafford. The atmosphere out there is unbelievable. It was better than anything I've ever experienced in all my days at Old Trafford. I had goosebumps on my arms. I could barely hear the Champions League song because there was so much noise from our fans. That's the kind of memory that a football player never, ever forgets. I've played in some huge games for United – we beat Juventus and other big teams at home – but this was something extra-special.

Stuttgart were a talented young team who were riding high in the German League when they faced Rangers in their opening group game. They had gone five consecutive games without conceding a goal, and when they scored through Kevin Kuranyi at Ibrox it did not look good for Rangers. But halfway through the second half, the game exploded into life when Christian Nerlinger equalised, sending the home fans into raptures. Ibrox was still bouncing five minutes later, when Lovenkrands fired home the winner.

Andreas Brehme (Kaiserslautern/West Germany) ahead of Rangers v Kaiserslautern, UEFA Cup, November 2001:

I've played here myself and I know what kind of atmosphere to expect, so I will be telling my players to approach the match without any fear. If you hide at Ibrox then you have no chance. Therefore that's why we will come here and attack so we can keep the tie open for the second leg. The Ibrox crowd is fantastic, and playing in front of an audience like that makes you want to perform. I think most players would prefer to play in front of 50,000 fans than 5,000.

Having been knocked out of the Champions League, Rangers dropped into the UEFA Cup, where they faced FC Kaiserslautern. Coached by former Bayern Munich defender Andreas Brehme, the Germans were beaten 1–0 at Ibrox but triumphed 3–0 in the second leg.

Ronald De Boer (Rangers/Holland) after Rangers v Sturm Graz, Champions League, September 2000:

The thing I've noticed since coming here is how noisy the crowd is. You can always hear them shouting and singing – even when we're behind. The atmosphere at Ibrox is better than it is in the Nou Camp – Tuesday's match against Graz proved that. It was incredible. In Barcelona, when there's 100,000 against Real Madrid, it's a special occasion, but apart from that it can be quiet during games. Maybe the fans get a little spoiled. But here you can feel the passion from the stands even though the stadium is only half the size.

Signed from Barcelona in the autumn of 2000, Ronald De Boer produced a virtuoso performance to give Rangers their biggest Champions League group-stage victory. He scored one goal and pulled the strings as Rangers cruised to a 5–0 win at Ibrox.

Rangers went on to secure a superb 1–0 win in Monaco against the French champions, but away defeats to Graz and Galatasaray and two draws at home to the Turks and Monaco put paid to hopes of qualification for another season.

Stefan Wessells (Bayern Munich) after Rangers v Bayern Munich, Champions League, September 1999:

> *The noise and the atmosphere were incredible and I couldn't even hear myself think. But I feel the Rangers fans inspired me. The crowd were very partisan but they were also very fair.*

Stefan Wessells's mother after Rangers v Bayern Munich, Champions League, September 1999:

> *I can't believe that these people could be so hostile to my boy. They did not stop whistling and shouting at him, but he had done nothing to them. I don't know how he managed to concentrate on playing football when people were being so horrible to him.*

Due to a series of injuries, fourth-choice goalkeeper Wessells found himself thrown into this Champions League group match. To say it was a baptism of fire would be something of an understatement. The atmosphere at Ibrox was red-hot, and Rangers were on top form. But however much Frau Wessel did not like it, the young 'keeper seemed entirely unaffected.

The home team had a whirlwind start, with the pace and movement of forwards Michael Mols and Jonatan Johansson causing massive problems for the German defence. A goal was inevitable, and it came through a trademark left-foot drive from Jorg Albertz. Despite piling on the pressure, Rangers could not add to their tally, and there was a sense

Inside the Ibrox dressing room. It has not changed much since the stand opened in 1929.

of inevitability when Bayern scored an undeserved equaliser in the final minute. The fact that the goal came from a deflected free-kick that should not have been awarded in the first place just added to the frustration.

Gaizka Mendieta (Valencia/Spain) after Rangers v Valencia, Champions League, October 1999:
The atmosphere was like hell and we turned in an outstanding, professional and brave performance to beat Rangers. It was the most difficult game we have had to play this season because the Rangers support was right behind their team all the way. They spurred their players on and made it very difficult for us. I wasn't intimidated by the atmosphere, but in some moments of the game I felt the pitch moving as they cheered their side on.

Valencia's first-half performance at Ibrox was one of the best seen from a visiting team for many years, and Mendieta was instrumental. Knowing that a victory would take them into the next round, the Ibrox crowd did their best to inspire the home team but the Spaniards were too fast and too strong. The game was effectively over at half-time, after Claudio Lopez put Valencia 2–0 ahead. A second-half header by Craig Moore gave Rangers some hope, but an equaliser never looked likely.

Claudio Reyna (Rangers/USA) after Rangers v Parma, Champions League qualifier, August 1999:
I've never experienced an atmosphere like that. The crowd lived every single pass, every single moment. They were never quiet throughout the entire match, and I had goosebumps at times. That definitely helped us, and I think it gave them a communication problem. When you can't hear your teammates, it throws you off a little and makes you hesitate. You could tell that happened with them a few times. On the other hand, if one of our players didn't hear someone shouting 'man on' then we heard the crowd shouting it for us.

Inspired by a raucous Ibrox crowd, Rangers overwhelmed Parma in this Champions League qualifier. Dick Advocaat's team played a thrilling brand of high-tempo passing football that the Italians simply could not cope with.

As Rangers piled on the pressure, the crowd responded by raising the decibel levels even further. A clearly rattled Cannavaro was sent off for two fouls on Rod Wallace and soon after, Rangers took the lead. Australian international Tony Vidmar was the unlikely scorer, sparking scenes of wild celebration in the stands. The pressure continued into the second half and paid off when Claudio Reyna scored a second.

It was a memorable night for the fans who had suffered so many European disappointments over the previous decade. In the second leg, after soaking up incessant pressure from Parma, Rangers escaped with a 1–0 defeat and moved into the group stages.

Chris Woods (Rangers/England) after Rangers v Dynamo Kiev, European Cup, September 1987:
It was the best crowd I have ever played in front of. It was amazing. I couldn't hear myself shouting instructions, the noise was so deafening. They were another player for us and it gave all of the boys a lift. Although Old Firm games were always noisy I think that night surpassed that.

In their first European Cup tie for nine years, Rangers could not have been given a more difficult task. But a 1–0 defeat to the USSR champions in Kiev was overturned on a dramatic night in Govan, with Mark Falco and Ally McCoist scoring the vital goals. The roar when the second goal went in shook the ground to its foundations, and many players, including McCoist and Serie A veterans Trevor Francis and Graeme Souness, considered it to be the best atmosphere they had ever performed in.

Robert Prytz (Rangers/Sweden) after Rangers v Inter Milan, UEFA Cup, November 1984:
The fans were unbelievable, and to this day I honestly remember that game as one of my best in Europe; it even surpasses the European Cup Final.

After a 3–0 first-leg defeat in Milan, few gave Rangers much of a chance in the return game against Inter's superstars at Ibrox, despite brave words from manager Jock Wallace. But when Australian forward Dave Mitchell scored with a header at five minutes, the supporters dared to dream. Hopes seemed to be dashed when Altobelli equalised, but just two minutes later, record signing Iain Ferguson put Rangers in front again with a spectacular 20-yard shot. Just after half-time, he headed home a third and suddenly the impossible was within Rangers' grasp. Driven on by the Ibrox crowd, the home team piled forward but could not break down the Italian defence.

Although Rangers were eliminated, the 3–1 victory was a highlight of what was generally a depressing time for the club's followers. Swedish international Prytz had played for Malmo in the European Cup Final and had starred in Serie A and the Bundesliga, but he counts the home game against Inter as one of the highlights of his career.

Jimmy Greaves (Tottenham Hotspur/England) after Rangers v Tottenham Hotspur, European Cup-Winners' Cup, December 1962:
When the teams took to the pitch the noise was deafening, the atmosphere intimidating in the extreme.

Rangers had been beaten 5–2 at White Hart Lane in the first leg of this Battle of Britain, but a crowd of 80,000 still turned out at Ibrox for the return, in the hope that they could somehow retrieve the tie. At nine minutes, Greaves silenced the partisan Rangers fans when he shot past Billy Ritchie. Although the home team battled hard, they ended up losing the game 3–2.

IBROX ROCKS

For all the international superstars who have graced the Ibrox pitch since the ground was opened more than 100 years ago, none could get even close to the worldwide fame of the man who appeared at the stadium on 12 June 1990. Cruyff, Di Stefano, Puskas, Beckenbauer, Gascoigne and Ronaldinho were all household names around the world but all bowed before the legend that was Francis Albert Sinatra.

Sinatra may have been past his best by the time he performed at Ibrox. His show may have been overpriced and something of a shambles. But as events go, it was up there among the most memorable ever to take place at the stadium. Sinatra himself, even at the age of 74 and after five decades in showbusiness, was moved to tears. For the audience, many of whom had waited a lifetime to see Old Blue Eyes in the flesh, it was something akin to a religious experience. After Sinatra's death in 1998, *Sunday Times* journalist Allan Brown described the concert as 'like a bingo night in the Sistine Chapel'.

When the revamped Ibrox was completed in the early 1980s, Rangers were determined to make the most of the new facilities. It was confidently predicted that the days of football stadiums lying empty in between games were over. All sorts of non-football events took place at the stadium – the Boys' Brigade centenary celebrations in 1983, Jim Watt's world title fight and a huge Rotarians conference all attracted tens of thousands of people to Govan. But it was a series of concerts by some of the world's biggest rock and pop stars that demonstrated that the stadium had the potential to be the sort of modern, all-purpose venue that the Ibrox directors envisaged. In addition to Sinatra, global stars like Billy Joel, Elton John, Bryan Adams and Jon Bon Jovi have performed sell-out shows, but fittingly it was football-loving rocker Rod Stewart who kicked it all off.

Despite posing in a Rangers strip in the 1970s alongside John Greig, London-born would-be Scot Stewart makes no secret of the fact that he supports Celtic. However, his love for his favourites did not prevent him from choosing the home of their rivals for the only Scottish show on his 1983 world tour. Stewart was promoting his critically-panned album, *Body Wishes,* and was not enjoying the best of times in terms of record sales. A planned tour of British football grounds was scrapped, with only Ibrox remaining from the original itinerary.

It was the stadium's first show as a rock concert venue, and it proved a major success. On a gloriously sunny June day, Rod played up to his playboy image, with a huge cartoon image of a scantily clad woman holding a football framing the Govan Stand. Fans who paid up to £10 for a place on the pitch were rewarded with a strange array of support acts before the main event. First on stage were local band Passionate Friends, plucked from relative obscurity by promoter Harvey Goldsmith. One-hit wonders the Jo Boxers were next up, followed by veteran glam-rocker Gary Glitter. He was a huge hit and got such a massive reaction to his 1970s hits that he overran his time.

Rod and his band turned up minutes before they were due to go on stage, with their luxury tour bus pulling up outside the main entrance on Edmiston Drive. They went straight on stage, performed and then went straight back onto the bus. But the show went down a storm with his fans, as Stewart – dressed in full Highland regalia – performed many of his biggest hits, including crowd-pleasers like *Tonight's The Night, I Don't Want To Talk About It, Maggie May* and *Sailing.* Despite his Celtic allegiances, Rod must have enjoyed the Ibrox experience, as he returned in 1995 to play another show 'in the round' with a 22-piece orchestra.

The next major concert at Ibrox took place in June 1986, and ironically a Celtic supporter was centre stage again. Jim Kerr's band Simple Minds were Scotland's biggest rock act of the era, having hit the top in both America and Europe, and their two nights at Ibrox came on the back of the massive success of their *Once Upon A Time* album. Kerr had carved a career as a right-on rock star, giving his backing to Amnesty International and the campaign to abolish apartheid in South Africa, but he was clearly not above the petty point-scoring of the Old Firm fan. Ahead of the show, he supposedly sprinkled holy water on the Ibrox goalmouth, presumably in an attempt to scupper the home team's chances of success. With Graeme Souness about to embark on his first Championship-winning season, it obviously failed to work.

In front of a home-town crowd of 30,000, Kerr was more diplomatic, telling the audience during the show 'The greatest thing about tonight is that instead of two sides singing different songs, you're all singing one.' The now-defunct music paper *Melody Maker* also focused on religion in its lukewarm review of the show:

The home of Glasgow Rangers football team is a Protestant club for Protestant people. Coming down from the main road, you see this massive red-brick building in front of you, more like a mill than a football ground, the very last place you would expect to find anything even close to entertainment…Inside, it's all narrow corridors, plush chairs and portraits of the greats throughout the ages. The pitch itself is surrounded by grandstands on all sides so that instead of the traditionally seething Kop ends behind either net, the hapless striker here must feel he's running into massive banks of seats that stretch somewhere into the sky…The basic argument against Simple Minds is that there is a great conceit at the heart of their music, which then touches everything they do. At Ibrox Park, that didn't really seem to matter so much as the fact that this band seemed hard-pressed to communicate their genuine enthusiasm at performing in front of their own people in this magnificent setting.

In 1990 Glasgow was enjoying something of a renaissance. Forever plagued with the *No Mean City* image of razor gangs and random violence, Scotland's industrial capital had suffered badly from the decline in manufacturing in the 1970s and 1980s and was in real need of an economic boost. The International Garden Festival of 1988, held on the southern banks of the Clyde, not far from Ibrox, was the first step on the road to recovery.

Two years later the makeover was complete, when Glasgow was named European City of Culture. A year-long festival of culture ensued, which did much to change the outside world's perception of the city, although critics argued that there were few benefits for the impoverished local population.

For many, the highlight of the festivities was Frank Sinatra's show at Ibrox. The man, considered by many to be the world's greatest singer, had not played in Scotland for almost 40 years, after a series of disastrous concerts in the 1950s when his career had temporarily gone into free fall. By the time he returned at the age of 74, he had assumed legendary status.

Tickets for Ibrox were not cheap, with some fans paying £60 each for premium positions in front of the stage. Even the cheapest seats were £35, and the promoters soon realised that the projected sales of 33,000 were never going to materialise. The decision was taken to only use the Govan Stand and the capacity was cut to just 11,000. Fans who had bought tickets for other parts of the ground had to be allocated new seats, meaning some who had paid £60 were put in cheaper areas. Queues began to build up outside the stadium, and thousands were locked out of the ground as Sinatra started his performance. Some fans did not get inside until the fifth or sixth song, while others had to wait even longer. Refunds were handed out to dozens of devastated fans, but it was scant compensation for missing the show. Even Rangers manager Graeme Souness was affected – he discovered his £60 seats were occupied by someone else and ended up watching from an Ibrox hospitality suite. Those who had got through the gates earlier were treated to support performances by Glasgow jazz singer Carol Kidd and, bizarrely, a stand-up act by local comedian Arnold Brown. But there was no question who the crowds had come to see.

Dressed in a dinner suit and black bow tie, Sinatra – performing on a stage set up in the middle of the pitch, miles away from the audience – opened with *You Make Me Feel So Young*. It set the tone for the night. He rolled back the years, performing many of his classics like *I Get A Kick Out Of You*, *Strangers In The Night*, *Bewitched*, *Mack The Knife*, *My Way* and *New York, New York*.

The stage set-up lacked intimacy, but the chemistry between performer and audience was so strong that the distance was barely noticeable. Tom Gardner and his wife were among those who had paid the top price for a ticket. He remembered:

Our seats were supposed to be on the pitch directly in front of the stage and cost £60 each. On the day they changed all the arrangements. Our new seats put us at the edge of the Govan almost where we normally sat on match days. We went back and complained and got centre-front seats. I think we were ahead of the disaster that then occurred when queues lasting several hours formed... The show started promptly at 7.30pm with some female singer, who was on for about

20 minutes. Then we got a 'comedian'. He died a death. Frank came on at roughly 8pm, and I remember he travelled across the pitch in a little golf buggy.

Sinatra performed for more than an hour, then he left the stage as he approached the end of the show. To the shock and delight of his fans, he appeared on the track in front of the Govan Stand and began shaking hands with members of the audience. Sinatra enjoyed the performance so much that he performed a rare encore, coming back onstage to perform a rendition of *Where Or When*. Tom continued:

Just as he finished his encore, an old woman squeezed in and sat down beside us. First thing she asked was did we know when he would be coming on. She burst into tears when we told her the show was finished…I believe many refunds were given out, and the council lost a fortune in the end. But it was a great show and for a 74-year-old his voice was pretty good. It does remind me that my mother also saw him play the Glasgow Empire back in the 1950s during one of his unpopular phases. The hall had less than 100 people in it.

Sinatra's English driver and friend, Dennis Parker, later revealed how much the Ibrox show had meant to the singer. 'He hated being so far away from them,' Parker told newspapers. 'Halfway through, he grabbed a hand mic and walked off stage to get close to the crowd. It was completely unrehearsed. The emotion that passed between artist and audience that night was magical. Afterwards, back at the hotel, tears started running down his cheeks, he had been so affected by it.' Sinatra later told his entourage 'In all my time in showbusiness I have never had such a stupendous feeling. I have never been so moved by anything in my life before.'

Walter Smith would not be many people's idea of a rock fan. In fact, with his grey hair and trademark cardigans, you could be forgiven for thinking Sinatra was more his scene. But when Bon Jovi performed at Ibrox in 1996, the Rangers manager was one of the 44,000 fans that packed out the stadium. He had been introduced to the band's music by Terry Butcher and Chris Woods when they played for Rangers in the 1980s and, to his surprise (he described himself as 'an ageing hippy'), became a huge fan and jumped at the chance to meet them after their Ibrox show. Given the work ethic he demands of his players, it is not surprising that Smith's admiration was based on their 'sheer professionalism'.

IBROX IN THE 21ST CENTURY

On a sun-bathed afternoon of nerve-shredding tension came the most dramatic moment of all. A hush fell over Ibrox as Mikel Arteta placed the ball on the penalty spot. With the scoreboard clock reading 90 minutes, a goal would almost certainly clinch the League title for Rangers. In the stands, 50,000 fans held their breath, many of them unable to watch. Even Arteta's teammate Ronald de Boer stood with his back to the action as the young Spaniard began his run up. He did not need to watch. The roar that erupted around Ibrox seconds later was enough to tell him that the ball had hit the back of the net. Minutes later Rangers were officially Scottish Premier League champions, as confirmation came through that Celtic had only beaten Kilmarnock 4–0.

It was the conclusion of one of the most remarkable days Scottish football had ever seen. Rangers and Celtic had gone into their final matches of the 2002–03 season neck and neck. After 37 games, the Old Firm were level on points and on goal difference. Rangers held the slimmest of advantages, having scored one more goal than their rivals, but after a long, hard season the destination of the SPL trophy was going to come down to a 90-minute shoot-out.

With Celtic away to Kilmarnock and Rangers at home to Dunfermline, the Ibrox team were favourites to win the race for goals, and they got off to a flying start. Just two minutes into the game, Michael Mols turned and poked the ball past the Dunfermline 'keeper Derek Stillie after receiving a pass from Claudio Cannigia. Rangers were ahead on points, goal difference and goals scored. It was the perfect start and the home supporters settled down for a deluge of goals.

However, in football, things have a habit of not going quite to plan. Nine minutes later Ibrox was stunned as Jason Dair equalised for Dunfermline. Down the A77 in Kilmarnock, the Celtic fans celebrated as the news came through. Their joy was to be short-lived though. Five minutes later, Cannigia put Rangers back in front. Seconds later Chris Sutton scored for Celtic to break the deadlock at Kilmarnock. Both teams were now level on points and goal difference, but Rangers were two ahead on goals scored.

In the 29th minute, Dunfermline managed to repel yet another Rangers attack. The ball ran out towards the touchline in front of the west enclosure. It looked like a lost cause, but Rangers centre-half Lorenzo Amoruso refused to give it up. He chased down the ball, stopped it from going out of play, then steadied himself to hit a beautiful cross that Davie Cooper would have been proud of. Shota Arveladze dived in to head the ball past Stillie – 3–1. There were no more goals at Ibrox before half-time, but at Kilmarnock Sutton kept Celtic in touch with a second goal.

Seven minutes into the second half Alan Thompson scored a penalty for Celtic and put *them* ahead on goal difference. Suddenly the mood darkened at Ibrox. For the first time that afternoon, Rangers were behind in the title race. And it could have got even worse, with only a brilliant save by Stefan Klos denying Dunfermline a second goal from Craig Brewster. The tension was becoming unbearable.

Then, just as the pessimists in the stands began to fear the worst, Ronald de Boer scored with a superb header to give Rangers the initiative once again. And when Steven Thompson added a fifth, three minutes later, it looked like Rangers might have done enough. Celtic were now behind on goal difference and on goals scored, and when news filtered through that Alan Thompson had missed a penalty there were scenes of euphoria at Ibrox.

It looked done and dusted, but still the drama was not over. With eight minutes to go, Petrov scored at Rugby Park. As it stood, Rangers were still two goals in front, but they knew that it would not be beyond Celtic to get the two goals they needed in the time remaining.

Into injury time at Ibrox, and with nerves still jangling Neil McCann was brought down in the penalty area. Referee Stuart Dougal immediately pointed to the spot. There was a lengthy delay as the Dunfermline players protested the decision, before Arteta, the coolest man in the stadium, finally stepped forward to take the kick and ensure Rangers would emerge from an amazing afternoon as the champions.

Even after the final whistle blew at Ibrox, there was an agonising wait for the match at Kilmarnock to finish. Eventually, manager Alex McLeish got the message from a rock steady steward that it was all over and the celebrations could begin. In its 104 years, Ibrox had never seen a day like it. There had been titles won at the stadium before, and there had even been final-day dramas like the match with Aberdeen in 1991, but nothing came close to matching the roller coaster of emotions endured by the supporters that afternoon.

Earlier in the season, Duncan Stewart had given up his season ticket to a friend because of work commitments and on the last day of the season found himself desperately trying to find a ticket. 'I pulled in a couple of favours and ended up sitting right in the front row of the enclosure, virtually on the track. It was a bizarre view, but the ticket only cost me £8 – I hadn't paid that little to see a game since Graeme Souness arrived. There was a guy sitting a few seats along from me who had a radio, and I spent almost as much time watching his expression as I did watching the game. The thing with trying to follow other matches on the radio is that there's always the chance you'll pick up something wrong. The trick is not to pass on the wrong information to anyone else, but unfortunately I did just that. When Celtic got their fourth goal, somehow I actually picked it up that Kilmarnock had scored and told the guy beside me just that. He passed it around and soon everyone around me was cheering and hugging each other. When the truth eventually came out, I was not a popular man. Thankfully, it all came good in the end, but if it had ended badly I think I might have had to make a run for it.'

Coming after two successive Celtic Championships, the last-day title win was welcomed, but it disguised a deep malaise within Ibrox. The club had run up massive debts during Dick Advocaat's reign as manager, spending far more on transfer fees and wages than could be afforded by a club operating in Scotland. The total debt at the end of the 2002–03 season was estimated to be around £80 million. McLeish had taken over as manager from Advocaat in 2001 and had inherited a team packed with talent that had lost its way. He managed to steady the ship and, while the League was already beyond him by the time he took over, he won the two domestic cup competitions in his first season and secured the treble in his second.

However, the financial issues blighting the club undermined the manager's efforts. Several of his best players, including captain Barry Ferguson, Dutch international Arthur Numan and Claudio Cannigia, left the following season and their replacements were simply not good enough. The result was that Celtic regained the title and Rangers endured a painful European campaign. The signing of Croatian forward Dado Prso on a Bosman and the return of Barry Ferguson half way through the season inspired McLeish's team to another dramatic final-day title win in 2005, but the following season saw another slump, only progress to the last 16 of the Champions League saving Alex McLeish from the sack. Rangers finished in third place behind Celtic and Hearts – their lowest League position since 1988 – and it was only then that McLeish finally walked away from the post.

TRIBUTE TO A LEGEND

Frenchman Paul Le Guen was brought in to replace McLeish in the summer of 2006. He was considered one of the most sought after young coaches in Europe, having led Lyon to three successive French League title wins. Le Guen brought his own coaching methods and arrived with a reputation as a tough disciplinarian. His appointment was met with a wave of optimism among the support, although early results were not promising.

In September 2006 Rangers paid tribute to their greatest-ever manager, Bill Struth, by renaming the Main Stand in his honour. It was not the first Ibrox tribute to the legendary figure. The previous year, a bust of Struth had been commissioned and put on display on the famous marble staircase. However, with the 50th anniversary of his death approaching, it was felt that something more should be done and the decision was taken to name the stand in his honour. It was a fitting tribute to the man who had been largely responsible for driving forward the building of the stand in the 1920s.

The celebrations took place before a League match against Falkirk. Ahead of kick-off, fans unfurled a 50ft banner as a plaque was unveiled by John Greig, and at half-time, the big screens showed a video celebrating Struth's career, while some of the surviving stars of the Struth era took to the pitch. The Rangers chief executive Martin Bain paid his own tribute: 'The word legend is often overused these days, but Bill Struth deserves the title as the man who set the standards and traditions at the club for others to follow.'

On the pitch Le Guen was struggling to settle and results were not good. A CIS Cup defeat to First Division St Johnstone was the low point. The majority of his signings failed to meet the standards required and his methods failed to win over the existing Scottish players in the squad, most notably Barry Ferguson. Just six months into his reign, Le Guen declared Ferguson was being put on the transfer list. It was a brave, some would say foolhardy, move.

Days after the announcement it was Le Guen, not Ferguson, who left Ibrox. He returned to France with his reputation damaged and left behind a club in turmoil.

WALTER'S RETURN

After almost a decade away, Walter Smith returned to the Ibrox hot seat in January 2007. His time as manager of Everton was not considered a massive success by fans on Merseyside, but his reputation was enhanced considerably by his time as Scotland manager. Smith had taken over as national team boss in the aftermath of the disastrous Berti Vogts era. Vogts had become a joke figure and Scotland had plummeted in the world rankings during his time in charge. Smith stopped the rot and set about restoring some credibility to the Scotland set up, with the highlight of his time in charge being a victory over World Cup runners-up France at Hampden.

He arrived back at Rangers facing a similar job. With the League title already gone, his first task was to steady the ship and instil a team spirit that had been lacking under Le Guen. Having achieved that, the next aim was to win trophies. Rangers had gone two seasons without winning any silverware, a completely unacceptable state of affairs to the fans. By the end of the 2007–08 season Smith's team had won the Scottish Cup and the League Cup but lost out on the League to Celtic on the last day of the season. Having been in an almost unassailable position, they suffered an alarming slump in the closing stages of the season, not helped by a lengthy injury list and a crippling fixtures pile-up, caused in part by the team's unexpected run to the Final of the UEFA Cup, and exacerbated by the SPL's refusal to extend the season to accommodate the extra games.

Smith had taken a lot of criticism during his first period as manager for Rangers' repeated failures in Europe. This time around he had clearly learned from past mistakes. His approach was to make the team incredibly difficult to beat by packing defence and midfield and leaving just one man up-front. Having narrowly missed out on qualifying for the knock-out stages of the Champions League, Rangers dropped into the UEFA Cup and embarked on a run that may not have pleased the football purists, but it certainly pleased the Rangers fans.

Rangers were drawn at home for the first leg of each round, starting with Panathinaikos. A 0–0 draw at Ibrox did not seem a great result on the surface, but the important thing was that Rangers did not concede a goal at home. In the second leg the Greeks scored early, but Nacho Novo's late equaliser demonstrated just how important that Ibrox clean-sheet was, putting Rangers through on away goals. Germans Werder Bremen were defeated 2–1 on aggregate in the next round thanks to home first-leg goals from Daniel Cousin and Steven Davis and another Ibrox clean sheet. In the quarter-final Sporting Lisbon were confident after securing a goalless draw at Ibrox, but Rangers produced a classic counter-attacking performance in the return match, with goals from Jean Claude Darcheville and Steven Whittaker clinching a deserved 2–0 win.

Against all the odds, Rangers were in the semi-final of a European competition for the first time in 36 years. The opponents were Fiorentina, evoking memories of the 1961 Cup-Winners' Cup Final. If Rangers were to progress they would have to overcome a team that were heading for the top four in Italy and featured numerous internationals, including the former Chelsea star Adrian Mutu.

The first leg at Ibrox was a momentous occasion, and one which many Rangers fans thought they would never see. The sense that this was history in the making was enhanced as some of the stars of the 1961 Final took to the pitch before kick-off and received a rousing reception. Rangers were weakened by a combination of injury and suspension, but they frustrated the Italians, allowing them plenty of possession but preventing them from creating any clear-cut chances. The Scots played the game as if they were the away team, and although they did not create much themselves they succeeded in blunting the threat of *La Viola*. Yet again, the match ended 0–0, but this time the Rangers fans knew their team was capable of getting a result in the away leg. And so it proved. In Florence Rangers held out against the predicted Italian onslaught to win the tie on penalties. Nacho Novo scored the winning kick that put Rangers into the Final at the City of Manchester Stadium against the Russian champions Zenit St Petersburg, now coached by Dick Advocaat.

An estimated 200,000 fans went to the north west of England for the occasion, the biggest travelling support in history. Most travelled without a ticket, aiming to watch the game on big screens set up in Manchester city centre. Back in Glasgow, another 30,000 watched the match on screens at Ibrox. In the end Zenit had too much for Rangers, their inspirational playmaker Andrei Arshavin the key difference between the two teams. Rangers simply did not have anyone approaching his quality. The 2–0 defeat was a disappointing end to what had been a thrilling campaign.

THE FUTURE OF IBROX

If Bill Struth had somehow found himself transported through time to the modern Ibrox, he would have discovered some things have not changed much since his day. Millions of pounds have been spent transforming other parts of the ground, but the grandstand on Edmiston Drive, that he was so instrumental in creating, has survived. Of course, even it has changed over the years, most strikingly with the addition of the Club Deck tier. The blue gates that once stood at the bottom of the Copland Road terracing have been moved and a new pair has been added for symmetry at the Broomloan Road end, and the row of turnstiles providing access to the terraces have long gone. But otherwise Struth would not notice many changes. The red-brick frontage and the main entrance, with its RFC mosaic crest on the floor and its heavy wooden doors and etched glass windows, are exactly as they were when he last visited more than 50 years ago. The no-smoking signs might take him by surprise, but it is likely he would approve.

Inside, the famous marble staircase still leads up to the Blue Room where the manager used to play the piano for guests after matches. Next door is the manager's office where Struth spent many an hour, often working late into the night. These days the Rangers manager bases himself at the training complex at Auchenhowie, but the old office remains much as it was during Struth's reign. The Trophy Room was added after Struth's death, but he would recognise many of the items contained within it, and he could not fail to be impressed by the glittering array of honours and gifts amassed by the club since his passing.

It would not be until he made his way from inside the stand to his seat in the directors' box that Struth would become aware of the dramatic changes to Ibrox. Directly opposite the Main Stand, instead of the covered, standing enclosure, is the Govan Stand, with seats for around 11,000. Each is allocated to a season-ticket holder, who gains access to the stand with an electronic smart card. Behind the goals, the huge banks of terracing are gone, replaced with smaller versions of the Govan Stand, each holding 7,500. In the corners are two enormous television screens showing highlights of previous triumphs as a state-of-the-art sound system blasts out pop hits and Rangers songs.

Around the directors' box, the well-heeled supporters would take their seats as kick-off approached, many of them having enjoyed the lavish hospitality that is now available for those who are willing to pay. Ibrox caters for more than 1,200 on a match day in hospitality suites named after some of the club's legendary players of the past. In Struth's day, a handful of the directors' special guests would have been treated to a hot meal followed by drinks served up from the art-deco cocktail bar. Sadly the bar no longer exists, and a public appeal for its return a few years ago was unsuccessful.

So what would Struth make of the 21st-century Ibrox? His reputation as a traditionalist might lead some to assume that he would disapprove of developments, but in essence Struth was an innovator and a forward thinker, as demonstrated by his close involvement in the Ibrox sports and the development of the Main Stand, which in its day was a state-of-the-art facility. He would certainly be fascinated by the way Ibrox has embraced modern technology without abandoning the past, and, as someone who insisted on nothing but the best for the club, he would surely appreciate that the new Ibrox was built to the highest of standards.

Struth would also understand the notion that nothing lasts forever. Almost 30 years after the redevelopment of the stadium was completed, there is a growing feeling that Ibrox is now in need of a major facelift. The current capacity of around 51,000 is considered to be too small. Many Rangers fans will always judge the club on how it compares to their Old Firm rivals, and are uncomfortable with the fact that Parkhead is capable of housing 9,000 more spectators than Ibrox. But it is not just a question of one-upmanship, there is a financial side to the argument as well. A rough calculation based on £25 for a ticket, would suggest Celtic could generate an extra £4 million, over the course of a League season, through their ground's extra capacity. The gulf in income becomes even greater when the Champions League and domestic Cup competitions are added into the equation.

There have been piecemeal developments over the years aimed at increasing the Ibrox capacity. The filling of the corners in 1996 took the number of seats up to 50,444, and another 600 were added 10 years later, with the addition of three new rows of premium seats at the front of the upper tier of the Govan Stand. The most recent increase also saw the opening of an exclusive hospitality area called Bar 72, themed around the European Cup-Winners' Cup victory of 1972.

Unfortunately the design of Ibrox makes any large-scale capacity increases impossible, at least at a realistic price. The solution would be either a brand new stadium on a new site, or a wholesale redevelopment of the existing ground. Those in favour of a completely new stadium believe it would be better to start with a blank canvas rather than try to make the design fit an existing space. In response to those who believe Rangers are inextricably linked to the Ibrox area, they point to the fact that the current Ibrox is the club's fifth home.

In January 2008, in response to a Sunday newspaper article, Rangers announced that they were looking at a series of options to redevelop Ibrox and the surrounding area. Three 'strategies' were being considered, the most radical of which would see the total rebuilding of the stadium, while retaining the historic Main Stand. According to the media reports, this would cost more than £700 million and would result in a 70,000 capacity and a return to the 'bowl' shape that was abandoned in the 1970s.

The area surrounding the ground – currently in a run-down state – would be transformed into an Ibrox 'village', featuring at hotels, apartments shops and restaurants. The inspiration for that comes from the Chelsea Village around the London club's Stamford Bridge home.

Corporate investors would help fund the scheme, the reports said, with naming rights being one of the key ways of raising cash – much in the way that the Emirates airline helped pay for Arsenal's new home in return for attaching its name to the stadium.

The reports suggested Rangers were just weeks away from making an official announcement on the development, and in March chairman Sir David Murray confirmed that details of the proposals would be revealed soon. 'I'd hope by the start of May people will know our options,' he was quoted as saying as he announced a freeze on season ticket prices. 'We are very enthused by the level of interest from partners, funders and investors. I don't want to give away our plans but it's not just a football stadium, it's an events centre. If it does come to fruition, football would probably only be 20% of revenue because you would be bringing in boxing, business seminars and other things.'

By autumn of that year, however, the stadium redevelopment plans were on hold as the economy plunged into recession. Planning permission was granted in October 2008 for proposals to redevelop land around the ground, replacing the existing, delapidated flats with a luxury hotel and retail outlets. Glasgow City Council agreed to transfer land to Rangers, noting the £350 million project would make a significant contribution to its own redevelopment plans.

Sir David said he was beginning a search for partners to back the development but conceded the economic climate could make that difficult, and at the time of writing (December 2009) no further details have been revealed. Rangers' own financial difficulties, which saw Sir David stand down as chairman and put his majority shareholding up for sale, would suggest that such a scheme may never see the light of day, certainly in the short term.

Sir David's successor as chairman, Alastair Johnston, told the club's AGM in December 2009 that, whatever the club's financial problems, naming rights to the Ibrox were not up for sale. The club have also given assurances that Leitch's historic stand would form the centrepiece of any future development. After Arsenal's move away from the similarly historic Highbury, it would be a sad loss if Rangers were ever to abandon Ibrox. The red brick façade on Edmiston Drive remains one of the most imposing and distinctive in football, and the famous foyer within cannot be matched anywhere in the world for its rich history.

For the 50,000 who attend every home game, Ibrox is more than just a stadium. It is a temple of football, the place where they come to worship their idols and pray that they fulfil all their dreams. It also stands as a memorial to dozens of men, women and children who lost their lives simply because they chose to watch their team play on a Saturday afternoon. Whatever the future holds for Ibrox, it is essential that these people are never forgotten.

BIBLIOGRAPHY

Blue Heaven: The Ibrox Trophy Room by Willie Thornton (1991)

Rangers: The Managers by David Mason (2000)

Engineering Archie by Simon Inglis (2005)

Scottish Football by Kevin McCarra (1984)

The Roar of The Crowd by David Ross (2005)

The Football Grounds of Great Britain by Simon Inglis (1993)

The Story of The Rangers: Fifty Years of Football by John Allan (1923)

Rebirth of The Blues by Chick Young (1986)

Legend – Sixty Years At Ibrox by Bob McPhail with Allan Herron (1988)

Rangers – The New Era by William Allison (1966)

Playing For Rangers No 3 by Ken Gallacher (1971)

Follow On: 50 Years of Rangers in Europe by Iain Duff (2006)

The Little Wonder by Rob Hadgraft (2004)

Your Fathers The Ghosts by Tom F. Cunningham (2007)

The Second City by C.A. Oakley (1946)